The European Union and East Asia

The European Union and East Asia

Interregional Linkages in a Changing Global System

Edited by

Peter W. Preston and Julie Gilson

Department of Political Science and International Studies, University of Birmingham, UK

Edward Elgar

Cheltenham, UK • Northampton MA, USA

Published by
Edward Elgar Publishing Limited
Glensanda House
Montpellier Parade
Cheltenham
Glos GL50 1UA
UK

Edward Elgar Publishing, Inc.
136 West Street
Suite 202
Northampton
Massachusetts 01060
USA

A catalogue record for this book
is available from the British Library

Library of Congress Cataloguing in Publication Data

The European Union and East Asia : inter-regional linkages in a changing global system / P.W. Preston and Julie Gilson (eds.).
    p. cm.
    Includes index.
    1. European Union countries—Foreign economic relations—East Asia. 2. East Asia—Foreign economic relations—European Union countries. 3. European Union countries—Foreign economic relations—Asia, Southeastern. 4. Asia, Southeastern—Foreign economic relations—European Union countries. I. Preston, P. W. (Peter Wallace), 1949- II. Gilson, Julie.

HF1531.Z4 E185 2001
337.405—dc21

2001033427

ISBN 1 84064 394 3

Printed and bound in Great Britain by MPG Books Ltd, Bodmin, Cornwall

Contents

PART V   CONCLUSION

Figures and tables

FIGURE

TABLES

Acronyms

AEAF	Asia-Europe Agricultural Forum
AEBC	Asia-Europe Business Conference
AEBF	Asia-Europe Business Forum
AECF	Asia-Europe Cooperation Framework
AEETC	Asia-Europe Environmental Technology Centre
AEFGC	Asia-Europe Forum of Governors of Cities
AEITTP	Asia-Europe Information Technology and Telecommunications Programme
AEM	Asia-Europe Management
AEMM	ASEAN-EU Ministerial Meeting
AEPF	Asia-Europe People's Forum
AEUP	Asia-Europe University Programme
AEVG	Asia-Europe Vision Group
AEYLS	Asia-Europe Young Leaders Symposia
AFTA	ASEAN Free Trade Area
AIM	Asian Institute of Management
APEC	Asia-Pacific Economic Cooperation
ARF	ASEAN Regional Forum
ASEAN	Association of South East Asian Nations
ASEF	Asia-Europe Foundation
ASEM	Asia-Europe Meeting
ASEP	Asia-Europe Parliamentary Partnership
BSECZ	Black Sea Economic Cooperation Zone
CCP	Common Commercial Policy
CFSP	Common Foreign and Security Policy
CIS	Commonwealth of Independent States
CTBT	Comprehensive Test Ban Treaty
DIPECHO	Disaster Preparedness Programme of the European Community Humanitarian Office
DPP	Democratic Progressive Party
EAEC	East Asian Economic Caucus
EANICs	East Asian Newly Industrialized Countries
EBICs	European Business Information Centres
EC	European Community
ECJ	European Court of Justice

ECO	Economic Cooperation Organization
EEC	European Economic Community
EMEAP	Executives' Meeting of East Asia–Pacific Central Banks
EP	European Parliament
EU	European Union
FEER	*Far Eastern Economic Review*
GATS	General Agreement on Trade in Services
GATT	General Agreement on Tariffs and Trade
GITIC	Guangdong International Trust and Investment Corp
IBRD	International Bank for Reconstruction and Development
IMF	International Monetary Fund
IPAP	Investment Promotion Action Plan
IPR	intellectual property rights
JCC	Joint Cooperation Committee
KEDO	Korean Peninsula Energy Development Organization
KMT	Kuomintang
LTICs	local trust and investment corporations
NIC	Newly Industrialized Countries
OECF	Overseas Economic Cooperation Fund
OEM	original equipment manufacturing
MFA	Multi-Fibre Arrangement
MFN	most favoured nation
PMC	Post-Ministerial Conference
PRC	People's Republic of China
QMV	qualified majority vote/voting
QRs	quantitative restrictions
RFU/RL	Radio Free Europe/Radio Liberty
RIET	Regional Institute for Environmental Technology
SAARC	South Asia Association for Regional Cooperation
SAR	Special Administrative Region
SCAP	Supreme Commander for the Allied Powers
SEANWFZ	Southeast Asia Nuclear Weapons-Free Zone (Treaty)
SEZ	Special Economic Zone
SMEs	small- and medium-sized enterprises
SOEs	state-owned enterprises
SOM	Senior Officials Meeting
SOMTI	Senior Officials Meeting on Trade and Investment
TFAP	Trade Facilitation Action Plan
TNAS	Towards a New Asia Strategy
WTO	World Trade Organization

Contributors

Professor Peter W. Preston, Department of Political Science and International Studies, University of Birmingham, United Kingdom.

Dr Julie A. Gilson, Department of Political Science and International Studies, University of Birmingham, United Kingdom.

Professor Stephanie Lawson, School of Economic and Social Studies, University of East Anglia, United Kingdom.

Professor John Clammer, Faculty of Comparative Culture, Sophia University, Tokyo, Japan.

Professor Hans-Dieter Evers, Sociology of Development Research Centre, University of Bielefeld, Germany.

Dr Markus Kaiser, Sociology of Development Research Centre, University of Bielefeld, Germany.

Dr Paul Lim, European Institute for Asian Studies, Brussels, Belgium.

Dr Sum, Ngai-Ling, Department of Politics, University of Lancaster, United Kingdom.

Dr Zhao, Chenggen, Department of Political Science and Public Administration, University of Beijing, People's Republic of China.

Sean McGough, Department of Political Science and International Studies, University of Birmingham, United Kingdom.

Tseng, Su-Ling, Department of Political Science and International Studies, University of Birmingham, United Kingdom.

Professor Tong, Jia-Dong, Centre for European Studies, University of Nankai, Tianjin, People's Republic of China.

Preface

The global system has seen sweeping changes in recent years. The economic, social and political dynamics of that system, the nature of the regions within it and the implications of these changes for the governments and peoples of individual countries have become key questions for the social sciences. In turn, there is increasing interest in the interchange between the internal dynamics and regional interlinkages of the European Union and East Asia. A series of formal and substantive issues can be identified: firstly, the task of establishing an agenda of enquiry where divergent cultural expectations, intellectual traditions and political concerns militate against any simple declarations; secondly, clarifying the nature of political-economic, social-institutional and political-cultural linkages within the context of the developing global system; and thirdly, detailing the political processes central to the development of linkages between the European Union and East Asia. The editors hope that the papers collected in this volume will contribute to clarifying these issues.

Acknowledgements

The present volume had its origins in a conference organized and funded by the Asia Research Centre of the School of Social Sciences of the University of Birmingham. The conference was held in the summer of 1999 and was attended by colleagues from England, mainland Europe and East Asia. We should like to thank all those colleagues who participated in the conference and contributed to its success.

PART I

Introduction

1. Europe-Asia: regional interlinkages, mutual definitions and formal mechanisms

Peter W. Preston and Julie A. Gilson

INTRODUCTION

The chapters in this volume are concerned, one way or another, with the interchange between the internal dynamics and regional interlinkages of the European Union and East Asia.[1] Collectively they address the ways in which patterns of life within one region are shaped by their contacts with the other region. It is a process of mutual exchange and definition. At the present time a series of complex changes within the global system can be identified: (i) the very sharp reforms to the hitherto state-socialist countries of Central and Eastern Europe; (ii) the accelerating integration of the member countries of the European Union; (iii) the slow relative decline of the USA; and (iv) the sequence of broadly integrative changes in East Asia. It is within this general context that an intense interest in the global system and the role of regionalism has developed. In turn, within this context, there is an increasing interest in the interchange between the internal dynamics and regional interlinkages of the European Union and East Asia.

These interlinkages may be understood from a number of perspectives. They represent historical developments in interchanges between the two regions, which, in turn, have influenced the unique formation of Asia and Europe. This history could be read as a simple narrative, or as an archaeology of the present, illustrating how the past is inscribed in the routines and ideas evident today. These interlinkages could be understood in their contemporary form and, from this perspective, they embrace economic, social, cultural and political interaction through the media of trade, people-to-people exchange, the spread of ideas and the signature of treaties and agreements. In today's global system, summit meetings between heads of state, international business deals, the diversification of foreign direct investment, cultural exchanges and the mass communication of popular culture all have their place in creating and sustaining region-to-region linkages. This introductory chapter will endeavour to introduce these complex issues. We will begin by establishing an agenda both in terms of a series of key issues and, more substantively, in terms of recent developments. In particular, we will consider material interlinkages, discourses and formal mechanisms: ways in which the interchange has been vehicled, construed and ordered. The historical development of the interchanges will frame our enquiries into current concerns. We will offer an anticipatory review of the work of our contributors and offer a conclusion which suggests that there is much to do in clarifying this long-established, deepening and important interchange.

ESTABLISHING SOME ELEMENTS OF THE CORE AGENDA

The European Union and East Asia are linked in a number of ways. Historical linkages of the two regions embrace patterns of ancient trade (the old Silk Road), the more recent episode of colonial rule (which began with European trading voyages around the Cape of Good Hope to India, Southeast Asia and China, and which deployed, thereafter, its characteristic admixture of development and exploitation), together with continuing economic, political and cultural legacies stemming from that period. Substantive contemporary linkages embrace the economic (trade, investment and financial flows), the social (migration, diasporic networks and tourism) and the cultural (law, language, custom and memory). Formal linkages embrace interstate relations, treaty organizations and the various consultative fora.

It is clear that the countries of the European Union and East Asia are presently experiencing extensive change as the global system structures which enfold these areas and countries reconfigure. In some cases there has been institutional acknowledgement of these trends; for example, APEC, AFTA or ASEM [2], or, indeed the quickening drive for integration within the European Union. It is clear that the two regions are different, have differing dynamics within the developing global system and have differing impacts, one upon the other, through their established and developing pattern of linkages, yet the interchanges are helping to shape internal regional dynamics in an extensive practical and cultural process of mutual definition.

In the case of the countries of Europe, a series of concerns centred upon the further economic, social and cultural integration of the European Union, within the shifting circumstances of the post-cold war period, can be identified: (i) the dynamics of European-level economic restructuring, currency union and the development of the machineries of European Union-level economic regulation; (ii) the dynamics of European-level social interchange, such as employment, leisure and welfare; (iii) the dynamics of

European-level culture, including the issue of identity; and (iv) the dynamics of European political institutional change at subnational, national and EU levels.

At the same time, in the post-cold war era the peoples of East Asia have been confronted with the task of responding to a dynamic situation, the difficulties of which have been compounded in recent times by financial crises. A series of issues can be identified: (i) the dynamics of East Asian economic networks, including flows of trade, investment and aid; (ii) the dynamics of East Asian social interchange, including travel, tourism, kin networks and migration; (iii) the dynamics of East Asian cultural interchange, including great traditions, arts and the popular cultural realm of media and consumption; and (iv) the dynamics of East Asian regional political life, which combines cooperation and continuing conflict.

It is within this very broad framework that the core elements of the intellectual agenda that animates the chapters comprising this volume must be established. Three initial areas of work can be identified: material inter-linkages (vehicled), discourses (construed) and formal mechanisms (ordered); followed by a fourth; current concerns.

Material Interlinkages

The first area of concern relates to the material interlinkages of the two regions. Such material interlinkages have developed as a result of a long history of sporadic encounters and sustained intervals of cooperation and conflict. Historically, Europeans made contact with Asia through travellers, merchants, missionaries, soldiers, adventurers and administrators. These different groups of people, exposed to different tracts of the Asian continent in various stages of expansion and development, left imprints upon their often reluctant hosts as far-reaching as political systems and religious beliefs and as incidental as contemporary fashions. Peoples within Asia received these interlopers with a range of reactions, from respect for an elite civilization to repulsion at barbaric invasions. However it is interpreted, the legacy of European colonialism in Asia continues in many parts of Asia to impose western demands on systems often ill-equipped or unprepared to fulfil them.

Concurrently, Asian influences on Europe have been varied. One only need peruse late nineteenth century art to find *japonaiserie* in fashion and the *Mikado* offering a convincing representation of Asian exotica for European tastes. A half-century later, however, Asia had become a threat, the rise of militarism in Japan and of communism in China and beyond providing proof that this continent could not be ignored.

Today, linkages between Europe and Asia are sustained through economic, political and social channels. On the economic level, trade flows in both directions continue to increase, whilst the donor–recipient relationship has eroded in favour of a flurry of two-directional investment. On a political level, the ASEAN Regional Forum (ARF), its Post-Ministerial Conference (PMC) and the Asia–Europe Meeting (ASEM), as well as various bilateral agreements, ensure that leaders and other official representatives of the two regions encounter each other regularly to discuss matters of mutual interest and concern. At the third ASEM summit in Seoul in October 2000, the twenty-five participants from Asia and Europe (plus the president of the European Commission) agreed to continue cooperative efforts to address subjects of mutual concern, such as the fight against drugs smuggling, money laundering, the smuggling of immigrants and other forms of international crime. Added to these dimensions, growing tourism and the influence of mass communications and high technology ensure that people-to-people exchanges continue apace. These material linkages are underpinned by new and developing sets of ideas and discourses.

Discourses

As the peoples of Asia and Europe came into contact with each other over the centuries, various idea-sets were formed in respect of the two regions. Later, as material linkages took root more widely, and as colonialism came to be established, images shifted. Europeans began to replace ideas of Asia as a fabulously wealthy continent of exotic spices with an image of a decadent East. Asians, for their part, were increasingly forced to regard Europeans as their colonial overlords. Different forms of mutual recognition came to characterize different periods, these including: (i) the significance of memory, formed from periods of psychological and long-lasting importance, such as the opium war, unequal treaties and humiliation in China, or the halcyon days of late empire (typically the 1920s and 1930s for Europe); (ii) the role of mutual ignorance, as ensured by US hegemony in Asia and Europe during the last half of the twentieth century; and (iii) the importance of current exchanges in trade (material goods, consumption styles), travel (diasporic networks, immigration trends and tourism), and policy (the expectations of policymakers). These various forces have ensured that Europe and Asia have meant different things to each other at different stages of their development. The expansion of material linkages and 'real time' contact, however, have not reduced the impact of mutual perceptions of Asia and Europe today. Rather, continuing stereotypes are frequently reinforced in trade disputes, political wrangles and cultural misunderstandings, these making it imperative for studies of interregional contact to take into account the discursive patterns which underpin and hinder or facilitate them.

Formal Mechanisms

Historically, incoming Europeans made local treaties with the Asian rulers they encountered, the adoption of which became more widespread as the slow process of colonization advanced. The cumulative result of such formal structures was to solidify the status of colonial rule across the Asian continent. The structures and influences embedded within colonialism also harboured the seeds of formal decolonization which followed it. As a result, a postcolonial era saw the spread of new nation-states, with exchange governed by a range of interstate treaties.

Since the end of the cold war era, these interstate treaties have proliferated to establish a whole network of intra- and extra-regional activities. Within Europe, the EU continues to further its integration processes, with the result that plans towards membership expansion and a single currency are accompanied by both political and security projects of deeper cooperation. The Common Foreign and Security Policy (CFSP) of the Union continues to be governed by interstate bargaining, but now also comprises a High Representative to act as the foreign policy face of the EU where appropriate. Common goals have also been expanded in the field of security cooperation, as the structures of the Western European Union (WEU) become integrated into the EU framework itself and as the European contingent of NATO attempts to deal by itself with issues in its own backyard. Although the format of integration and collective behaviour in Asia is qualitatively different from that in Europe, there are nevertheless a number of frameworks within which intra-Asian cooperation is now formulated. The oldest current example of formal channels of dialogue is ASEAN, which was established in 1967 to counter cold war trends but which today has a greater range of activities to address. Its existence is variously strengthened and threatened by the establishment of other fora in the region, such as the ARF and the PMC, ASEM and APEC, and it has pinned its future sustainability most notably upon the development of an ASEAN Free Trade Area (AFTA) to increase and consolidate intra-ASEAN trade.

The fora in which ASEAN members participate also include Japan, China and South Korea. Japanese formal ties with other nations and regions developed in the 1970s in order to provide frameworks through which to negotiate thorny trade conflicts and tensions. South Korea followed later, but China's participation in formal arrangements within and beyond its own region is, for the most part, a novel phenomenon. China's membership of a number of formal processes ensures that all the countries of East Asia (excepting North Korea, which, nevertheless, has embarked upon historic formal discussions with the South) are now integrated into structured dialogues. The trend towards formal mechanisms of exchange has been precipitated by a changing global system characterized by the need to respond collectively to issues which transcend national borders, and by the inevitable rise of regionalization as one way of forming such collectives.

Current Concerns

These three dimensions of regional interaction demonstrate the underlying premises of contemporary regional engagement. However, the day-to-day interchange involving representatives of nations and regions is, in fact, a practical endeavour, one shaped by both pressing and banal events which must be negotiated by different groups of representatives. These groups may be classified as political actors, non-political actors and analytical observers.

Political actors now have to address contemporary realities shaped by a post-cold war shift in political interests from geostrategic to geoeconomic problems. As a result, the familiar political agendas of the countries of Europe and Asia, within the realms of internal as well as international politics, are being reoriented to embrace the shifting structural patterns of power within and between regions. These shifting patterns are challenging the role of the state, and facilitating greater political participation for non-state actors. At the same time, observers of particular or general dimensions of these processes of change help to shape underlying debates concerning the very nature of contemporary international relations. These observers, from within units of policy analysis as well as academic institutions, are concerned with delineating and defining the nature of contemporary exchanges in their various dimensions. Their interventions also serve to sustain debates concerning the nature of regions.

The European interest in the post-cold war global system has opened up a debate about the nature of regions. There are a number of theories of regions and they have been variously applied in Europe and Asia, both to the European Union and to East Asia. There is a related debate concerning the relationship of the global system, regions, nations and subnational units. In Europe and Asia the issue of the particularity of regions has been addressed (in terms of economic, social, cultural and political logics). In turn, the contested claim that regions are elaborate constructions has opened up a debate about the diversity of routes to the modern world. More formally, the claim that theorists, policy analysts and political actors will have to learn how to act within a multipolar global system has reopened debate about the limits of received traditions of social scientific reflection, as well as the related substantive issue of handling the diversity of extant forms of life.

In sum, this is evidently a complex set of core concerns and the following section examines possible means of ordering investigations.

DEVELOPING THE AGENDA

The mixture of material basis of interchange, the discursive construction of these exchanges and the formal institutional machineries ordering these exchanges could be reviewed in a number of ways. The strategies of historical narrative and archaeology have already been mentioned. Here, we will borrow from the classical European tradition, recently represented in the guise of critical/structural international political economy, in order to elucidate the dynamics of complex change in the ongoing shift to the modern world. These intermingled matters can be formulated as a sequence of historical phases which create a framework within which we can consider the contemporary expression of the three dimensions of interaction outlined above.

The phases would be these: (i) the extension of European power in Asia; (ii) European domination and the demands of empire; (iii) European eclipse, US hegemony and Asian recovery; (iv) Europe/Asia rising; and, finally, and most importantly, (v) Europe/Asia relations in the contemporary global system.

The Extension of European Power in Asia

A. G. Frank[3] writes about the period before European expansion and argues that Asia was the core of the global economy. The Europeans were marginal to the Asian economic system. However, the Asian system was conservative, and decisions to turn inwards, in particular by China and Japan, allowed the Europeans, at the time just beginning to acquire the means and disposition to trade overseas, to expand within the Asian economic sphere. Thereafter, European persistence, aggression and some technological advance allowed Europe to expand its activities within the Asian economy. It was this trade which allowed the development of Europe. In Frank's version of history – a global-centric vision to replace more familiar Eurocentric schemes – the European economy grew as a result of trade with the richer Asian economy which, thereafter, it systematically entered, and this process of expansion was to eventuate in the construction of formal colonial empires. If we examine these matters from the three perspectives outlined above (material interlinkages, discourses and formal mechanisms) a number of important points are raised.

The material interlinkages of this early period of interaction were facilitated by the activities of travellers and traders. There was an overland route, the old Silk Road, and later there was the sea route via the Cape of Good Hope which led to India, Southeast Asia and China. The Europeans who travelled along the Silk Road traded with Central Asia and China. Those who travelled around the Cape traded with India, Southeast Asia and China. In these early exchanges the number of people making such journeys was small. The civilizations they encountered were rich and prosperous. The early European travellers and traders made little significant impact upon the Asian civilizations. At this time the economic, social and cultural gradient ran from Asia to Europe, not the other way round as it has for most of the modern period.

The discursive frameworks tentatively established during this phase had aspects which were to endure and which can be recognized today. The early European travellers brought back their tales and, in general, their image of Asia was positive. Since the cultural gradient ran from Asia to Europe, Europeans were meeting more advanced civilizations. The reaction of the various Asian peoples reflected this situation. As the Europeans made their first trading contacts they were merely one more group of traders, indeed a small and rather marginal group. However, as trade developed the European presence became more problematical and came to be read by elites as a threat, and in northeast Asia a series of countries closed themselves to contact with the outside world: China in the mid-1500s; Japan in the early 1600s; and Korea, from around the 1600s.

These early exchanges were ordered in terms of the resources of local political structures. In Europe, at this time, the economy was primarily agricultural. The political system was still largely feudal. The key to political power was control of land and peasants. However, merchant groups existed and the trading cities of medieval Europe, located in (modern) Italy, Spain and the Netherlands, were developing extensive competing trading networks which, in due course, reached out beyond Europe. On the other hand, in East Asia, the political organization was different. There were dynastic empires – a decentred feudalism – in China, Korea, Japan and Vietnam. These roughly comprised the area of China's influence. The Sinocentric system bound countries into a system centred on China, and the political and economic link was via tribute. In Southeast Asia there was a mixture of Malay land-based sultanates and shifting fluid Malay maritime sultanates. The exchanges undertaken by the European traders were ordered by the sets of expectations current within those Asian trading networks within which they now moved.

Europe and the Demands of Empire

The development of mercantile and later industrial capitalism within Europe was to have profound consequences not only for the peoples of Europe but also, in time, for the peoples of East Asia. The theorists of the early modern period, the late eighteenth and early nineteenth century, correctly observed that the capitalist system within which they lived had two key characteristics: it was both extremely dynamic and progressive (which is to say that it continually increased the demands it made upon its existing population and also sought to expand so as to draw in further populations). In simple terms, the system became more efficient at home and expanded overseas.

The irruption of the mercantile and, later, industrial capitalist system within East Asia remade the economies, societies, cultures and polities of the existing countries. The same process that remade medieval Europe went on to remake the ancient civilizations of East Asia. The whole process, in both regions, can be characterized as the shift to the modern world. In Europe this was achieved at the behest of rising social groups, (merchants, traders and the inhabitants of urban centres) whereas in East Asia the key actors were outsiders; the traders, missionaries, functionaries and so on of European powers.

The material interlinkages of this period involved the slow deepening of trade relations. The European interest in East Asia began with trading voyages in the late medieval period, around the fifteenth century. The products brought back were exotic, high-value goods such as spices, silks and other tropical products. The Europeans primarily traded precious metals for these (as they had no other goods to trade). At this time the Europeans represented marginal players within the Asian trading pattern. However, the expansion of mercantile capitalism in Europe generated a wider spread of tradable goods – some metal manufactures, for example – and technological advance, in particular in military matters, which allowed the Europeans to assert themselves within the East Asian region. The original voyages of trade had involved a few ships, calling at established local ports and then leaving. The presence of Europeans was thus a minor and temporary matter. However, as the European economy developed they were able to sustain larger trading links and steadily establish more permanent bases in East Asia.

The key shift in the material interchange between Europe and Asia came, in two phases, where local patterns of production were altered to provide greater supplies to Europe. The first phase encompassed the assertion of European political/administrative power in the region (with moves towards what was to become the colonial system) which allowed the development of a plantation agriculture based on established crops. The second phase saw the development of industrial capitalism in Europe, which generated a new schedule of demands upon the East Asian economy; for example, plantation agriculture, with new crops such as rubber, or the development of mines to exploit local minerals. The slow process of European expansion within East Asia had serious implications for the elites and for the peoples of East Asia. There was a developing schedule of manufactured goods from Europe and a range of recreational narcotics (tobacco, alcohol and opium). The process of inter-change became asymmetric, the cultural gradient running steeply from Europe to Asia. The Asian economies were reconstructed (in places at great cost to the local people, as with the substitution in India of local cloth production with imports from Lancashire, or in Java where the Dutch system of producing sugar came to be characterized in the USA as analogous to slavery). One aspect of this reconstruction was the flow of migrants within East Asia to work in the new European-sponsored industries.

The discursive shifts during this period involved the creation of a new elaborate colonial discursive framework, whereby the 'exotic other' within the ancient sophisticated civilization became the 'degraded other', a mere servant of European masters. The cultural gradient was reversed. The process can be elaborated into a series of elements, the tales told by various agent groups: traders, missionaries, administrators, soldiers, adventurers, politicians and so on. The whole ensemble develops over time into the bombastic jingoism of the later years of the colonial era; the period when, as Barraclough puts it, 'Asia seemed to have gone under for good'.[4] However, the reaction of the Asian peoples was not passive. In East Asia we find the local counterpart, the discourses of reaction to the demands of incoming mercantile/industrial capitalism. If we distinguish mass and elite, the former work within the sphere of everyday resistance, they deploy the 'weapons of the weak'. As for the elite, there are a variety of responses: incomprehension, resistance and accommodation.

In China the dynastic centre did not understand the implications of the arrival of the Europeans. It sought to involve them in the Sinocentric tribute system. The Europeans used war to force trading treaties on the Chinese government. A key trading good was opium. Chinese government resistance met with further wars and the country was slowly made into a quasi-colony. A series of reactions was produced: the self-strengthening movement; the Boxer Rebellion and the nationalism of Sun Yat-sen. A similar situation prevailed in Japan, where the existing Shogunal government could not contrive a plausible response to the demands of the foreigners. However, Japanese political agents had the lesson of China to consider and argument moved from an anti-barbarian stance, to accommodation/conciliation, through to emulation. After the regime collapsed, the incoming Meiji government inaugurated a programme of national economic and security development. A series of strands of thinking can be identified: samurai reaction ('expel the barbarians'); Shinto nationalism, emperor worship and, later, state Shinto; the progressive stance of Fukuzawa; early pan-Asianism (the business of 'Japan's orient'[5]) and the pragmatic borrowing of the Meiji state (economic, military, social and political modernization). After the triple intervention, there came a renewed nationalistic response and the first step towards the militarized society of the 1930s, the consequences of which resonate down to the present day.

In the other parts of East Asia we can find a similar pattern. In Korea, the country resisted the outsiders and then became a sphere of contestation between China, Russia and Japan. The latter was successful, and the Korean shift to the modern world was initiated in the context of a Japanese colonial system. Modern Korean nationalism thus began as resistance to Japanese colonial rule. In Southeast Asia there were similar reactions: in the Philippines, with discussion of identity looking to disentangle the American and the Filipino; in the Dutch East Indies, with the PKI and Serekat Islam looking for independence; and, in Malaya, the early growth of Malay nationalism in the late 1930s.

The formal mechanisms saw the slow process of establishing colonial rule. The nature of colonial rule varied in details but it invariably privileged the European/American ruling minority. There were some concessions, such as indirect rule or a variety of accommodations (for example, the system in Singapore of a 'Chinese office' to control immigration, prostitution and link-up to secret societies, or the continuation in Malaya of Sultanates and religious law) but the core of the relationship was clear, colonial overlordship.

European Eclipse, American Hegemony and Asian Recovery, Phase I: The 1950s

The Pacific War inaugurated the final phases of colonial empire in East Asia: for the Europeans, the disruptions of war dispossessed them; so too the Americans; and, for the Japanese, military success was short lived. In the period of confusion a new balance of political actors emerged. The European withdrawal from empire took place over the late 1940s and 1950s. The hegemony of the USA was extended throughout non-socialist East Asia. The period also saw the start of East Asian economic reconstruction and political recovery, as a group of indigenous nationalist leaders emerged to take power within a region which was now quickly subject to one overriding divide: that of the cold war division between an American-centred sphere and a socialist sphere centred on China.

The material interlinkages of this period saw the beginnings of the development of the East Asian regional economy, which involved extensive US aid to Japan, South Korea and Taiwan. In Southeast Asia decolonization began. Thereafter, European involvement in the development of the region was slight. A key economic relationship began after the 'reverse course' between the USA and Japan, which marked the beginnings of economic recovery and advance in Japan. The Japanese model of national development came to be influential around the East Asian region.

The discourses of the period involved, for Europeans/Americans: (i) the rhetoric of cold war (defending the free world); (ii) the rhetoric of decolonization and nation-building (discharging a responsibility); and (iii) the rhetoric of internationalism (in the context of early UN-focused optimism). Thereafter, the US had specific exchanges with South Korea, Taiwan and Japan. The ensemble of preoccupations had, of course, an Asian counterpart. The discourse of the period for East Asians involved: (i) aspirations to nation-statehood (for those looking to decolonization); (ii) aspirations to socialism (for China, after 1949); and (iii) an economic nationalism in Japan, (including aspirations to regional leadership, 'flying geese', and claims to non-Asian semi-Western status) which later proved influential throughout the region.

There were formal mechanisms: (i) new relationships of new nation-states; (ii) SEATO (Southeast Asia Treaty Organization); (iii) Japan–US treaty; and (iv) in Europe, the EEC was established in 1957 (a development of the earlier coal and steel community) to address the realities of the need to pool resources and prevent a recurrence of war in Europe.

Europe/Asia Rising; From the Sixties to the End of the Short Twentieth Century

The end of the Second World War saw the USA as the pre-eminent economic, military and political power within the global system. In both Europe and East Asia the USA was a key centre to which all shades of domestic opinion looked. It was an economic centre, a military centre, a political centre and a cultural centre. However, the period of US pre-eminence came to an end. One contributory factor was the rise of powerful economies in both Europe and East Asia. In the former, a key vehicle was the machinery of the European Economic Community and, in the latter, it was the role of Japanese capital and, later, Chinese capital within East Asia. As Eric Hobsbawm's 'short twentieth century' came to an end, it became apparent that the bipolar cold war world was giving way to a more complex pattern involving multiple powerful centres.

The period of 'Europe/Asia rising' saw a series of significant shifts in the global political–economic balance. The countries of East Asia continued the economic rapid advance of earlier years. The Japanese economy emerged as a regional core with linkages throughout East Asia. The role of Japanese and NIC (newly industrialized country) capital in building regional production networks has been highly significant. Yet, this is not the only significant circuit of capital. The role of Chinese and overseas capital in the region, which has tended to flow into commercial activities of a more service-oriented kind, has also been very important. Over this period, the relationship between East Asia and both the USA and the European Union has developed. The USA has provided a relatively open market for East Asian exports over the years, although with Japan, in particular, there has been significant trade friction. The East Asian region has also run surpluses with its European trading partners. In this case it is important to note the early role of the EEC in encouraging intra-European trade. The European Union now constitutes a powerful economic bloc. As yet, however, the linkages between Europe and Asia are relatively weak.

The discursive pattern of the period can be summarily grasped in terms of a trio of interacting schemas, each with their changing institutional vehicles: the US-sponsored discourse of cold war, the free world versus state socialism; the Asian discourse of national development and the rise of the notion of the developmental state; and the newer discourses of regionalism, certainly crucial in the European Union. The discourse of cold war offered an interpretive and legitimating framework for US involvement in East Asia throughout the 1950s and 1960s. However, the defeat in Vietnam led to revisions in US thinking, including a partial rapprochement with China. The policy shifts inaugurated by Deng Xiaoping entailed a further diminution of the salience of the rhetoric of cold war. The key terms in which changes in East Asia were understood, increasingly came to centre on economic advance; in particular, the developmental state-ordered pursuit of export-oriented industrialization. The end of the cold war in Europe, an historically abrupt episode, saw a further diminution in the significance of cold war thinking and, as commentators looked for new patterns, the importance of regionalism was grasped. It is this discourse which, in significant measure, now shapes contemporary debate.

Europe/Asia Relations in the Contemporary Global System

The nature of the contemporary global system is still being debated, while its contours continue to alter and present policymakers, analysts and peoples of Asia and Europe with new sets of issues and concerns. More than a decade has already passed since the end of the cold war was heralded by the destruction of the Berlin Wall in 1989, and yet the 38th parallel dividing the two Koreas (North and South) remains to be breached at the beginning of the 21st century. At the same time, however, East Asia and Europe are frequently referred to as two key pillars in the contemporary global economy, and their mutual identification as regions is rarely challenged. Nevertheless, that they constitute different forms of region is frequently acknowledged: the European Union accommodates a coherent integrative framework (embodied in its Commission, Parliament and Council) in which supranational structures sit alongside continuing intergovernmental processes; while Asia houses only loose regional structures, the representatives of which eschew European-style integration.

The material linkages which now bond European and East Asian networks are plainly evident: trade between the two regions by the mid-1990s surpassed that of Asia and the US, while foreign direct investment had reached an all-time high. When the European Union became involved in the Korean

Peninsula Energy Development Organization (KEDO) in 1995 and, in the same year, published its *Towards a New Asia Strategy* document, it was clear that European concerns extended beyond their own backyard. Asian governments, for their part (especially Japan), took part in international efforts to assist in post-conflict nation-building following crises in Bosnia and Kosovo during the 1990s. Such cooperative initiatives were undertaken not only in order to secure future economic advantages in those regions but also in recognition of the globalized nature of contemporary issues, from regulating international trade and finance, to the prevention of environmental degradation, to the need for regional and interregional stability (in dealing with issues such as East Timor and Aceh in Indonesia, tensions between China and Taiwan, and the possible reunification of North and South Korea). At the same time, the Internet, mass and cheaper transport capabilities, the widespread availability of the national and international media, phenomenal flows of migrants and tourists within and across continents, and the global export of national consumer products from Scottish whisky to Pokemon have expanded the material conditions for Europe–Asia interaction to levels previously unimaginable.

These changing conditions have been accompanied by a novel contradiction in the discourses which underpin region-to-region exchanges. Previous phases witnessed the shift from one set of discursive patterns to another, whereas the current system houses multiple discourses simultaneously. It does so because different levels of understanding and recognition belong to diverse modes and principles of engagement. On an economic level, the rise of the Asian tigers and rapid developments seen in Asia during the 1980s evoked ideas of Asia as a threat and challenge to European trade interests, as well as notions of an equal partnership to harness mutual interests. However, whilst the postcolonial discourse of donor–recipient relations was said to be obsolete, European reactions against Asia's apparent 'crony capitalism' during the financial crises after June 1997 reinforced earlier stereotypes. In terms of the idea of 'region' itself, moreover, the partnership of equals recognized within the ASEM process is not replicated in intraregional interpretations of the term; indeed, Asian representatives frequently portray Europe as the legalistic opposition to their own attempts to create a unique region imbued with 'Asian values'. The current period, in this way, represents a time of negotiation, rather than compromise, between different conceptualizations of the development of region, as both consequence of, and resistance to, globalizing trends. These forces of tension are subsumed within the idea that Asia and Europe sit at the base of an isosceles triangle of economic and political interests in some kind of new tripolar world. In those trilateral terms, not only are the kinds of region left unproblematized, but Asia–Europe relations will continue to be viewed as the poor relation to US–Asia and US–Europe affairs.

The growing number of exchanges between representatives of Asia and Europe, and the different discourses which underpin them, are mediated by an increasing number of formal mechanisms, within and between Asia and Europe. In the 1990s alone, the ASEAN Regional Forum and the Asia–Europe Meeting (ASEM) have ensured regular high-level discussion between officials from most East Asian and EU states. These developments have also represented the formation of an increasingly significant voice for the organs of the EU itself, particularly the president of the European Commission, and demonstrate the gradual development of a 'European voice' as the EU more and more becomes synonymous with the idea of Europe itself. As it expands to include up to ten new member states in the next few years, very few parts of the European continent will, in fact, be left out of the Union's structures.

Within Asia, there is debate as to whether the proliferation of regional and subregional formal groupings contributes to, or potentially threatens, the further consolidation of existing fora such as ASEAN. The formation of the ARF and ASEM, as well as participation by East Asians within other meetings such as APEC, gives greater weight to the existence of an Asian grouping that comprises ASEAN alongside China, Japan and South Korea: the so-called 'Asian Ten'. Once representing the membership only of Malaysian Prime Minister Mahathir's contentious East Asian Economic Caucus (EAEC), this identification of Asia has now become formalized within other groupings, to the extent that Japanese reticence has been overcome and legitimacy sought for it to represent a distinctly 'Asian Way' of doing business. The necessity of competing with other regional groupings such as NAFTA (as well as groups within Latin America and Africa) enhances the demand for collective action at the regional level. Both Europe and Asia, in different and unique ways, are responding to that challenge and, in the process, have established a regular multilevel dialogue between themselves.

Developing the Agenda: in Summary

The relationship between Europe and Asia has developed over a long period of time. A key vehicle for reflection on the issue, in the years following the end of the cold war, has been the notion of regionalism and regional interlinkages. At this point we can turn to consider just what is seen to be at stake in these debates.

CURRENT CONCERNS

The foregoing material enables a final set of reflections, covering much of the same ground but focused on three questions: (i) the nature of current concerns;

(ii) who is concerned with the matter of regional interlinkages?; and (iii) what are the implications of ongoing research?

The schedule of current concerns is large. They can be schematically ordered around the interests of three key groups; political actors, policy analysts and scholars.

In the wake of the end of the cold war and the shift in political and policy scientific interest from geostrategy to geoeconomics, the familiar political agendas of the countries of Asia and Europe (internal and international politics) are reorienting to embrace the shifting structural patterns of power within and between the regions.

There is a series of policy-analytic debates running in both regions (although it must be noted that East Asia does not have the elaborate formal institutional mechanisms of consultation and decision which are found in Europe): (i) how to conceive and order economic exchanges (trade and financial links); (ii) how to conceive and order social exchanges (patterns of migration, diasporic networks and travel); how to conceive and order security issues (patterns of treaty obligations and the balance of forces within the regions) and cultural issues (the implications of transnational or transregional patterns).

In respect of the ongoing debate about regions and their interlinkages it seems that we can draw out a series of lessons.

In the realm of political life we are reminded that competition between powerful political actors will continue to define and order the future of the European and East Asian regions.

In the territory of policy analysis we are reminded: (i) that economic interchange between discrete regions is a matter of negotiating 'deep access'[6]; (ii) that the ill-advised and disruptive US drive to secure its Enlightenment project of a global market–liberal system has not been discontinued[7]; (iii) that, as the region develops, the issue of dealing with interregional and trans-regional social networks becomes more important; and (iv) that in the sphere of cultural exchange we are reminded that the assumptions of the priority of the USA/West, which have been familiar in the recent past, are now untenable.

In the territory of scholarship we are reminded of a clutch of awkward problems, which include (to cast the matter in terms of the classical European tradition) the fact that social scientific analysts inhabit discrete cultural and intellectual traditions, the conceptual vocabularies of which are the basis for exercises in argument making, where such arguments are oriented to a variety of tasks. In summary, a necessary condition for scholarship is reflexive criticism. It can be argued that this implies (for Europeans and those working with reference to these materials) a return to the resources of the classical European tradition as the basis for new analyses of shifting patterns of complex change.

THE CHAPTERS IN THIS VOLUME

The roles of regions and their interlinkages have become an increasingly salient part of contemporary political, economic and social interaction, and the foregoing sections have demonstrated that greater social scientific reflections will be required to make sense of them. It is to this task that the current volume turns its attention, by offering a series of chapters which address the issues sketched above from a number of perspectives. They are grouped around a series of key issues and, while they deal with specific elements of Asia–Europe interlinkages, they contribute as a whole to the greater understanding of the multifaceted nature of interregional linkages today.

Part I sets up the nature of the debate, with papers by Stephanie Lawson and John Clammer each addressing the cultural dimension of Asia–Europe relations. Lawson reminds us that 'to speak of Asia–Europe relations is to speak of thousands of years of history', and insists that the concepts of 'Asia' and 'Europe' cannot be understood without problematizing the 'historical particularities' and 'cultural specificities'. Clammer reminds the reader that identity 'in any simple sense has been shattered by the cultural impact of globalization'. These two contributors thus establish some of the principal discursive parameters for the rest of the volume.

Lawson considers the difficulties of analysing the linkages between Europe and Asia in an intellectual environment that has moved away from the received universalist aspirations of conventional Western scholarship and has moved on to stress, and perhaps overstress, the particularity of local cultures. The problem of adequately grasping the complex logics of discrete forms of life which nevertheless engage with regional and global structures is pursued against a background of recent debates in international relations. Lawson suggests a 'cultural politics' approach that looks at the ways in which the distribution of ideas through the social world mirrors (and indeed contributes to maintaining) the distribution of power through that society, the result being that patterns of power within the social world find parallel expression in the familiar discourses of social life. The changing values of the terms, Western, European or Asian can be tracked in terms of the notion of cultural power, and insight gained into new constellations of power within the European and Asian spheres.

Clammer picks up these themes and looks to rework the ideas of culture and global system such that the nature of culture (the production and reproduction of meaning in the context of ordinary life) and the deeply interrelated nature of the emergent global system can be acknowledged. Clammer draws his reflections from the spheres of anthropology and sociology and, in particular, engages with debates relating to postcolonial theory, the world system, globalization and the local reception of translocal cultural flows. The global system can be read as a hugely complex network of material and cultural flows. It is within this polycentric context that people make their own lives. The issue becomes, in this discussion, one of deciphering the ways in which local logics, the processes vehicling local cultures and forms of life, negotiate the demands of a protean capitalism.

Part II of the book turns to the material linkages which characterize contemporary political, economic and social relations between the two regions. Hans-Dieter Evers and Markus Kaiser integrate discursive and material dimensions of Asia–Europe linkages by examining the comparisons and contrasts between the old and new forms of the Silk Road. Paul Lim and Julie Gilson examine the institutional dimensions of contemporary Asia–Europe linkages. Lim describes in detail the background to the most recent forms of institutional developments within the Asia–Europe Meeting (ASEM), while Gilson assesses how ASEM contributes to regional identification through functional institutional formation as well as through cognitive integration.

Evers and Kaiser turn to a novel area of concern in a post-cold war development: the process of the reconstitution of the old Silk Road. As with the other chapters in this volume, Evers and Kaiser are clear that identities, linkages and regions grow out of the mundane business of ordinary life and they therefore apply the intellectual resources of the actor–network approach in order to detail the business of the reconstitution of the Silk Road, a long trading network which links Europe and Asia not along the familiar trade routes around the Horn of Africa and through the archipelago of Southeast Asia but along a land bridge that runs through the geographical heart of the Asian continent. The trade link is segmented: traders work along a part of the route, passing goods and ideas along a network which, in significant respects, remains concerned with international petty trade. However, against this, there are larger-scale activities, ranging from oil-pipeline plans to further rail links and developing patterns of investment, as money from Europe and Asia moves along the network to find work in the newly opened areas of Central Asia. It may be that a new macroregion, a new geocultural space, 'Eurasia' is in the process of being made but, as yet, it has no obvious vehicles. Evers and Kaiser find no evidence of the discursive or institutional vehicles of macroregional construction; there is no 'European Union' or 'Asia-Pacific' in prospect in the activities of the traders along the new silk road.

Lim directly addresses the matter of elite macroregional definition in his treatment of the Asia-Europe Meeting (ASEM) as displaying both the concerns of actors within the sphere of high politics and the quite particular character of elite-level institutions. It is a world remote from the sphere of petty trade but it does have its own constitutive routines. Lim recalls that ASEM was proposed by Prime Minister Goh as a way of establishing a link between Asia and Europe that would balance the links both had with North America. The first meeting was held in Bangkok in 1996, the second in London in 1998 and the third in Seoul in 2000. Lim details the elite political players in ASEM – foreign ministers, European Union representatives and numerous officials – and considers the extent to which ASEM has developed an institutional structure notwithstanding its characterization as an informal meeting. It is clear that a minimum coordination is a necessary condition of its functioning, and it is equally clearly developing an elaborate agenda of topics for discussion. However, Lim notes that interest in ASEM is uneven; that is, some countries in Europe and Asia pay more attention than others. For both Asia and Europe the focus is ostensibly pragmatic, that is related to trade, but the wider concerns and consequences of the meetings cannot be disregarded. Lim points out that ASEM has called into being Mahathir's EAEC, since the countries with which the European Union talks are precisely the Asian countries of East Asia. It may well be that ASEM will continue to act as a low-level catalyst in the development of both Europe/Asia relations and the further crystallization of identities within each region.

Gilson pursues the implications of the institutionalization of ASEM in terms of the intellectual varieties of institutionalization on offer and their implications for the future of ASEM. Looking to the resources of international relations, she distinguishes what, for present purposes, we can call functional and cognitive institutionalization. The former looks to organizational machineries – meetings, secretariats, agendas and so on; the latter looks to the development of mutual understandings of common activities and shared problems. The history of ASEM can thereafter be reviewed in these terms, in order to discover how the two versions of institutionalization function and what they imply for the future of ASEM. Gilson argues that the sphere of elite-level macroregional identity construction is best understood as a cognitive endeavour. It can be granted that some functional integration is needed, else the meetings will not take place, but this risks allowing debates and exchanges to become fixed in received terms, whereas the real value of ASEM might just be that it opens up new ways for the participants to interact in the slow process of interregional definition. Gilson suggests that what is needed may be a notion, borrowed from the politics of ASEAN, of the 'ASEM Way'.

Part III addresses the politics of economic linkages, with five chapters covering specific aspects of their relations in order to highlight the different forms activity takes. Sum, Ngai-Ling takes an explicitly material–discursive look at the formation of the 'Asian Crisis' through the interplay of competing actors and discourses as part of the restructuring of the global–regional–national political economy. Zhao, Chenggen and Sean McGough focus upon some of the principal difficulties found during attempts to restructure the

Chinese economy, and offer a salutary lesson in the need to accommodate specific historical and socioeconomic contexts for a deepening of Europe–Asia linkages to take place. They assess the need for the continuing role of a strong state in the economic reform and development of the country, even in the face of contrary demands. Tseng, Su-Ling offers an examination of two of the major actors that contribute to the formation of material and institutional linkages by looking at the European Union's commercial policy towards China. Tong, Jia-Dong contrasts 'institutional'- and 'market'- oriented models of economic integration and considers how they relate to EU–China trade. Finally, Peter Preston turns to the challenge of understanding the competing national, regional and global factors that constitute East Asia in the new millennium.

Sum analyses the politics of economic interchange in a discussion of the Asian financial crisis. The material–discursive approach allows an analysis of the changing balance of political–economic power within the region and between the region and the global system to be examined. The key actors can be identified and the political–cultural projects they are variously pursuing can be detailed. The out-turn of these politically mediated processes constitute the familiar world of regional and interregional political–economic activity. In this perspective, the recent financial crisis should be explained neither in terms of crony capitalism nor global financial system failures – the two most familiar contending tales – but rather as the result of the unstable relationship between a Japan-centred regional production network and the US-centred financial system (a dollar bloc). A series of adventitious circumstances, in particular the emergence of China and the downturn in the domestic Japanese economy, contributed further strains, and when the Thai economy ran into difficulties the entire regional/transregional structure failed. Sum argues that the interesting question for the future is how the different visions for the future of the region will be resolved. It is clear that Japan and China have ideas about how the region might develop, and equally clear that these ideas are at variance with the US/IMF neoliberal project.

Zhao and McGough consider the situation in contemporary China as the economic reform process inaugurated by Deng Xiaoping continues to unfold, bringing changes throughout Chinese society. The process of economic reform has been widely embraced, and as the state-directed system has declined the newer market-based activities have prospered. The changes have not been without cost, evidenced, for example, in rural–urban migration, increases in inequality within and between regions and, most broadly, a diminution of the established authority of the ruling party. However, Zhao and McGough point out that the changes unfolding within China were initiated by the ruling party, and they consider this apparent paradox in terms of the distinction between totalitarianism and authoritarianism. They argue that a key aspect of the reform programme of Deng Xiaoping was precisely the shift from a Maoist totalitarian state to the rational authoritarianism of Deng. The reform of the party and state was a priority for Deng and the upshot was that a number of reformers committed to economic development came to hold power. The authors comment that this rational authoritarianism has governed China's development over the last twenty years and is likely to do so for the foreseeable future. The heart of the Chinese government's project is thus a dual concern for stability and economic development.

Tseng turns to the detail of the politics of economic advance in a discussion concerning the ways in which the European Union formulates its commercial policy towards China. The economic exchange between the European Union and China has been growing in recent years and negotiations in respect of trade are crucial. It is on the basis of elaborate detailed agreements that trade relations are conducted. The process of policymaking is, therefore, of considerable interest. Tseng looks at the European Union's commercial policymaking and argues that it should be understood in terms of three levels of activity: first, the European Union level (the formal structure of decision making, the levels of relevant expertise and the efficiency of the organization); second, the Europe/China level (with formal commercial agreements and the more general context of relations); and, third, the global level (where GATT and WTO systems bind both the European Union and China. The process of commercial policymaking is both complex and contingent; the players in this particular game are many and their objectives shifting. It seems clear that any resultant statement or agreement in respect of policy will represent the contingent outcome of fluid and shifting political and policymaking processes.

Tong pursues the issue of trade relations by examining the linkages between the European Union and China through the prism of the debate among economists concerning the business of international economic integration. He distinguishes two models of integration: the institutional and the market. The former looks to build formal institutional structures to order economic integration amongst the participants. The participants derive benefits from the integration which are not available to non-participants. Tong points out that the greater the integration the more it becomes possible to extend the benefits of participation to non-participants. The alternative strategy is market integration, which proceeds not by formal institution building but by trade liberalization measures. These benefits can be extended to non-participants, as the 'disbenefit' of the free-rider phenomena can be disregarded. In terms of popular terminology, the distinction here is between closed and open regionalism. In this light, Tong considers the performance of the European Union and APEC, and commends the latter model to Europeans. A change in policy by the European Union, Tong argues, would encourage economic growth within Europe and foster more rapid growth in its trading partners.

Overall, Tong sees opportunities for economic growth in Europe, East Asia and China which are presently unrealized as a result of Europe's preference for closed regionalism.

Part IV concludes with a tentative assessment of the potential and need for further research agendas to deal with this important aspect of contemporary political, economic and social affairs. Preston returns to the earlier themes of establishing agendas of enquiry alongside the production of substantive statements. The recent intense interest in regional development is located in the shifting political environment of the post-cold war period, which has seen a wide-ranging debate in respect of the future of the global system. It is clear that some commentators are disposed to affirm the continuing (or enhanced) status of the USA (and its allies). The discursive construct of 'globalization' is yoked to this purpose. However, there is much evidence accumulating in favour of the importance of regions. It is now possible to point to economic, social, cultural and political networks which find increasing expression in discourses of regionalism. The relative eclipse of the USA is paralleled by the rise of the European Union and East Asia. The success of the EU is not in doubt. In respect of East Asia the recent financial crisis has been seen by some outside commentators as marking the end of the miracle but any even-handed overview of macroregional developments must issue in an optimistic view of the future. The countries of East Asia are economically powerful and are likely to become more so in the years ahead.

CONCLUSION: EUROPE/ASIA AGENDAS

The end of the cold war has allowed observers to register the growing tripolar character of the global system; the development of what has been termed the dollar, yen and euro zones. In each zone, or region, there are powerful national economies, which are increasingly trading amongst themselves. There are also distinctive patterns of social life as well as elites increasingly disposed to view regionalism as an element of their political–cultural projects. This realization manifests itself differently in the different regions.

In Europe it is a positive matter, as the continent moves towards integration at home and emerges from the shadow of the USA on the global stage. It is clear that the detail of the political–cultural project of the European Union is in many respects either not worked out or represents merely an agglomeration of elements taken from various places/times (for example, the French statism of the Brussels machinery (Larry Siedentop's point[8]), or the Thatcherite neoliberal flavour of the move to the single market). A strong argument has been made for the 'democratic deficit' in Europe – both institutionally and in terms of the construction of a European public. Be this as it may, the overarching tendency of the European Union seems to be towards a federal system. Over the long years of the Union's construction this has been the abiding political goal of the elite.

In the USA the tripolar system seems to be viewed as a threat. As the cold war came to an end, the neoliberal idea of globalization came to fill the now vacant political/ideological space. The notion of globalization posits a future convergence of presently diverse economies, societies, cultures and polities upon the model of free-market liberal-democratic industrial capitalism. The USA intends to sit at the heart of a spread of institutional vehicles, all turned to the neoliberal project, such as NAFTA, APEC and the redirected machineries of the old Bretton Woods system; the IMF, IBRD and WTO. However, it is difficult to see the Europeans and East Asians collaborating in a project designed, in essence, to make the world safe for American multinational companies. One might, therefore, anticipate that there will be more conflicts between the USA and those cast in the role of partners in the great neoliberal project. One area of conflict will be trade relationships; indeed, these are already visible in familiar US complaints about Japan and, by process of extension, in the new patterns of dispute with the European Union.

In East Asia the debate about the future of the global system seems, in contrast to the Europeans and Americans, to be somewhat clouded. It is true, crucially, that East Asia is the least integrated of the three regions; indeed, it is possible (if implausible) to make an argument in favour of increasing regional disharmony and conflict. It may well be that the extent of formal regional integration is slight in comparison with Europe and the USA but the development of regional economic, social and political networks continues apace. It is on the basis of these pragmatic routine linkages that discourses of regional integration could develop. One could argue that the first signs are already visible. The Asian financial crisis has shown the regional elites just how vulnerable they are to uncontrolled global financial flows. It has also shown them that the USA – hitherto regarded as a benign hegemon, at least by sometime cold war allies – was perfectly happy to pursue its own neoliberal agenda without concern for the domestic Asian implications. One might expect to find a diminution of hitherto expressed enthusiasm for deregulation and privatization – those key neoliberal shibboleths – and an increased interest in regional solutions to regional problems (as with the idea for an AMF).

It is in this novel tripolar global context that the linkages between the European Union and East Asia assume importance. The elucidation of these linkages – material and discursive – is a key task for social scientific analysis. The editors appreciate that these are difficult issues but hope that the material in this volume will make some contribution to the debate.

NOTES

1. The member states of the European Union are as follows: Austria, Belgium, Denmark, Finland, France, Germany, Greece, Italy, Ireland, Luxembourg, the Netherlands, Portugal, Spain, Sweden and the United Kingdom. The region of East Asia includes: Brunei, Burma, Cambodia, China, Hong Kong SAR, Indonesia, Japan, Laos, Malaysia, Philippines, Singapore, South Korea, Taiwan, Thailand and Vietnam.
2. Respectively, Asia Pacific Economic Cooperation (APEC), ASEAN Free Trade Area (AFTA), Asia Europe Meeting (ASEM).
3. A. G. Frank (1998), *Re-Orient: Global Economy in the Asian Age*, Berkeley, Ca: University of California Press.
4. G. Barraclough (1964), *An Introduction to Contemporary History*, Harmondsworth: Penguin.
5. S. Tanaka (1993), *Japan's Orient: Rendering Pasts into History*, Berkeley, Ca.: University of California Press.
6. J. Zysman (1996), 'The Myth of a "global economy": enduring national foundations and emerging regional realities', *New Political Economy* **1** (2).
7. J. Gray (1998), *False Dawn: The Delusions of Global Capitalism*, London: Granta.
8. L. Siedentop (2000), *Democracy in Europe*, London: Allen Lane.

PART II

Setting Up the Debate

2. The cultural politics of contemporary Asia–Europe relations

Stephanie Lawson

INTRODUCTION

> The rise of Asia is dramatically changing the world balance of economic power. The World Bank estimates that half the growth in the global economy will ensure that, by the year 2000, one billion Asians will have significant consumer spending power and, of these, 400 million will have average disposable incomes as high, if not higher, than their European or US contemporaries.[1]

This statement, contained in a report commissioned by the European Union (EU) in 1994, demonstrates a focus fixed squarely on Europe's economic future in the Asian region. Since then, a fomalization of Asia–Europe relations has emerged in the form of an Asia–Europe Meeting process (ASEM), first convened in Bangkok in 1996. ASEM involves all member countries of the EU on the one side, and Asian countries from Burma through to Japan on the other. The original idea for the Bangkok summit had been hatched by the Singaporean Prime Minister, Goh Chok Tong, in October 1994 – barely three months after the release, in July, of the EU Commission's report – and it is partly through Singapore's activism that the other ASEAN countries and, subsequently, the leading East Asian nations of Japan, China and South Korea were drawn behind the project.[2] Just as notable are the countries excluded from the process: in Europe, all non-EU members have been left out and 'Asia' does not include the South Asian countries of India, Pakistan, Sri Lanka and Bangladesh nor, on the other side of the region, Australia and New Zealand.

The new interest in Asia–Europe relations and linkages, including issues of inclusions and exclusions, has brought into focus a number of important conceptual issues for scholars as well as for the policy community. Beyond the pragmatic salience of security and economic interests, the contemporary phase of Asia–Europe relations is also underscored by broad historical and 'civilizational' issues. Indeed, to speak of Asia–Europe relations is to speak of thousands of years of history, with themes ranging from the political economy of exploration and trade to formal colonialism and Orientalism, and thence to postcolonialism, Occidentalism and the prospect of a coming 'Pacific Century' in which the Asian region has been envisaged as displacing Europe or 'the West' as the dynamo of global economic activity.

These issues have also been highly influential in shaping contemporary questions about culture, identity, values, legitimacy, authenticity and representation, especially as they relate to regionalism. As Camroux and Lechervy have remarked, 'if it is accepted that a sense of Asian regionalism also involves questions of identity, values and a sentiment of being "neighbours", then the question of what is Asia takes on a fuller and deeper dimension'.[3] And we might well ask, at the same time, what constitutes 'Europe' as well as the broader entity known as 'the West' against which contemporary 'Asia' is so often constructed.

Such questions obviously cannot be answered by reference to any straightforward criteria provided by physical geography, or even by reference to political entities such as the European Union. 'Europe' is certainly much more than this late twentieth-century political construct. Nor can such questions be addressed by some simplistic reference to culture or civilization. While these criteria are certainly part of any definitional strategy, they are inevitably mediated by the political aspects of identity formation and representations of region – both of self and other – and a context of postcolonialism in which Eurocentrism and Orientalism, Occidentalism and a 'new Asianism' are key themes. These issues are also implicated in communitarian and cosmopolitan approaches to contemporary normative international relations theory.

The purpose of this chapter is to not so much to 'deal' with these issues as to identify some of the major problems that have been generated by them. In doing so, I shall look also at an approach to the study of Asia–Europe relations that incorporates a 'cultural politics' perspective. This approach is generally concerned with the exposure of implicit power relations in social, economic and political structures and institutions, especially in terms of inclusions and exclusions. Since the concept of 'culture' underscores all these issues and approaches, I shall start with a brief account of this concept, and how it relates to 'values', for these are clearly important for understanding the 'Asian values' debate, which, in turn, forms a central component of a 'new Asianism'.

CULTURE AND VALUES

There is now an abundance of contemporary literature on the culture concept, thanks largely to the significant expansion over the last twenty years or so of cultural studies. This follows an even more abundant anthropological literature that has been growing steadily for more than a hundred years and which itself has fed into the field of cultural studies. The culture concept has also come to occupy a central place in much contemporary international relations theorizing, and there seems little doubt that anthropological conceptions have had a strong influence here. I say conception*s*, in the plural, because I want to avoid the impression that there is a single anthropological conception of culture. Yet, however varied these may now be, a common point of departure shared by many traditional anthropological conceptions is that the notion of culture denotes a *whole* way of life as well as a *particular* way of life. The application of the term in this sense extends, of course, beyond the individual person. That is, 'culture' does not refer to the way of life of an individual, nor even of a family group – its application is reserved almost exclusively for a 'community'.

This much does not seem especially controversial, at least not until we come to defining the entity 'community' and determining what 'particularities' might attach to it, as well as the degree to which its 'wholeness' is compromised by the inevitable internal contradictions and tensions that mar the apparent homogeneity and equilibrium of practically any social formation. However, the most controversial issues that have usually been raised by the culture concept, especially in terms of normative international theory, derive from the relativizing properties that the concept now possesses. More specifically, it is an anthropological doctrine of cultural relativism, especially when pitted against universalist positions, that has underscored contemporary normative discourses about human rights, democracy, sovereignty, nationalism and self-determination: all of which are major issues in contemporary Asia–Europe relations.

Critics of cultural relativism note that it entails a tendency to totalize and reify 'culture', relying on a nineteenth-century notion of the concept as 'discrete and homogeneous, as the product of isolation, and as the basis of all difference and similarity between human beings'. It is constructed as 'internally uniform and hermetically bounded', and referred to 'as an entity, not as a process; as a noun, not a verb'.[4] 'Culture' is also seen as the sole source of moral and other values. So, in terms of normative issues – such as notions of what constitutes crime and appropriate punishment, how the community should be governed (and by whom), and how rights and duties are to be understood – the moral values that underscore these are seen as deeply embedded in the particular cultural properties of any given community. While some supporters of this view might mitigate the emphasis on difference between human communities that it entails with an acknowledgement of the presence of significant similarities across cultures and attendant moral value systems, the most radical version of cultural and moral relativism would see such value systems as ultimately incommensurable.

Whereas conventional anthropology has structured the world into local communities, conventional international relations theory has structured the world into sovereign states, and recognized these as the principal (if not the only) effective agents in an international sphere characterized by anarchy. Morality in this sphere, according to traditional realist theory, has no purchase. Morality can only be grounded within authoritative entities that not only set standards of behaviour in accordance with local normative values, but can also enforce them. Only entities possessing sovereign power – that is, states – can effectively do this. Morality is thus relative to the internal standards of each state in the international system. Realists therefore share with cultural relativists a theory which founds morality in particularistic entities (communities or states). And the idea that states are, in some sense or other, containers of culture is reinforced by common discursive practices. We often take the name of a state, say Thailand or Australia or Japan, and then speak of 'its' culture; that is, 'Thai culture' or 'Australian culture' or 'Japanese culture'.

A relativistic conception of culture and morality, which tends to conflate community and state, has also come to underscore at least some communitarian positions in international theory. 'Communitarianism' as a moralistic political doctrine has been promoted in recent years by a range of writers on state and society, including Amitai Etzioni, Daniel A. Bell and Henry Tam. The latter says that communitarianism sets itself against both authoritarianism and individualism and calls for a new agenda for politics and citizenship focusing on a more inclusive form of community.[5] Etzioni's emphatic call is for the restoration of civic virtues: 'for people to live up to their responsibilities and not merely focus on their entitlements'.[6] Michael Walzer is firm in his insistence that members of an 'historical community' inevitably shape their own institutions and laws and will 'necessarily produce a particular and not a universal way of life'.[7] Daniel A. Bell, writing with Kanishka Jayasura, looks specifically at the Asian region and invokes a general communitarian framework to provide a critique of the assumption that Western liberal-democratic models of government and politics, mired as they are in a strong tradition of individualism, are not necessarily appropriate for non-Western societies, like those found in East Asia, which carry an 'alternative cultural baggage'.[8] In normative international theory, communitarianism also stresses the idea of cultural difference. Once again, individualism is rejected as a basis for normative theory and communitarians argue from the premise that 'the self is embedded within a concrete set of social relations'. In turn, this means that 'the central source of moral values inheres in particularistic communities'. One conclusion to be drawn from this is that 'the demands of socially located ethics override the demands of abstract cosmopolitan morality'.[9]

Needless to say, all the theoretical positions outlined above – from the anthropological doctrine of cultural relativism, to realism in international relations, and to communitarianism in normative theory – are ranged against universalist versions of morality. I will not spend a great deal of time here setting out the basics of universalism. Suffice to say that universalism, as embodied in the cosmopolitan approach to normative international theory, repudiates the notion that morality resides only in specific historical communities or 'cultures' and cannot transcend the boundaries of these entities. Cosmopolitans are committed to the basic idea that, by virtue of their common humanity, people everywhere share attributes and needs and that this creates a common moral bond.[10] This by no means entails an absolutist position, nor does it commit cosmopolitans to adopting rigid universals in the application of moral theory. Indeed, both moderate cosmopolitans and communitarians tend to converge around a pluralistic median. But cosmopolitans certainly reject the one universal that is logically embraced by strong versions of relativism: and that is the relativity of all moral standards.

To summarize briefly, some of the implications of the general positions adopted by communitarians and cosmopolitans – especially in terms of international relations – as well as for the general themes of the present discussion are as follows. First, the 'political community' which communitarians endow with moral authority in international relations relates, generally speaking, to sovereign states. This accords with conventional realist theory, which similarly endows states with primacy both in terms of their status as actors in the international system as well with respect to their status as the only realm within which morality is possible. Supporters of the anthropological doctrine of cultural relativism do not necessarily endorse the legitimacy of states in this manner; indeed, anthropologists themselves have generally looked to far smaller, localized entities as the bearers of 'a culture'. Nonetheless, doctrines of cultural relativism are now commonly deployed at the level of the state. Cosmopolitans, on the other hand, while acknowledging that states have a certain legitimacy as actors in both domestic and international contexts, do not concede that states hold an automatic moral high ground on any given issue. Moreover, cosmopolitans will be among the first to point out that people are at most risk of violence and other abuses from the very state governments that are supposed to value them as human beings as well as members of 'the community'. And states – or at least their governments – while often claiming to encapsulate 'a culture' are most likely to do violence to the many small local communities or minority groups within their borders.

Beyond the level of the state or community, however, it has also become increasingly common to speak of much larger entities. Now, whole regions such as 'Asia' or 'Europe', or entities of even greater abstraction such as 'the West', are seen as possessing certain defining 'cultural' or 'civilizational' characteristics. Such characteristics have very significant implications for politics. 'The West', for example, is often depicted as the ultimate source of individualism, of liberal democracy, of 'Enlightenment values', 'rationalism', and so on. Thus, writers like Bell and Jayasura have argued that the entrenchment of liberalism prior to democratization gave Western liberal democracy its 'historically specific form', namely, a democracy 'shaped and structured within the limits set by liberal values and assumptions'.[11] Apart from the gross reduction of influences on the development of democracy to 'liberal values' – as if socialism, conservatism, nationalism and other ideologies have had little or no impact – 'the West' is presented as a simplified entity with definite characteristics which can be held up in contrast with an equally simplified depiction of Asia. For example, Bell and Jayasura say that 'Western' political understandings may be contrasted directly with those of East and Southeast Asia where much greater value is evidently placed on 'a substantive moral consensus' that denies or suppresses tendencies to moral pluralism and social diversity.[12]

The gross cultural entities on which such claims rest bring to mind Edward Said's well-known critique of Orientalism which deals with the mechanisms through which such constructs are imagined, manipulated, falsely opposed, and so on. It is also important to note that Huntington's 'clash of civilizations' thesis and his prognostications concerning the future bases of international conflict also depend on the positing of such entities. And the same devices are clearly evident in the 'Asian values' debate as well as a broader 'Asianism' which depends almost entirely on a dichotomous (re)construction of 'Asia' *vis-à-vis* 'Europe' and/or 'the West', but in terms which invert Said's original categories thereby giving rise to 'Occidentalism'. We shall look at some of these themes shortly but, before doing so, a few words on what is meant by 'cultural politics' are necessary.

THE DOMAIN OF CULTURAL POLITICS

'Cultural politics' is an approach to the study of power relations which has been applied in the study of such phenomena as class, gender and race. According to Jordan and Weedon, the authors of a major book on the subject[13], the 'culture' in cultural politics is most appropriately understood as encompassing literary and intellectual work, which, in the contemporary era, increasingly includes popular culture and the mass media. Jordan and Weedon are concerned to expose how culture, defined in these terms, has worked to exclude or marginalize certain classes of people. This focus has led the authors to reject other formulations of the culture concept as inappropriate or at least marginal to their specific concerns. The broad anthropological conception of culture as 'a particular way of life', they say, is not especially relevant. Given some of the problems with this conception, as outlined above, perhaps this is a good thing. But to ignore its influence – and indeed some of the important issues that it raises – is to confine the scope of a cultural politics approach far too narrowly.

Another important point arising from Jordan and Weedon's work, although not specifically stated, is that their analytical framework assumes that the domain of cultural politics is more or less contained within the boundaries of the state. That is, it is concerned largely with national societies. In this respect, it accords with traditional approaches to political science and international relations in which state boundaries have worked to define specific fields of enquiry and which have certainly separated issues into domestic and international realms. Yet some of the most important questions raised via a cultural politics approach transcend conventional boundaries. This is especially so when we look at the very perceptive way in which power relations are understood in a cultural politics approach:

> Whose culture shall be the official one and whose shall be subordinated? What cultures shall be regarded as worthy of display and which shall be hidden? Whose history shall be remembered and whose forgotten? What images of social life shall be projected and which shall be marginalized? What voices shall be heard and which be silenced? Who is representing whom and on what basis? THIS IS THE REALM OF CULTURAL POLITICS.[14]

Each one of these questions is vital, for example, to studies in the genre of Edward Said's *Orientalism*[15] as well as postcolonial studies more generally, both of which clearly transcend the sphere of 'national society'. Many of the same limitations apply in other fields as well, including cultural studies. An important recent exception comes from scholars working largely in the Asia-Pacific region.[16] The editor, in fact, states that:

> [H]aving persistently questioned cultural relations of power in local social formations for the past forty years, cultural studies is now undergoing a critical phase of internationalization ... very much in response to the changing dispositions and structure of global forces such as the transnationalization of culture of capital [and] the realignment of national states into regional super-states in the so-called post-Cold war era.[17]

Among this group, moreover, is a critical focus on what many of them perceive as a very strong element of ethnocentrism in both British and American cultural studies. But the most important point to note for present purposes is that the contributions to this volume give a much clearer sense of an approach which makes a concerted effort to transcend the national state and deal with issues that have salience beyond its borders.

The final point that needs to be made here is that what is common to both cultural studies and cultural politics is that 'culture' is political. It is not an innocent or neutral category: it is used as tactic, strategy and weapon in virtually all areas of political debate and struggle and all geopolitical arenas, including local, national, regional and global. Nowhere is this more evident than in the new Asianism – a phenomenon which arises from the historical and political context of Asia–Europe relations and which will undoubtedly influence many aspects of relations or linkages for some time to come.

THE NEW ASIANISM

According to Tessa Morris-Suzuki, the image of 'Asia' has come to possess an especially potent presence in the rhetoric of international politics in the post-cold war era. Of course, it has a much longer history, stretching back to at least the 1920s and 1930s when a pan-Asianist vision was shared by a number of thinkers from Japan through to the Dutch East Indies, India and Turkey. But in the 1990s, she says, a new version of pan-Asianism has emerged and is especially strong in East and Southeast Asia.

> While prewar pan-Asianism focused on the idea of a struggle for political liberation from Western imperialism, the new Asianism builds above all on the concept of an underlying set of shared cultural values: values which are believed to give a distinctive character to both the political and the economic destiny of the region.[18]

The new Asianism[19] embraces a number of elements, not all of which are necessarily compatible – and this is in the nature of any diffuse social movement. The idea of 'Asian values' is one component, and a significant one at that, but its role is limited to the extent that the 'Asian values' debate has been devoted largely to promoting a specific political agenda designed to delegitimate certain allegedly 'Western' values in defence of authoritarian political practices. Of course this is not how the actors themselves depict their motives and actions. Proponents of 'Asian values' are ostensibly concerned with countering hegemonic 'Western' discourses which they see as undermining the legitimacy and inherent worth of 'Asian' cultural traditions in many spheres of life. The general call is for the establishment of an alternative and ultimately more 'authentic' approach to a range of normative issues. This involves, among other things, setting out a working theory of cultural, and therefore moral, particularism based on a sense of 'Asian-ness'.

The intellectual resources for this are, somewhat ironically, provided by traditional anthropological approaches to culture and morality – in other words, by the resources of 'Western' social science itself. As a colleague and I have noted in a previous work, there is a strong case for arguing that the concepts which underpin 'Asian values' and identity are constructed very largely on the edifice of the 'Asia' studied by Western scholars. In looking at the concepts underpinning interpretive analyses of 'Asian political culture', for example, it is clear that these have been carried out mostly by Western scholars, and then imported back into the 'Asian values' paradigm by the political elites who promote it. The subject point promoted through this paradigm is, in fact, the product of revitalized traditional images that derive substantially from Western studies of the Orient.[20]

In any event, the new Asianism is wider than the 'Asian values' debate, for it embraces not simply the authoritarian defenders of non-democratic regimes, but a broader spectrum of actors who are concerned with establishing, in one way or another, an 'Asian' subjectivity. Moreover, whereas a major theme in the Asian values debate has been the cultural relativity of values, some strands of Asianism have promoted the superiority of Asian culture and values over and above those of the West. This is something which represents a repudiation of the basic premises of cultural relativism: that all cultures are 'different but equal'. Instead, the West has recently been depicted as an entity in serious social, political, economic and moral decline in contrast with a vibrant, dynamic Asia buoyed by solid and stable cultural values. These ideas have been most clearly evident in the polemical work co-authored by Dr Mahathir of Malaysia and a former Liberal Democratic politician from Japan, Shintaro Ishihara (now Governor of Tokyo).[21] The blurb encapsulates the basic tone of the book very clearly, as any good blurb should, and stands as something of a monument to contemporary Occidentalism. It is therefore worth reproducing (almost) in full.

> The future belongs to Asia.
> Resolute economic advance coupled with a firm sense of social order have, over, the past several decades, transformed East Asia. A new assertiveness characterizes opinion from Singapore and Malaysia, China and Japan. In *The Voice of Asia*, two of the most outspoken proponents of an Asian model of capitalism challenge Western domination and celebrate the renaissance of the region's ancient civilizations.
> A provocative dialogue … the *Voice of Asia* gives unprecedented insight into what Ishihara calls 'the paramount reality of the mid-1990s – the retreat of the West and the increasing dynamism of Asia' … Mahathir claims that Japan provided the model for Malaysia's development; Ishihara urges his country to leave off deferring to the United States and return to the Asian fold. Can the West take up this challenge, or is the Asian era really at hand?
> Here is a world-view as foreign to the Western reader as most Western values are to Asians. But as the balance of economic power slips inexorably toward the East, there is a greater need than ever to come to grips with an emerging Asian ethos. *The Voice of Asia* is the best briefing available.[22]

So, while the phenomenon of Asianism does not necessarily require that Europe or the West be depicted in negative oppositional terms, this is in fact a prominent feature of at least some Asianist discourses. This is also what is partly behind the exclusion of Australia and New Zealand, as 'European civilizational outposts', from the 'Asian' side of the ASEM process. While countries like Japan are supportive of inclusion, the main political obstacle is Mahathir, whose opposition to their inclusion is based on a long-standing hostility to Australia in particular, a country which the Malaysian leader has often depicted as culturally insensitive to 'Asian-ness'.[23]

It is also worth noting here that although the 'Asian values' debate has been somewhat muted by the recent financial crisis, as is talk of the Pacific Century, it is by no means a dead issue in the region. Richard Higgott argues that the crisis has prompted some leaders in the region 'to rediscover the rhetoric of popular nationalism' and that this serves as a means of deflecting critical domestic responses. But beyond the nationalist formulations lies a broader regionalist line as well. As Higgott says, a discourse of 'robbery', or a 'new imperialism' – not heard since the years of the immediate postcolonial era – has been voiced very strongly across most of the affected states. This has occurred not only in Malaysia where Mahathir has argued that Western governments and financiers 'have deliberately punished Asia for its arrogance and refusal to converge more quickly towards Anglo-American liberal approaches to democracy, market opening, labour standards and human rights.' He says these themes have also been voiced in Thailand, the Philippines, South Korea and Indonesia.[24] This brings us to some of the issues raised by postcolonialism – in both academic theory and political practice – which I shall mention, at least briefly, as an important subtext in the new Asianism.

A NOTE ON POSTCOLONIALISM

The persistence and strength of Asianist rhetoric is, in part, attributable to the fact that it is part of a broader postcolonial discourse – or perhaps, more accurately, an ideology of postcolonialism – which will almost certainly continue to mediate relations within and between the regions well into the foreseeable future. 'Postcolonialism' is, however, a term which introduces a further set of confusions and contradictions. First, it must also be noted that despite the 'post' in postcolonialism, it is arguable that colonialism or imperialism has scarcely ceased to exist merely because the national institutions of government are now formally under local control. Some would suggest that more insidious forms are now thriving through the control mechanisms of global capital as well as institutions such as the World Bank and the International Monetary Fund. This is in addition to the moral and epistemological imperialism that is believed to be clearly manifest in the attempted imposition of 'Western' human rights standards and models of democratic government on certain countries in the region. These factors feed directly into many aspects of contemporary Asianism.

In her recent exploration of colonialism and postcolonialism, and all the difficulties of defining the terms and field(s) of study, Ania Loomba suggests that it is probably most helpful to think of postcolonialism 'not just as coming literally after colonialism and signifying its demise, but more flexibly as the contestation of colonial domination and the legacies of colonialism'. This position, she says, allows us to incorporate diasporic movements as well as 'the history of anti-colonial resistance with contemporary resistances to imperialism and to dominant Western culture'.[25] But there is also a warning about some of the dangers of using an all-encompassing term like 'the postcolonial', especially when it is taken to signify an oppositional position. In this case, she says, 'it has the effect of collapsing various locations so that the specificities of all of them are blurred'.[26] Asianism does precisely this, and in much the same way as Orientalism.

Eagleton identifies another problem with postcolonialism – or at least with the way in which it is often put forward – in that it embraces a 'theoretical agenda' which is hostile to the idea of a 'general common humanity'. The latter construct, he says, is criticized as a form of 'essentialism'. It is also condemned as a 'liberal humanist stratagem for suppressing cultural difference'. Thus 'postcolonialism', at least in this form, is 'a brand of culturalism' which works to inflate 'the significance of cultural factors in human affairs' – certainly to the extent that what comes to be seen as the real set of issues at stake between north and south really does revolve around 'questions of value, signification, history, identity, cultural practice rather than arms, trade agreements, military alliances, drug trafficking and the like'.[27]

In treating postcolonialism as an ideological construct, it is therefore possible to recognize the extent to which the 'culturalist' elements work to obscure other issues. It is also important to be alert to the way in which postcolonialism is generally positioned in opposition to Europe or the West.[28] There is, of course, a certain logic to this positioning – after all, the colonizing powers in Asia (and elsewhere) were largely European. With respect to this last point, however, it is just as pertinent to look today at the phenomenon of internal colonialism and the extent to which it remains a problem throughout most regions of the world.[29]

Looking to wider structural issues, Chen identifies transformations occurring 'from territorial colonialism to neo-colonialism under the stamp of globalization' signalling the 'shifting gravity of colonialism' from Western Europe and North America to the 'Inter-Asia continent'.

Throughout the Inter-Asia region, he notes, there is a weird sense of 'triumphalism' directed against the 'West', despite 'internal' antagonisms: the twenty-first century is 'ours'; 'we' are finally centred. Wherever one is geographically positioned, there is an emerging, almost clichéd formula: 'Asia is becoming the centre of the earth' ... This is where history comes in. Contrary to the now fashionable claim that we have entered the postcolonial era, the mood of triumphalism as reaction and *reactionary* to colonialism indicates that we still operate within the boundary of colonial history in which all of us are caught up.[30]

This lends support to one of the main points developed in this paper. Because it is embedded in an ideology of postcolonialism, Asianism – and the symbols of regional identity and representation that underscore it – must be understood in terms of the reactive nature of the project. Therefore we must look at how the constituent elements of the entity 'Asia' have been selected and constructed against its opposing image: 'Europe', or, more generally, 'the West'.

CONSTRUCTIONS OF REGION

It has been noted that writers like Spengler, Toynbee and Wight, in attempting to understand and explain world politics, were influenced by ideas about culture or civilization as a way of classifying large systems, rather than states. Pasic says that 'civilization studies' were grounded in the work of earlier philosophers such as Herder and followed by the cultural historians and cultural anthropologists of the nineteenth and early twentieth centuries. She says these studies 'reveal how the essentially mythological and value-laden cultural construct of "civilization" became a referent for the unity of large political systems'.[31] Europe, or more especially Western Europe from which 'the West' is derived, grew out of an older notion of 'Christendom'. But questions about what actually constitutes 'Europe' or 'the West', either historically or currently, are vexed questions – certainly not settled ones. Michael Wintle, in discussing whether or not there is such a thing now as a 'European cultural identity' says that one response is to say that it consists simply of 'modernity', and that this is sometimes taken to be the 'essence' of European civilization. But Wintle, in showing how this assumption works through to other issues, points out that critics like Said and other opponents of Eurocentrism have had an important assumption in their sights which goes well beyond this:

> The assumption under attack is that Europe has been the cradle of civilization from the beginning of recorded history, and that European civilization stretches in an unbroken line from the ancient Greeks ... right down to the present day; that unbroken line represents the nurturing and gradual refinement of the most important

institutions, values, ethics, and culture which the world has today ... This offensive view of Europe, as the fount of wisdom and educator of the world through 'modern' and 'western' civilization, has of course been heavily criticized ... it has also been taken to pieces from within, as it were, by European scholars demonstrating that the long, unbroken development of any sort of civilization in Europe is a nonsense, or at best a myth.[32]

These views have done much to inspire various forms of Asianism, both past and present, although it should be noted that critiques of the rampant Eurocentrism that underscores such views are as often as not found within Europe (or the West more generally) as well – especially in universities, and especially among students of postcolonial and cultural studies. But the question of how to approach both arrogant forms of Eurocentrism and aggressive Asianist postures is not an easy one. This is evident from various criticisms that followed the publication of Said's *Orientalism*, and I will turn briefly to his work to illustrate some of the problems.

Edward Said speaks of the perceptions of qualities possessed by 'the West' and the way these have been contrasted with those assumed to characterize 'the East'. He points out that such perceptions are 'as intrinsic to Orientalism as they are to any view that divides the world into large general divisions, entities that coexist in a state of tension produced by what is believed to be radical difference'.[33] And that, says Said, is the main intellectual issue raised by Orientalism. He continues:

Can one divide human reality ... into clearly different cultures, histories, traditions, societies, even races, and survive the consequences humanly? By surviving the consequences humanly, I mean to ask whether there is any way of avoiding the hostility expressed by the division, say of [people] into 'us' (Westerners) and 'they' (Orientals). For such divisions are generalities whose use historically and actually has been to press the importance of the distinction between some [people] and some other [people], usually towards not especially admirable ends. When one uses categories like Oriental and Western as both starting and the end points of analysis, research, public policy ... the result is usually to polarize the distinction – the Oriental becomes more Oriental, the Westerner more Western – and limit the human encounter between different cultures, traditions, and societies. In short, from its earliest modern history to the present, Orientalism as a form of thought for dealing with the foreign has typically shown the altogether regrettable tendency of any knowledge based on such hard-and-fast distinctions as 'East' and 'West': to channel thought into a West or an East compartment.[34]

These thoughts, although arising directly from a critique of Orientalism, are clearly just as applicable to Occidentalism. Moreover, as James Clifford points out, Said's critique at times indulges in such sweeping and categorical generalizations about the 'Orientalist' and 'Orientalism' that it sometimes appears to mimic the essentializing discourse that it attacks.[35] In this respect, there is always the danger that critiques in the style of Said's will themselves lapse into an 'Occidentalist' mode in which a grossly homogenized and reified entity called 'the West' will be subject to the same simplifications. This is, to a very large extent, what has been happening in the Asianist discourses, for many of these amount to little more than anti-Westernism.

A third style of discourse, which is not Asianist so much as simply anti-Western, comes out of an intellectual branch of postcolonialism and bears the imprimatur of cultural studies. In looking at this style, I refer, in particular, to an essay by Ien Ang in Chen's recent collection of cultural studies essays mentioned earlier.[36] The essay starts with the following observations, which, as far as they go, promise a fresh critical look at some problems in tackling a European brand of ethnocentricity. These observations also reveal some aspects of the politics of theorizing in the academy.

> 'Eurocentrism' has become a guaranteed term of abuse in cultural studies and postcolonial studies today, a bad Other against which good, 'politically correct' positions often impulsively define themselves. Yet, as with all terms of abuse, the meaning of the term is rarely clarified. All too often, to be accused of Eurocentrism is rather simplistically to be charged with racism, white supremacism, a Western superiority complex and complicity with colonialism, all at one go. In such discursive assaults a militant, self-righteous, hyper-oppositional stance serves only to deflate itself through the unproductive demonization of a grandiose, abstract, Euro-Other.[37]

What follows this initial insight, however, lapses straight back into a stance which produces yet another 'demonization' of Europe and Europeans and which therefore replicates the Occidentalist discourses outlined above. Ang's stated purpose in this essay is 'to re-establish the relationship between Eurocentrism (as a particular discourse on world history and culture) and the European subject of that discourse, "Europe" as the concrete, culturally and geographically specific site where this discourse has been historically produced and still is produced today'. Ang goes on to assert that 'Europeaness' and Eurocentrism are often self-identical; 'most Europeans are unthinkingly Eurocentric because Eurocentrism is, in a fundamental way, formative of and crucial to the European sense of cultural identity'. Moreover, Eurocentrism is not merely manifest in generalized discursive structures but, crucially, it takes the form of an 'historically sedimented mode of subjectivity'. The final seal of Ang's disapproval is provided by the European subject's sense of self, for according to Ang, 'the paradigmatic European subject' is 'the bourgeois male'.[38]

In parts of the essay, however, Ang does qualify some of these sweeping generalizations: 'Of course, I am not saying that all Europeans are the same, nor that they all equally inhabit the dispositions of European subjectivity.' And further: 'It is clear that to speak of "Europe" as if it had an "identity" and a "culture" in any essentialist, homogeneous and singular sense would be to run the risk of reproducing precisely the abstractions of European discourse itself.' She also admits that 'Europeaness' does not completely 'saturate the subjectivity of actual Europeans' who, after all, differ along the lines of class, gender, ethnicity, regional and religious background and so on. But she maintains that 'a "European subjectivity" may still be talked about as a culturally particular, historically constructed, psycho-social affective formation which informs, in subtle and elusive ways, what it means to be European'.[39]

Towards the end, Ang writes that Europe's time as the dominant entity is drawing to a close. 'World history', she says, 'is no longer explainable from an exclusively Eurocentric point of view', and she invites us to consider 'the spectacular rise of East Asian capitalism as a significant step in the plural history of modernity'.[40] And quoting Göran Therborn:

> For the first time since the Industrial Revolution there has emerged in East Asia a kind of rich and developed society owing virtually nothing to Europe ... To the Europeans the legacy of a specific history ... will remain important. Its sediments, from Antiquity to the industrial class struggle, are built into the European House. To the rest of the world, however, the lights of Europe are growing dim.[41]

There are a few problems in this, for one message that seems to come across is that it is because East Asia has come to look more *like* Europe in terms of 'development' that it no longer needs to look towards it. More to the point, however, is that like Said in his attack on Orientalism, Ang is unable to avoid the very same errors of gross essentialization that lends a distinctly Occidentalist quality to her critique. In consequence, her critique contributes directly to the new Asianism.

SOME CONCLUDING THOUGHTS

My point in setting all this out is to demonstrate the extent to which discourses about culture in the international sphere, especially those which continually talk about the 'historical and/or cultural specificity' of groups, countries, or even regions – and take this kind of 'specificity' as an unquestioned given, often remain mired in an Orientalist/Occidentalism framework. In their efforts to defeat any form of universalism, far too much has been invested in 'specificity' as well as in categories such as 'the West' and 'the Orient' or 'Europe' and 'Asia', and this has continued to reinforce polarized distinctions. This applies as much to some of the positions taken in cultural and postcolonial studies as it does to the more conservative culturalist approaches typified by the communitarianism of Bell and others. It also applies just as well to the equally conservative and culturalist – but also conflictual –

approach to international relations set out in Huntington's 'clash of civilizations' thesis.

It follows that a viable cultural politics approach to the study of Asia–Europe relations must be fully alert to these problems, and must be prepared to ask critical questions about what, exactly, it means to talk about 'historical particularities' and 'cultural specificities', especially when these terms are applied to 'Europe' or 'Asia' or 'the West'. Apart from the lack of specificity that these entities actually possess, the terms themselves are too often used in a highly clichéd way, and sometimes, it seems, more as a signal about the political speaking position of the author than as terms carrying significant analytic weight. Moreover, the way that these terms are used in distinguishing between 'Europe' and 'Asia' tends to gloss over much more pertinent questions about power relations, not only within regions and countries but within local communities as well.

NOTES

1. European Union (1994), 'Towards a New Asia Strategy', COM (94) 314, p. 1.
2. David Camroux and Christian Lechervy (1996), '"Close encounter of a third kind?", the inaugural Asia–Europe Meeting of March 1996', *The Pacific Review*, **9** (3), 443.
3. Ibid., p. 448.
4. Richard A. Wilson (1997), 'Human Rights, Culture and Context: An Introduction' in Richard A. Wilson (ed.), *Human Rights, Culture and Context: Anthropological Perspectives*, London: Pluto Press, p. 9.
5. Henry Tam (1998), *Communitarianism: A New Agenda for Politics and Citizenship*, London: Macmillan, p. 2.
6. Amitai Etzioni (1995), *The Spirit of Community: Rights, Responsibilities and the Communitarian Agenda*, London; Fontana, p. ix.
7. Quoted in Stephen Mulhall and Adam Swift (1996), *Liberals and Communitarians* (2nd edn), Oxford: Blackwell, p. 129.
8. Daniel A. Bell and Kanishka Jayasura (1995), 'Understanding Illiberal Democracy: A Framework', in Daniel A. Bell, David Brown, Kanishka Jayasura and David Martin Jones, *Towards Illiberal Democracy in Pacific Asia*, New York: St Martin's Press, p. 3.
9. Mark Hoffman (1994), 'Normative International Relations Theory', in A.J.R. Groom and Margot Light (eds), *Contemporary International Relations: A Guide to Theory*, London: Pinter, pp. 29–30.
10. See Joseph Boyle (1992), 'Natural Law and International Ethics', in Terry Nardin and David R. Mapel (eds), *Traditions of International Ethics*, Cambridge: Cambridge University Press.
11. Bell and Jayasura, 'Understanding Illiberal Democracy', pp. 2–3.
12. Ibid., p. 8.
13. Glenn Jordan and Chris Weedon (1995), *Cultural Politics: Class, Gender, Race and the Postmodern World*, Oxford: Blackwell.
14. Ibid., p. 4, emphasis in original.
15. Edward Said [1978] (1995), *Orientalism*, London: Penguin.
16. Chen Kuang-Hsing (ed.) (1998), *Trajectories: Inter-Asia Cultural Studies*, London; Routledge.
17. Chen Kuang-Hsing, 'The Decolonization Question', ibid., p. 3.
18. Tessa Morris-Suzuki (1998), 'Invisible countries: Japan and the Asian dream', *Asian Studies Review*, **22** (1), pp. 5–6.

19. The 'new' in the 'new Asianism' is intended to distinguish the broad contemporary movement that I'm attempting to describe here from previous terms or usages such as 'pan-Asianism' or 'greater Asianism'. See, especially on the former, Morinosuke Kajima (1973), *The Road to Pan-Asia*, Tokyo: Japan Times Ltd. On p. 19, Kajima mentions Sun Yat-Sen as advocating a 'Greater-Asianism' in Kobe in 1924.
20. Miyume Tanji and Stephanie Lawson (1997), ' "Democratic Peace" and "Asian Democracy": a universalist–particularist tension', *Alternatives,* **22** (2), 147.
21. Mahathir Mohamad and Shintaro Ishihara (1995), *The Voice of Asia.*
22. Ibid., inside front cover.
23. This was highlighted, in particular, by the infamous diplomatic incident when the former Australian Prime Minister, Paul Keating, called Mahathir 'recalcitrant' for declining to attend the APEC summit in Seattle in 1993. For some interesting comments on how this incident was played out in the 'image wars' in the region, see Michael Byrnes (1994), *Australia and the Asia Game*, St. Leonards: Allen & Unwin, esp. pp. 169–173.
24. Richard Higgott (1998), 'The Asian economic crisis: a study in the politics of resentment', *New Political Economy*, **3** (3), 347.
25. Ania Loomba (1998), *Colonialism/Postcolonialism*, London: Routledge, p. 12.
26. Ibid., pp. 16–17.
27. Terry Eagleton (1998/9), 'Postcolonialism and "Postcolonialism" ', *Interventions*, **1** (1), pp. 25–6.
28. This is a tentative formulation which obviously requires much more filling out.
29. I searched for a reference to 'internal colonialism' in the Loomba book but it did not appear in the chapter sub-headings, nor was there a single reference in the index.
30. Chen, 'The Decolonization Question', p. 2.
31. Sujata Chakrabarti Pasic (1996), 'Culturing International Relations Theory: A Call for Extension', in Josef Lapid and Friedrich Kratochwil, *The Return of Culture and Identity in IR Theory*, Boulder: Lynne Reinner, p. 98.
32. Michael Wintle (1996), 'Cultural Identity in Europe; Shared Experience', in Michael Wintle (ed.), *Culture and Identity in Europe,* Aldershot: Avebury, p. 11.
33. Edward Said ([1978] 1995), *Orientalism: Western Conceptions of the Orient*, London: Penguin, p. 45.
34. Ibid., pp. 45–6.
35. James Clifford (1988), *The Predicament of Culture: Twentieth-Century Ethnography, Literature, and Art*, Cambridge, Mass.: Harvard University Press, pp. 261–2.
36. Ien Ang, (1998),'Eurocentric Reluctance: Notes for a Cultural Studie of "The New Europe" ' in Kuan-Hsing Chen (ed.) *Trajectories: Inter-Asia Cultural Studies*, London: Routledge, pp. 87–108.
37. Ibid., p. 87.
38. Ibid., pp. 88–9. It's worth noting here that Ang does fill us in on how she comes to have the authority to make such pronouncements, or what her 'speaking position' is. Having been born and having spent her early childhood in Indonesia, but then moving to Amsterdam for twenty-five years as a 'participant observer' of Europe and 'Europeaness', and now living and working in Australia, Ang says she now speaks to us as both an 'insider' and an 'outsider': a doubly privileged position in anybody's hermeneutic scheme.
39. Ibid., pp. 88–102.
40. Ibid., p. 103.
41. Göran Therborn quoted ibid., p. 103.

3. Beyond Orientalism? Culture, power and postcolonialism in Europe–Asia relations

John Clammer

INTRODUCTION

Linkages between Asia and Europe exist, and have long existed, at a number of levels – economic, political and social. Underlying and reflecting these is the cultural level – the perceptions and representations of Asia by Europeans and of Europe by Asians. There are older and now, perhaps, less sophisticated models for characterizing this mutuality (often a distorted one based upon differential access to power), notably 'Orientalism'[1] and 'Occidentalism'[2]. Both these approaches assume (as does the even older field of 'International Relations') two broadly defined blocs or entities between which interchange takes place.

The limitation of such conceptualizations is that they predate or deflect the immense shifts in the understanding of the concept of culture itself which have accompanied late modernity and the globalizing forces that it has set in train. Leaving aside for the moment the disputes about the precise meaning of the term 'globalization' and its significance for the critical analysis of the contemporary world system, most commentators would agree that it contains and implies profound implications for culture, whether this is understood in terms of the migration of peoples, symbols or objects, of attitudes to selfhood and subjectivities or of the implications for everyone of such powerful Eurocentric concepts as 'development'.[3] The concern is not only that of establishing the place of culture within globalization but, more profoundly, that of questioning the meaning of culture itself in these new circumstances.

While the argument for the centrality of culture to the framing of questions in political economy is not a new one[4], it has re-entered debate through the three portals of postmodernism, anthropological disputes over the means (and the legitimacy) of the representation of the 'Other'[5], and attempts to create a new vocabulary to ensnare the phenomena that have emerged out of postcolonial studies, the study of international migration and 'travelling cultures', and the increasing visibility of transnational communities such as the Overseas Chinese - a vocabulary that now contains such celebrated and disputed terms as 'hybridity' and 'creolization'. The cumulative effect of these conceptual and methodological shifts has been to both recentre culture in debates about the nature of the world system and, at the same time, to problematize the concept of culture itself, by seeing it as no longer the relatively fixed possession of spatially and temporally bounded groups but as a processual and highly dynamic strategy of identity negotiation, by its nature open-ended and without points of closure.

The primary consequence of this is that to talk at all about cultural relations between Asia and Europe it is necessary to reframe the debate. The outline of how this might be done constitutes the body of this chapter; an endeavour which involves essentially the attempt to formulate a new vocabulary as a consequence of the fact that the study of European–Asian cultural relations needs resiting in the context of the realities of globalized cultural complexity. This must necessarily bring into question the langauage of 'flows', 'values' and 'identities' and, especially, of the whole language of 'development' through which the formally postcolonial West has continued to impose itself on the rest of the world in the postwar decades.

To undertake this critique and to suggest an alternative conceptual reconstruction, there are four elements that need to be taken into primary account. The first of these is the notion of postcoloniality. There are those in Asia[6] who argue that understanding decolonialization is the key question for cultural studies in the region. The basis for this claim is not only the huge empirical impact of colonialisms on Asia economically, politically, linguistically and institutionally, but also the continuing impact of colonialism long after its formal demise in the creation of mindsets, definitions of reality and creation of institutional forms, and in the guise of 'development' programmes. Postcolonial theory, while it has certainly taken its own peculiar polemical turns, raises some fundamental questions not usually addressed in the context of the globalization debate.

The second element to consider is the notion of contemporaneity: the coexistence of cultures and social systems in what is actually a single world system.[7] Western anthropology, in former incarnations at least, was inclined to treat 'other cultures' as spatially remote examples of the temporal past, of its own social evolution. Now, it increasingly recognizes that supposedly 'other' cultures are, in fact, deeply implicated with its own, through their real, even if remote, relationships created by the world system and through the mental means through which it constructs those 'others' and through which it, itself, is reciprocally constructed. There are not simply 'relationships' between 'East' and 'West': those relationships are constructed and mediated today largely by the social 'sciences', which purport to study, but in fact simply tend to construct, models of the societies in question and their supposed linkages. The assumptions that the East somehow represents the Other of the West, and that, from the perspective of the East, the West necessarily represents its future, are deeply questionable. The 'reality' of these societies, and their challenge epistemologically and politically to the West's philosophical and historical hegemony (largely expressed through colonialism), is a necessary precondition for any talk of 'relationships'.

Thirdly, and related to the foregoing, is the whole question of globalization as the West's modernizing project – a project founded, in fact, on the assumption of a Westernizing and homogenizing civilizational process. Such a conception has, of course, not only sparked debate about the extent to which globalization spawns intensified localization but also raised the question of alternative modernities at the macro level; modernities which may take the form of reactions to globalization in such forms as the Islamic revolution in Iran[8] or the defining of routes to postmodernity which bypass modernity altogether, as in the case of Japan.[9]

Finally, the actual content of culture and of cultural 'flows' must be carefully examined. While Easterners do indeed consume the West (fashions, food, education, literature and film for example), the West now also increasingly consumes the East – both those same items and more, religion being a conspicuous example. This not only involves the wholesale export of spiritual alternatives (especially Indian forms of neo-Hinduism and Japanese new religions), but also the assimilation and transformation of Asian religious traditions into distinctly Western forms, as with varieties of Sufism now popular in the West[10] or with the emergence of a whole variety of Buddhism now called 'Western Buddhism'.[11] Just as indigenous intellectuals in the East have, in the past, negotiated, assimilated, rejected or modified the cultural offerings of the West, so now, as that process continues in Asia, a parallel process is occurring in the West in respect of Asian cultures, at an accelerating pace. At another level, film, literature and popular culture represent points at which complex cultural negotiation takes place on an everyday level in the attempt by Asian peoples to define postcolonial identities[12], something which also occurs in the context of everyday consumption activities[13]. Even as the Pacific war is being weekly refought (and won) in Japanese manga (or comic books), so housewives in Kuala Lumpur or Colombo daily negotiate their relationship to the world through the contents of their shopping baskets. The relationship, then, between Asia and Europe is not simply one of increased cultural flows; it is also and predominately an issue of the ways those flows are understood and assimilated into broader cosmologies. If globalization has changed the nature of culture, then a fresh appreciation of the subtleties of these changes on intercultural and international relationships has to be taken into account. Without this, new possibilities for regional cooperation will be fraught with representational problems not so dissimilar from those analysed in the older critical literature on classical Orientalism, but this time simply transposed into a postmodern key.

FRAGMENTATION OR CULTURAL FLOWS?

A by-now-conventional approach to the cultural situation of the world at large is to characterize it through a language of fragmentation.[14] But a more accurate picture would be not of disintegration but of new and unacknowledged patterns of flows, fresh recombinations of elements and, as chaos theory so tellingly suggests, of small differences in initial conditions leading to large differences in outcomes of situations. The high volume of travelling and physical interaction between Asia and Europe leads not only to the mobility of bodies but also to the travelling of images. A language of syncretism, however, is inadequate for describing the outcome of these interactions: some things blend, some are adapted, but also totally new cultural configurations emerge out of unexpected and almost random conjunctions of ideas, styles, events or modes of behaviour. A view of global culture as decentred assumes that there was originally a centre somewhere (presumably in the West?).

In fact, the Westernization of the world is paralleled by (and indeed contested by) the Japanization of the world, and attention to regional zones rather than to the total global system demonstrates more restricted but, on the ground, equally significant interactions. Hong Kong is, simultaneously, an heir to British colonialism, to Japanese popular culture and modes of consumption (the departmental store for example), and to linguistic and cultural (to say nothing of economic and political) input from mainland China, Taiwan and the Chinese of the diaspora. At the same time, Hong Kong exports itself through tourism, its large film industry[15], its global airline (Cathay Pacific) and its own substantial economic impact on the region. It is a society that both imports labour to serve its own middle and upper classes (Filipina domestics) and exports its skilled labour (to Singapore and elsewhere in Southeast Asia, Australia, Canada and the Gulf) and unskilled labour (as illegal migrants to Japan). Different, but structurally similar, models could be constructed for Singapore, Malaysia and other societies within Asia-Pacific. Star TV, transmitted from Hong Kong, is seen all over Asia, the Japanese NHK transmits to Europe, and CNN and BBC news can be viewed all over the region. On a Sunday morning anyone in the region with a satellite-equipped TV can watch the news in English, Japanese, Chinese, Korean, Russian, German, French and Spanish.

The question then becomes one of what all this means specifically for an analysis of 'cultural relations' between Europe and Asia. The basic assumption of classical Orientalist discourse was that it is the West that constructs the East, the East itself being essentially the residue; that which is left over beyond the edges of Western definitions of civilization. Postwar political and, more especially, economic changes that have led to Asia-Pacific emerging as a powerful bloc and international actor in its own right have profoundly changed and even reversed this: the progressive project and even modernity itself becomes an Eastern prerogative, and Europe and its erstwhile colonies or colonized spaces (such as those in Africa and Latin America) decline.[16] The daily cultural problematic of a worker in England, Ireland or continental Europe may be, whether consciously recognized as such or not, negotiation of Japanese culture and management techniques, assimilation of Indian or Chinese foods and mastery of Taiwanese technology, while planning meanwhile a holiday in Thailand. Globalizing images arise as much now in the East as they do in the West. The West's modernizing project, in other words, has effectively reached its end, an end signalled by its own internal exhaustion (of which postmodernism is the major symptom); the glaring ineffectiveness of 'development', its main postcolonial mechanism of influence on the non-Western world; and the reversal of cultural flows and economic power which, combined with sheer demographics and control of raw materials, places the definition of the global future effectively in the hands of the East.

This brings into play several new factors. Paramount amongst these is the perception that history is not only chronological, but also 'spatial and relational'[17], in which case the temporal metanarrative leading universally from premodernity through modernity to postmodernity, in which 'postmodernity is in effect accorded the status of being the latest stage in a master logic of historical development, notwithstanding all the obligatory homilies paid to the critique of development'[18], is lodged in Western experience. Societies which place themselves outside of this logic (Japan, Thailand, China, and Burma before the generals, would come to mind) create different historical spaces for themselves in which alternative projects of civilizational construction take place which are in no way Eurocentric but, on the contrary, are those on which the West impinges merely as a distraction and as the inappropriate route to the future.

Secondly, as Jonathan Friedman so cogently argues[19], analyses of creolization and hybridization have tended to concentrate on cultural artefacts and the ways in which they are 'transformed' through 'culture contact'[20], whereas if culture is to be seen as process rather than as substance, then the real focus of attention must be on cultural practices that produce and reproduce identity spaces of an ever-shifting nature. East/West cultural flows consequently need recasting in this form – not as the exchange of objects, or even of ideas, but as a complex network of identity strategies in which artefacts and commodities are employed not as 'essences' but as counters in a game with no fixed rules.

Thirdly, cultural analysis frequently ignores the underlying economic realities. In this context there are three such realities: (i) that it is international capital (both Eastern and Western) that currently dictates the fundamental context in which social and political action takes place (it is the locus of power in other words); (ii) that this power is not merely 'material' but takes symbolic forms, either in the creation of meaning systems and systems of values, or in the creation of symbols which are themselves commodities[21]; and (iii) that this capitalism is itself protean, diverse and possessed of distinct national characteristics (British, let us say, as opposed to Japanese capitalism). All debates about culture, and all debates about East/West relations, must be placed in this frame. The coding and decoding in which cultures and individuals are constantly engaged in a globalized world is not, as in a culturalist model, autonomous, but takes place in the context of the prevailing international political economy, which is a capitalist one.

Finally, there is little left, in a globalizing world, of 'pure' cultures, in which, despite a whole popularizing literature to the contrary (The Japanese Mind; Thai Culture; The Ways of Thinking of Eastern Peoples), the 'essence' of particular geographically defined cultures can be discerned and packaged. This is true of the West as much as of the East, and if the cultures of the Orient were transformed by colonialism, so the cultures of the West are being transformed by hybridization occasioned by the movement of artefacts, foods, symbols, peoples, literatures, arts and technologies from Asia, Africa, the Caribbean and Latin America. The actual polycentrism of the world system is matched by the actual hybridization of the cultures in each of these shifting 'centres'. Even under colonialism, seen by many largely as the self-export of the West to the rest, counterflows of resources, ideas, language, people, artefacts and arts occurred widely. Even (or especially) at moments of high imperialism, classical Orientalism not only failed to grasp the extent of these flows but also failed to realize the existence or extent of counter discourses. Subaltern studies is actually only the contemporary surfacing of a tradition which has long been present in Asian societies but which has only been able to fully articulate itself with the demise of colonialism and the conceptual decentring of the world system.

For this reason, postcolonial studies have come to occupy an important place in the intellectual landscape. The language of postcolonialism is also of significance for two other reasons. The first is that it represents the way in which the debate about East/West relations has been framed in much of Asia, especially in India and East Asia.[22] This is significant both as an indigenous discourse (however much it has been co-opted by Western scholars and publishers as a politically correct intellectual option – for example, Williams and Chrisman (1993), among many others) and to the extent that it avoids any of the language of 'development' so prevalent in the West. The second reason that postcolonial language is significant is that it allows into the discussion themes which have been largely excluded from conventional political science or sociological approaches to 'international relations' – such as memory, and the emotions of dispossession and domination. Europe in Asia is still a haunting legacy, and if Europe itself and its vaunted version of modernity still has to fully digest the implications of the Holocaust[23], so Asia still has to fully digest the experience of colonialism and to integrate it into a balanced understanding of the present and possible futures.

Significantly, postcolonial studies began in literary studies and, since then, has continued to be a discourse largely about culture and about the exclusion from the West's master narratives of modernity (for example, Habermas and Giddens) of any discussion of colonialism itself or of the profound cultural transformations that it wrought on subject peoples through its creation of massive diasporas and through its many and often subtle effects on the colonizers themselves.[24] It calls into question the universality both of the modernist project itself and of the notions of culture which it generated and which are themselves part of the technology of domination; notions which essentialized identities ('Japanese', 'Indian', 'Hindu') while actually displacing and confusing them through an inevitable process of hybridization. As Featherstone puts it,

> Here we think of the need to investigate the ways in which particular European notions of culture were generated within modernity which presented its culture as unified and integrated, which neglected the spatial relationships to the rest of the world that developed with colonialism, in effect the dark side of modernity that made this sense of unity possible.[25]

As Featherstone goes on to point out, sociology, the 'science' of this modernity, itself came of age in an era of the formation of nation-states and created a disciplinary culture which, passing through functionalism to structuralism via Talcott Parsons, revealed, like its sister science anthropology, a mania for discovering the principles of 'integration'. In an at least partially postnational world, in which global complexity has swept aside any simple notions of functional integration and in which the dark underside of late modernity itself (continuing global 'underdevelopment', Eurocentrism in social and economic theory, racism and other abiding social issues) both this disciplinary focus and the assumptions that underpinned it are obsolete. It is necessary to match this with new notions of culture, which are spatial as well as temporal, processual rather than categorical, and recognize hybridity rather than essence as the normal condition of being. This arises from the multiple understandings of modernity that conceptualize human subjectivities and understandings of selfhood differently and which, in many cases, are conflictual, in that they continually contest received notions of social reality (for example, new social movements in the 'South', Asian theologies of liberation, Buddhist socialisms, indigenous conceptualizations of identity such as the Japanese Nihonjinron), and are also based on fundamentally different philosophical premises from those of the Enlightenment project. Globalization itself is consequently a paradoxical phenomenon in that, while it integrates at some levels (primarily economic), it creates differences at others and, indeed, creates the pluralist context in which the previously subaltern can speak, and can expect to be heard, as equal voices, as occupants of different spaces, even if of the same time, as the colonizers.

What then, in summary, are the implications of postcolonial analysis for Europe–Asia relations? The first is not only the obvious one that flows of people, ideas, ideologies, religions, arts and material goods are from the former colonizers to the formally colonized, but that this flow is now not so much simply reversed as deepened in its complexities and ambiguities. There are more Muslims in Bradford than Christians in Kuala Lumpur; but there are also probably more Christians in Africa than there are in the whole of Europe. Turkish is the de facto second language of large areas of Germany, even as Mexican Spanish is of southern California. Identity, in any simple sense, has been finally shattered by the cultural impact of globalization. Secondly, this fact, together with expanding knowledge of Asia in the West and of the West in Asia, finally does away with any notions of cultural superiority or inferiority on either side. With probably more Westerners becoming Buddhists than Asians are becoming Christians, the very philosophical underpinnings of the Enlightenment model begin to dissolve. And since postcolonial theory has as a basic premise the assumption that academic knowledge – its nature, production and dissemination – have been historically involved in the colonial project, even as it is now implicated in the project of 'development', so Western academic study of the East faces serious questions as to its purposes, methods and political or business linkages. For scholars in Asian academies the problem is oddly similar; not that of simply reproducing a mirror-image of Orientalism in a reactive Occidentalism, but rather the more subtle danger of having so internalized the preconceptions of the West that the indigenous scholar becomes a postcolonial orientalist, reproducing and perpetuating European concepts of the East, not least because of the still Western-centred distribution of academic power, prestige and influence. Who, even today, will do his/her PhD at the University of Hanoi if he/she has the opportunity to do it at Harvard?[26]

The Eurocentric power to define, characteristic of both classical Orientalism and most of its successors (most notably 'development studies'), is also visible in much of the contemporary globalization discourse, which, while again purporting to generate a universalist theory, is often a triumphalist and (like its cousin, postmodernism) partial account of the world. The apparent globalization, as seen from Wall Street, looks a little different when seen from a Calcutta slum. A key lesson of postcolonial theory is that the vocabulary of differences must be, and must remain, critical and self-critical, since the language of Westernization and, to an increasing extent, of Japanization, is a pervasive one that has dominated Europe–Asia cultural relations for too long and that can easily reappear in new forms (such as in the domination of cultural studies by European modes of thought).

Postcolonial theory, then, sets out the basic model for examining relations between West and East, and must do so initially because it draws attention both to the structural levels (economic, political and military power), and to the cultural, not only in the sense of empirical flows but also of images, representations, memories, prejudices and subliminal linkages. Until the colonial is fully exorcised and relations can be established on a wholly equal basis, the critical dialogue embodied in postcolonial theory must continue. This is not to say, however, that it is the final model, for if the present is encompassed in a postcolonial framework, the future need not necessarily be so. Thus, while Kuan-Hsing Chen[27] unequivocally identifies the subject of cultural studies in Asia to be colonialism, he also admits that a postcolonial reaction, given the economic success of much of East and Southeast Asia (at least until the collapse of 1997), can easily be a facile triumphalism which simply replicates in reverse the earlier triumphalism and Eurocentrism of the past. But, having admitted this, Chen's own analysis of the alternatives is dated and anachronistic, leaning heavily on the discourses emerging from the colonial psychology/identification theories of Mannoni and Fanon on the one hand, and on the nativist and civilizational models of Memmi and Nandy on the other, leaving it a very open question as to whether these really constitute the basis for a fresh identity politics.

There is clearly no one unitary 'Asia' any more than there is a unitary 'Europe'. The main contemporary difference in political direction between the two broad areas is that, with the formation of the EU, Europe (or at least much of it) is striving through concrete institutional means (including a common currency) to bury old hatreds and to create a new collective identity. This is a very different model, for all its problems, tensions and degrees of commitment, from the 'pan-Asianism' of politicans like Lee Kuan Yew and Mahatir Mohammad who are attempting to create unity on the basis of 'Asian values' which clearly do not exist in any collective sense. So, while Asian leaders effectively seek to create Esperanto-like values, it is assumed, paradoxically both in Asia and in Europe, that pan-European values do exist, since these are thought to be precisely the philosophical foundations of the 'Enlightenment project', despite the obvious dangers of ascribing to a whole continent the same values, and the atemporality of somehow assuming that these values have remained constant since the 18th century despite the radical social changes that have taken place since then. In any case, a major flaw in both Eurocentric and pan-Asian models is that they ignore the presence of the United States, whose global presence is felt economically, militarily and culturally (especially in the area of popular culture) just about everywhere and which provides both a source of cultural and economic input, and a force to be opposed in both Europe and Asia.

EUROPE IN ASIA'S IMAGINARY

Chen[28] rightly suggests that 'The West has to be dealt with not so much as a geographical entity but as an emotionally charged imaginary' from an Asian point of view. The dynamics of identity politics within the EU consequently both resonate and contrast with formally similar processes in Asia. The 're-Europeanization' of Europe that some commentators see as being generated in the search for a collective European identity is part of this, but it is clearly not the whole story, as some Asian critics have effectively suggested. The 'new Europe' is not simply returning to its past: it is, to a great extent, engaged in exorcising that past (its old nationalisms, for example) while, at the same time, facing totally unprecedented new ones that have arisen in the search for a common political and economic (but not necesarily cultural or linguistic) identity – and these levels, while related, should certainly not be confused with each other. The new Europe is not only engaged in constant dialogue with its own past but also with its relations to the 'Rest', and especially to emergent Asia-Pacific, as well as to its 'Others within', many of whom are of Asian origin.

In this respect, the approach of some prominent cultural studies scholars of Asian origin (although revealingly not necessarily actually living in Asia) is subtly misleading. An excellent case in point is the acute but distorted analysis of contemporary Eurocentrism by Ien Ang[29], as she sees it located in, and indeed reviving in, the context of a Europe faced with the paradox of its own economic and international resurgence on the one hand, at the same time as its loss of transcendent superiority and the recognition of its own 'ordinaryness', with the demise of colonialism. Her argument is sufficiently important to deserve a little specific critical comment.

Ang is correct that Europe is engaged in a search for a new collective identity. This is indeed based on a kind of 'civilizational' approach (which, oddly, Chen Kuan-Hsing, earlier in the same book, sees as characteristic of Asian attempts to transcend the colonial era) as evidenced by EU reluctance to countenance the admission of Turkey on the grounds that it is not really

'European'. But this identity-seeking does not, as she implies, necessarily infer a new and revised edition of Eurocentrism. On the contrary, a substantial amount of humility is necessary to come to terms with Europe's own recent history and to confront, on the one hand, the political differences within the EU and the very real economic inequalities that still exist within the Union and, on the other, Europe's empirical place in an interdependent (read 'globalized') world system, of which Asia-Pacific is very much a major actor. This identity formation is itself hesitant and fitful, and has none of the neo-triumphalism that Ang seems to ascribe to it, nor does it involve any assertion of European cultural identity *vis-à-vis* the rest of the world, large minorities from which it harbours within itself, and many members of which are no longer 'African' or 'Asian' but are themselves hybrids of several generations depth, transformed by their own European sojourn into new Europeans themselves. So, while there are no doubt still individuals throughout Europe who decry the loss of their former colonies, these are an anachronistic minority, and to link a mythical resurgence of cultural superiority to a defensive posture resulting from this loss is strangely to impose on Europeans an inverted form of Mannoni's colonial psychology. In fact, in a tripolar world (in terms of economic power) a united Europe is operating from a position of strength, not of postcolonial demoralization, but Ang provides no evidence (other than that in the writings of a few European intellectuals) that this is accompanied by assertions of cultural superiority in relation to the rest of the world. By its very existence, the EU proves the presence of a hybrid place, a site of pluralism and an experiment in multiculturalism. Ang's subjective feelings of never quite belonging after a quarter-century of residence in Holland do not add up to a thesis about Europe as a whole. Indeed, her subsequent relocation to Australia is revealing: as a Chinese she would have no doubt discovered that a common Asianness did not necessarily protect her from discrimination in her own native Indonesia.

The idea that Europe is the sole motor of modernity, progress, historical change and economic leadership in the world is a straw man, not only given the contemporary role of the USA and Asia-Pacific but also because of all the contrary historical evidence ignored by cultural studies scholars but widely available; for example, studies of East Asian trading systems and their world role[30] or of complex systems of accounting and managerialism in South Asia and elsewhere.[31] Indeed, Frank's compendious demonstration that global trade based in Asia long predates or runs parallel to European commercial hegemony and that, even during high colonial times, the imperial economy was run largely on resources and networks centred in Asia, leads him to oppose what he calls 'real World History' to 'Eurocentric Social Theory'. The result, as he sees it[32], is globalism, not Eurocentrism, as the better factual description of the world economy, even during the heyday of colonialism itself.

That a certain subliminal Eurocentrism still shapes contemporary attitudes and thinking even after the demise of formal colonialism is not in doubt[33], but the very existence of postcolonial theory (amongst many other discourses, such as pan-Asianism) reveals that this is highly contested terrain, from within the European academies as well as from within the Asian ones. In fact, a more nuanced view sees Europeans as struggling to move beyond Eurocentrism of the superiority variety in both its practical manifestations (for example, racialism) and in academic discourse (vestigial Orientalism), just as Asians are hopefully moving beyond vacuous claims about 'Asian values' and what, elsewhere, Ang calls 'counter-othering'[34] to alternative and more open relations with the West with more realistic and less triumphalistic or subordinated searches for viable new identities. Europe's view of itself and its place in the world, then, does not directly parallel the search for 'Asian identity': the legacies and historical experiences have been too different, and the language of internal discussion is too different[35], especially when one listens to the discourse of the intellectuals as Ang does, rather than to the discourse of the politicans or, most important of all, to the discourse of actual average Europeans or Asians.

Even as the 'Asian subject' was undermined by the depredations of colonialism, so too the 'European subject' is being undermined from within by the spread of Asian religions and a host of Asian-inspired cultural movements in food, fashion, the arts and myriad other ways. The new non-transcendentally superior culture that Ang signals is, in other words, not brought into being by academic discourse but by cultural practices. To speak at all of 'European subjectivity' or of 'the European structure of feeling'[36] is, in fact, essentialist and grossly simplistic. European culture is already transformed by centuries of contact with the rest of the world and is deeply hybrid, whether it sees itself that way or not. The circuits of power in the modern world are now multiple, economically and culturally. Indeed, what is most conspicuously missing from the cultural studies approach is a grasp of political economy and of the intimate connections between cultural change and economic shifts, so it is to these now that we must at least briefly turn.

THE POLITICAL ECONOMY OF CULTURE

If it is a persistent shortcoming of economistic approaches to social transformation that they ignore culture, it is an equally persistent shortcoming of cultural studies that it ignores economics. As I have suggested elsewhere[37], the bringing together of these approaches, not through mere addition of one to the other but through genuine conceptual integration, is a major theoretical question for the contemporary social sciences. Preoccupation in cultural studies with issues of race, gender and multiculturalism has brought about huge theoretical (and political) gains but, to advance further these themselves need to be placed in the context of the new capitalisms that are currently, I would argue, the major determinants of discussions of cultural or other kinds of relationships between West and East. Indeed, I would also contend that most of the contemporary language of 'globalization', 'postmodernism', 'late modernity', 'risk', 'ambivalence' or even the 'third way' is actually a code for 'late capitalism'. Even as Frederic Jameson has argued that postmodernism is the cultural logic of late capitalism, I would extend this to suggest that all these key words of current cultural debate are, in fact, part of that same logic. The worldwide spread of commodity forms, the shaping of subjectivities and emotions through consumer capitalism, the penetration of capital into every kind of human culture and almost every form of relationship within those cultures, is symptomatic of this. What is new about this new capitalism is not only its increasing reliance on new technologies, especially those associated with information technology, but the fact that it itself takes cultural forms. Advertising is now regarded as art, 'lifestyle politics' have largely replaced emancipatory politics, entertainment is now almost wholly delivered through technology by corporations, and 'popular culture' is, in fact, mass-produced and mass-marketed. This new capitalism also penetrates the political, determines the parameters within which 'development' is supposed to occur, sweeps away traditional forms of life or co-opts them ('ethnic fashion'). To speak at all of 'cultural relations' in the absence of this overwhelming reality is meaningless.

To talk then of 'alternative modernities' is simply idealistic unless it is realized that these 'alternatives' are themselves varieties of capitalism – Japan pre-eminently, but also Taiwan, South Korea and the other little 'tigers' – and that those striving to join this club (Thailand, Malaysia, Vietnam, China) are paradoxically moving along exactly the route prescribed for them by the much-vilified modernization theorists of two or three decades ago. This route may not be seen as Westernization (since all these societies are eager to keep at least some of the trappings of their traditional cultures, without which the tourists do not come), but it is certainly capitalist. The 'failures' (Burma, Laos, Cambodia, the Philippines, Bangladesh and so forth) are not those who are cresting or discovering genuinely alternative routes for themselves but those which fail according to the criteria of World Bank- and IMF-defined 'development'. What has changed is the fact that this capitalist norm is no longer necessarily Western in origin, but is locally or regionally produced. 'Postcolonial' has unfortunately not translated into 'postcapitalist', and nor, except in microlevel social and economic experiments, is there any sign of it doing so. The failure to perceive this is the fundamental theoretical blindness of postcolonial studies. This is not to argue against either the profound effects of Western models (in particular Marxism and capitalism) or against the significance of local attempts to transform, adapt or reject these through social movements and religious and intellectual experiments, but rather to argue that 'alternative modernities' turn out to be primarily the local transformation of these macro forces into regional socialisms or into regional capitalisms and the subsequent historical ousting of the former by the latter.

Certain general conclusions can be drawn from this. The rather romantic idea of 'counter-modernity' held to characterize the postcolonial situation by some of its theorists[38] is not, in fact, except in some primarily religious forms, anything that really exists in this hegemonic context. Rather, forms and large pockets of 'underdevelopment' prevail within existing patterns of modernity. Sites of resistance to the dominant order do indeed exist, but the problems they face in transforming or displacing that order are largely themselves defined in terms of the nature of the order that they are struggling against (a consumer capitalist one). Change, of course, often begins with new ways of defining reality and this is what is happening within modes of critical theory that have been applied with telling results to 'development' discourse[39], which has developed a vocabulary of critical globalization, an analysis of regionalism within the current world system, and ways of seeing that system from outside the paradigms of modernity and developmentalism altogether.

The assumption that modernity began and expanded as a purely Western project (that famous Enlightenment one) is the final myth that needs to be exploded here. That idea is itself a profoundly Eurocentric one which overlooks the permanent historical polycentrality of the world. Models of Europe–Asia relations, which talk a language of flow in which a dominant West exported itself in the form of its religions, ideologies, arts (that is, classical Orientalism) but which now see that flow as being reversed (classical postcolonialism) are naive. What is dominant, undoubtedly, is the commonly shared idea that Western modernity was the only version available; an idea as much believed in the East as in the West, as the discourse of scholars like Ang so tellingly reveals.

The way beyond Orientalism is not by the blind alleys of triumphalism (based, like the 'Asian values' debate, on false premises), nor by the subtle self-denigration of Asian cultures by Asian scholars, but by a change of paradigm. That shift involves several elements: the recognition of historical polycentrism; the extent to which Western modernity, far from being a totalizing and successful world process, has been partial and uneven (including in Europe), and the fact that this modernity, from the beginning, contained the seeds of its own destruction. What has displaced it intellectually, however, has not been a model genuinely beyond the discourse of modernity but rather a language of postmodernity. This is simply a slippage, not a true revolution. What postcolonial theory has correctly grasped is that, while

Western modernity (and Western societies) saw themselves as primarily economic and political entities (hence the language of rights, democracy and power), Asian modernities were based on radically different principles – of society before the political, of the primacy of the cultural and of the subordination of economics to values instead of economics being the generator of values.

The shying away on the part of both postcolonial theorists and cultural studies specialists in and of Asia from the subject of religion is very revealing here, not only for its suppression of what is a vital element of life in many Asian societies, but because taking religion seriously would expose the real alternative cosmologies upon which differing civilizations have built themselves. A Buddhist epistemology is a much greater challenge to the philosophical assumptions of the West than any amount of political posturing by Asian Marxists, who, in reality, share a Western ideology. This is not, of course, to argue for a shift from a political–economy model to a 'pure' culture one – a move that would simply reinstate culturalism. It is to argue that these cultural processes have different relationships to the political and economic than do their putative counterparts in the West, the very definition of 'religion' itself, for instance, differing widely from one society to another. But, at the same time as these deep and essentially epistemological confusions and opportunities in dialogue between Europe and Asia need to be identified, clarified and absorbed into academic debate on the nature of the relationship and its future directions, it needs also to be recognized that the 'contemporaneity' of which Auge speaks is both made possible by global capitalism and is yet an ambiguous process. 'The world's inhabitants have at last become truly contemporaneous, and yet the world's diversity is recomposed every moment: this is the paradox of our day.'[40] The constant negotiation of that paradox is both the daily lot of modern people and the basis of a wider identity politics. As Allen Chun suggests in discussing identity politics in East Asia:

> If one can view discourses of identity as interpretative mechanisms through which specific people, institutions or cultures localize (or indigenize) diverse global flows in order to negotiate a meaningful life space or position themselves within a situation of power, then it would be possible to see how in different localities specific institutions and practices serve as strategic sites for meaning and power.[41]

This observation applies as much today to Europe as it does to Asia.

CONCLUSION

Discussions of 'relationships' are, in fact, discussions of identity. My purpose here has been to suggest that the specific field of Europe–Asia relationships cannot adequately be treated without what amounts to a politico-philosophical clearing of the ground. Failure to do this simply creates more empirically flawed studies and theoretically flawed assumptions. To blend the critical and deconstructive with the creation of new and constructive paradigms is not an easy task, but it is a necessary one if the fundamental heterogeneity but unitedness of the contemporary world is to be simultaneously grasped, while recognizing that the future itself, while constrained, is nevertheless fundamentally open to redefinition, through theoretical debate, certainly, but also through new forms of academic and social practice.

NOTES

1. Edward Said (1978), *Orientalism,* London: Routledge and Kegan Paul.
2. J. Carrier (ed.) (1995), *Occidentalism: Images of the West,* Oxford: Clarendon Press.
3. See J. Friedman (1996), *Cultural Identity and Global Process,* London: Sage; R. Robertson (1992), *Globalization: Social Theory and Global Culture,* London: Sage; A. Giddens (1991), *Modernity and Self Identity,* Stanford University Press.
4. J. Clammer (1985), *Anthropology and Political Economy,* London, Macmillan.
5. J. Clifford and G. Marcus (eds) (1996), *Writing Culture,* University of California Press.
6. See, for example, K.H. Chen (1998), 'The Decolonization Question', in K.H. Chen (ed.), *Trajectories: Inter-Asia Cultural Studies,* London: Routledge.
7. M. Auge (1999), *An Anthropology for Contemporaneous Worlds,* Stanford University Press.
8. P. Beyer (1997), *Religion and Globalization,* London: Sage.
9. J. Clammer (1995), *Difference and Modernity,* London: Kegan Paul International.
10. See, for example, L. Vaughan-Lee (1993), *The Bond With the Beloved,* Inverness, Cal.: The Golden Sufi Center.
11. Kulananda (1997), *Western Buddhism,* London: Harper Collins.
12. R. Chow (1998), *Ethics After Idealism: Theory, Culture, Ethnicity, Reading,* Indiana University Press.
13. J. Clammer (1997), *Contemporary Urban Japan: A Sociology of Consumption,* Oxford: Blackwell.
14. M. Featherstone (1997), *Undoing Culture: Globalization, Postmodernism and Identity,* London: Sage, p.1.
15. D.T. Lii (1998), 'A Colonized Empire: Reflections on the Expansion of Hong Kong Films in Asian countries', in K.H. Chen (ed.), *Trajectories.*
16. N. Sakai (1989), 'Modernity and Its Critique: the Problem of Universalism and Particularism', in M. Miyoshi and H.D. Harootunian (eds), *Postmodernism and Japan,* Duke University Press.
17. Ibid., p. 106.
18. M. Featherstone and S. Lash (1997), 'Globalization, Modernity and the Spacialization of Social Theory: an Introduction', in M. Featherstone, S. Lash and R. Robertson (eds), *Global Modernities,* London: Sage, p. 1.
19. J. Friedman (1997), 'Global System, Globalization and the Parameters of Modernity', in Featherstone et al.
20. Compare with J.J. Tobin (ed.) (1992), *Remade in Japan: Everyday Life and Consumer Taste in a Changing Society,* Yale University Press.
21. S. Lash and J. Urry (1994), *Economies of Signs and Space,* London: Sage.
22. H.K. Chen (1998), 'The Decolonization Question', in H.K. Chen (1998).
23. Z. Bauman (1989), *Modernity and the Holocaust,* Cambridge: Polity.
24. N. Thomas (1994), *Colonialism's Culture,* Cambridge: Polity.
25. Featherstone (1997), p. 12.

26. A. Behad (1994), *Belated Travels: Orientalism in the Age of Colonial Dissolution*, Cork University Press.
27. H.K. Chen (1998).
28. Ibid., p. 31.
29. I. Ang (1998), 'Eurocentric Reluctance: Notes for a Cultural Study of the New Europe', in H.K. Chen (ed).
30. A.G. Frank (1998), *Re-Orient*, University of California Press.
31. J. Goody (1996), *The East in the West*, Cambridge University Press.
32. Frank (1998), p. 8.
33. E. Shohat and R. Stam (1994), *Unthinking Eurocentrism: Multi culturalism and the Media*, London: Routledge.
34. I. Ang (1992), 'Dismantling Cultural Studies', in *Cultural Studies* **6** (3), 318.
35. See, for example, R. Kearney (ed.) (1992), *Visions of Europe*, Dublin: Wolfhound Press; E. Morin (1987), *Penser l'Europe*, Paris: UGE; C. Itty (1984), *Searching for the Asian Paradigm*, Bangkok; Asian Cultural Forum on Development; S. Sivaraksa et al. (eds) (1991), *Searching for Asian Cultural Integrity*, Bangkok: Sanit Pracha Dhamma Trust.
36. Ang (1998).
37. Clammer (1985).
38. For example, H. Bhabha (1994), *The Location of Culture*, London: Routledge.
39. For example, R. Munck and D. O'Hearn (eds) (1999), *Critical Development Theory*, London: Zed Books.
40. Augue (1999), p. 89.
41. A Chun (1996), p. 69.

PART III

Europe–Asia Linkages

4. Two continents, one area: Eurasia[1]

Hans-Dieter Evers and Markus Kaiser

INTRODUCTION: TWO CONTINENTS, ONE AREA

Europe and Asia: two continents, two civilizations, two vibrant economic zones, but one land mass, stretching from Madrid to Merauke, from Stockholm to Singapore, from Moscow to Madras, from Bonn to Beijing. You can buy a train ticket in Bielefeld to board a train for Beijing via Moscow or you can drive your car from Rome to Shanghai via Tashkent. The division of this vast area into two continents is a pure fiction of the human mind, a social and cultural construction of geographical space. The history of this division can be traced and historically explained, but still it is an imaginary, though powerful concept that draws boundaries and maintains distinctions. When Turkey applied for membership in the European Union it was at first rejected, officially on political (human rights) and economic grounds but it was alleged by the Turkish government, perhaps rightly, that some European politicians saw Europe as culturally distinct from an 'Asian' Turkey and therefore incompatible.

The orientalist construction of an 'Asian' culture as distinct from a European civilization that reached its peak during the colonial period, where it served to legitimize imperialist expansion, has by no means subsided. Good 'Asian values' as distinct from deteriorated 'Western values' are more recent inventions, based on similar strings of argumentation – but pointing in the opposite direction. For the past two decades Malaysia, like most other ASEAN countries, has 'looked East' in search of Asian values, production techniques, styles of governance and economic prosperity. Another forceful image of a region or continent has been constructed more recently, namely the so-called 'Asia-Pacific'. The term has been used to describe an area encompassing North America and East Asia, with some later extensions on both sides of the Pacific Ocean into Latin America and Southeast Asia. Since then it has become a powerful instrument to promote free trade, economic liberalization and the furthering of US interests. The vast streams of speculative capital flowing into the East and Southeast Asian part of the Asia Pacific area have brought boom and bust to the region. The devastating forces of speculative casino capitalism have been felt by Asian governments, corporations and, in a most severe manner, by the lower-income strata of East and Southeast Asian societies. 'Looking East', a policy prescribed by PM Mahathir of Malaysia, has come to an abrupt end. Perhaps it is timely to turn and look towards the long neglected North and West; to the vast tract of land of which Southeast Asia is, after all, an appendix.

Essentially, there have been two major routes connecting Asia and Europe: the ancient Silk Road and the sea route across the Indian Ocean. The latter is still used by modern shipping, but the old Silk Road has long lain dormant. Could it be revived?

EURASIAN TRANSREALITIES: REOPENING OF THE SILK ROAD

The Legacy of the Silk Road

The Silk Road from China to Europe could be analysed as being a geoculturally and geopolitically constructed corridor. Historically, long-distance trade (for example the Silk Road) was one mode of early globalization linking up different cultures, belief systems and networks of knowledge. The trading routes connecting Europe and East Asia have fascinated scholars, traders and adventurers throughout the centuries, and, of these, the Silk Road has been one of the world's oldest and historically most important intercontinental trade routes, its influences extending to the cultures of both Asia and Europe, the East and the West. From its emergence before Christ, through the golden age of the Tang dynasty in China, until its slow demise six to seven hundred years ago, the Silk Road[2] played a unique role in foreign trade and political relations, stretching far beyond the bounds of Asia itself. It left its mark on the development of civilizations on both sides of the continent.

Recent archaeological research in the steppes of Russia and Kazakhstan has shed new light on the domestication of the horse, the beginning of horseback riding, and the introduction of the chariot. These innovations in transportation were linked to the spread of ancient Indo-European languages, and to the opening of transcontinental trade and communication across the Eurasian steppes[3] establishing a Eurasian geocultural space. On the eastern and western sides of the continent, the civilizations of China and the West developed. The Silk Road was, for at least 4000 years, the main avenue of communication between the Mediterranean and China[4], linking two growth poles.

It is only with the hindsight provided by modern archaeological techniques, and access to historical documents from various Eurasian cultures, that we can form a picture of the vigour and constant motion of this trade system: 'The fragile threads of the Silk Road were always changing, waxing, and waning at the mercy of history. Roles changed as well as routes, as traders were joined by a motley crew of diplomats, invaders, refugees, pilgrims and proselytisers en route to outrageous new lands.[5]

According to Shimizu and Yakushik[6], in a geographical sense a route is a particular direction, a link. The historical Silk Road carries the notion of such a line on a map, just as the existing or planned infrastructure of pipelines, roads, air links, railway tracks, communication links and so on do today. Modern internal links within the Caspian Sea region inherited from the Soviet past, and external links with other regions are poorly developed, leading to the conclusion that the Caspian sea region in the twentieth century was cut off from the global economic and political systems in an unnatural manner.[7] Reconnecting Asia and Europe, and the natural neighbours of the former border zone of the once longest and most closed border of the world, is a result of the breakdown of the former Soviet Union.

The old and newly emerging system of transport for goods, persons and ideas suggests an interlinkage between, and an overlap of, Asia and Europe, facilitating a continual flow of money, goods, ideas, perceptions, discourses and persons. The circulating intermediaries allow networks to come into being by giving social links shape and consistency and, therefore, some degree of longevity and size. But they are not passive tools. For example, texts and technical artefacts can clearly define the role played by others in the network – both humans and non-humans. In other words, the 'material' and the 'social' intertwine and interact in all manners of promiscuous combinations[8] including the development of spatial conceptions. The 'material' might be loaded with different meanings, reflecting the transformation caused by market expansion on different levels. Goods might carry attached 'attitudes of consumerism' from the global economy which are recontextualized by the actors[9], thus integrating areas through a similarity of procedures. In short, localities are maintained while globalization takes place.

In the following paragraphs we will attempt to follow up the process of Eurasian integration, the construction of a region, along several dimensions. We shall not differentiate between physical and epistemological aspects of this process but, rather, combine the world of things with the world of meaning.

Transnational Trade

For some four millennia, trade connected Europe and East Asia, stimulating cultural creativity and economic growth. The recent opening of the borders of the former Soviet Union allowed access once again to the continental bridge of the Eurasian landmass, thus making it possible to reconnect the two economic growth poles of Europe and Southeast Asia for the potential benefit of Central Asia, as shown by Table 4.1 on the population and GNP per capita of respective countries. The table shows that the continental plateau of the Central Asian states has a comparatively small population with a low GNP per capita, constituting a development gap on a huge landmass. A development of this Eurasian corridor would most probably lead to a fast rise in economic performances along this Eurasian axis. This process has already begun.

Table 4.1   Eurasia: surface area, population and GNP per capita in selected areas, 1998

Region	Country	Surface area thousands of square km	Population (millions in 1998)	GNP (in billions of US$ in 1998)	GNP per US$ in 1998)
EU	15 member countries	3 244	375	8 261.9	22 032
Central Asia	Kazakhstan	2 717	16	20.6	1 310
	Kyrgyz Republic	199	5	1.6	350
	Tajikistan	143	6	2.1	350
	Turkmenistan	488	5	n. a.	640 (GDP)
	Uzbekistan	447	24	20.9	870
Total		3 994	56	45.2	807
Southeast Asia	Cambodia	181	11	3.0	280
	Indonesia	1 950	204	138.5	680
	Lao PDR	237	5	1.6	330
	Malaysia	330	22	79.8	3 600
	Myanmar	677	44	−33.4	n.a. (760 or less)
	Philippines	300	75	78.9	1 050
	Singapore	1	3	95.1	30 060
	Thailand	513	61	134.4	2 200
	Vietnam	332	78	25.6	330
Total		4 521	503	590.3	1 174
East Asia	China (incl. Taiwan)	9 597	1 239	928.9	750
	Japan	378	126	4 089.9	32 380
	Korea, RP	99	46	369.9	7 970
Total		10 074	1 411	5 388.7	3 819
NAFTA	Three member countries	21 293	397	8 914.4	22 454

Source: World Bank: World Development Report (2000).

There is already some tentative empirical evidence on how the newly emerging economic linkages facilitate Eurasian integration. Recent macro-economic data, presented in Table 4.2, show the establishment of an area as an alternative to 'Asia-Pacific'. Looking at the top ten countries and donors listed according to the amount of investments in Uzbekistan in 1997, one sees Europe and Asia meeting in Central Asia.

Table 4.2   Foreign direct investment, Uzbekistan 1997

Country	Percentage
United Kingdom	22.0
Malaysia	16.0
Turkey	12.6
USA	10.0
Japan	9.7
Korea	8.9
Germany	6.7
EBRD[10]	3.9
Indonesia	3.0
France	1.6

Note: The table displays the top ten countries and donors listed according to the amount of investments – including foreign direct investments, loans and financial liabilities under governmental warranty – in Uzbekistan at the end of 1997.

Source: Ministry for Foreign Economic Relations of the Republic of Uzbekistan (1998), p. 74.

Empirical research[11] in other regions of the world shows that, prior to a more formal regional integration, much more subtle and informal processes of integration foreshadow future trends.[12] In Central Asia, transborder petty trade has increased considerably after the demise of the Soviet Union. In Uzbekistan, our recent study showed that 83 per cent of goods imported by petty traders into Uzbekistan from outside the CIS originated from Asia. This might be taken as an indicator of the potential for a trans-Asian and Eurasian economic integration.

Central Asia's borders to China, Russia and the Near East are an important element in the development of trading there, as are the extensive informal networks and clan-style organizations that have developed new micro-structures in the context of the present postcommunist conditions.[13] Nevertheless, there are many factors in common with other postcommunist markets and trading arrangements, including the opening of borders leading to increasing day-to-day travel for the purposes of trade, the changing morality associated with trading and the embeddedness of market relations in distinctive social and cultural milieus which are, on the one hand, inherited from the Soviet times and, on the other, in the course of dynamic transformation.[14]

Existing parallels between current trading patterns and the 'Great Silk Road' strengthen the idea of its revival further. Earlier, hardship, banditry, time scales and common sense would obviously have made the conduct of transcontinental trading on a single track or network unlikely. It is reported that, even today, there are bandits operating on highways, while mafia groups are trying to get their slice of trading profits as well. Goods move in a stop-start fashion, and are exchanged from marketplace to marketplace. Similar to those old days, we see the emergence of trading posts and border markets on every major intersection of transnational roads and at national borders. In border towns, special container markets appear. In Chardjou, a town in Turkmenistan at the border with Uzbekistan, such a container bazaar came into existence as the Uzbek government allowed only smaller quantities to be imported.

Located in the countries of the CIS are major hubs for global merchandise. In Uzbekistan, it is the Ippodrom market in Tashkent, in the Ukraine it is Odessa, as a result of being located on the Black Sea coast. In the international markets, the inter-ethnic language is Russian. In Seoul – a centre for international shuttle-traders from all over the world – the Pusan (marketplace) is the centre for Russian and/or CIS shuttle-traders, and the Inchon (marketplace) is the centre for traders from China.[15] In Istanbul, ships are guided through its harbour by Russian traffic signs. A globalised Russianized infrastructure of hotels, restaurants, tourist agencies and so forth, in places like Bangkok, Istanbul, New Delhi, Kuala Lumpur, Seoul, Singapore and so on, emerged, serving the demand of the newly independent states of the former Soviet Union and Eastern Europe. In markets of a more regional importance, Russian is not that prominent any more. In Mazar-i-Sharif, Afghanistan, for example, shop-owners announce products with placards in Russian, but they have to ask someone else to write these for them since they do not speak Russian. The Cyrillic alphabet is just a symbol for trade in goods with a broader demand that attract people from the newly independent Central Asian states. Bargaining between shop-owners and shuttle-traders, however, is done in Tajik, Farzi, Uzbek or Turkmen. Using one of these languages would exclude the speakers from the others, since these languages are even written in different alphabets. Nevertheless, the Russian language is the *lingua franca* of cross-border trade to which all adjust, as did the merchants to the language of the Sogdian middlemen in the days of the Silk Road.[16]

Those findings coincide with the acknowledged increase of pilgrimage to Mecca by Muslims of Central Asia and China.[17] Nagata[18] provides a modern account of the interrelation of economic activity and religious matters. In Islam, economic activity is not viewed negatively and mobility is encouraged through the idea of transborder pilgrimage. To cite just one example from our field study, a pilgrim and small-scale trader stated, 'A pilgrimage to Mecca goes hand in hand with my business' (Ahmed, aged 42, Uzbek).

Generally the pilgrims are more wealthy and engaged in new economic activities. Many small-scale cross-border traders use the subsidized air fare on Uzbekistan Airways to join the hadsch to Mecca, and to stop over in Dubai, buying high-tech electronics along the way. Economic, cultural and spiritual integration is simultaneously taking place, constituting a Eurasian micro-structure of integration. Moreover, there is a flow of trans-Islam border-crossing movements, constituting a religious dimension of a Central Eurasian societal integration. Mobility in economic activities is a definite advantage, and religious mobility (for example, trips to Mecca) also implies social and economic prestige. The emergence of transnational Islamic connections is one effect of new religious movements.[19]

In this world on the move, distance becomes a category of social analysis. Distance, as well as borders, are at the same time obstacles and resources. Traders, for example, take risks and, therefore, are subject to exploitation by various kinds of people and different types of personalities. One resource for possible profit is the different prices in the various markets making up the market system. To the North of Tashkent, in Moscow, the prices are very high, becoming lower as one goes south. When flying from Almaty to Tashkent, prices are, on this axis, lower in Tashkent. In the producer countries in South-east and South Asia, commodity prices are even lower. National boundaries and economies are thus a resource for cross-border trading and travelling. National diversity, in other words, leads to the strengthening of integration.

Another question is whether there are developing transnational identities in relation to trade, or kinship networks among neighbouring countries. Our own studies give several examples of a tendency towards transnational linkages and family networks. The Chinese revitalized their old networks when they were allowed to travel to Kazakhstan again in 1986. As many goods are not produced in Xinjiang, there is an external influence anyway in the north-western Chinese province; for example, the fashionwear for women is Shanghai- or Singapore-dominated. Traders who have a base outside their home region, command female relatives to live at the trading post, or contract local marriages. This strategy, aimed at avoiding the reliance of other ethnic groups, seems to be a widespread pattern, as our field studies on Arab traders in Indonesia, and Chettiar moneylenders in Malaysia have shown.[20] Additionally, it offers the opportunity for a longer stay in foreign places for business reasons, and gives further evidence of translocalities emerging through economic reasoning.

Other examples of transnational identities are the typically hybrid joint ventures. UzDaewoo Bank, for example, was founded by a group of financial institutions together with several individuals. Fifty-five per cent of shares were held by Daewoo Securities, 10 per cent by Koram Bank, 25 per cent by the European Bank of Reconstruction and Development, 10 per cent by the National Bank for Foreign Economic Acitivity of Uzbekistan and Joint-Stock Bank of Consolidation Turon.[21] We regard this as an example of a newly emerged Eurasian banking institution.

In a way, the rise of new independent states in Central Asia, and the increasing importance of private trade and exchange of goods, led to a revival of the Silk-Road trade in the form of long-distance petty trade across the newly established borders of the new states of the former Soviet Union, as well as into other neighbouring countries including Turkey, Iran, Afghanistan, Pakistan, The Arab Emirates, Kuwait and China, and also India, Korea, Thailand and Malaysia. Turkish sources reported that the estimated annual turnover of the Turkish economy supplying trader-tourism from the former Soviet Bloc was in the region of ten billion US dollars.

Commodities: Asian Goods with a Western Accent

Transnational petty trade links different worlds and produces Eurasian products, markets and shops. It also promotes 'consumer attitudes' and a kind of consumerism that integrates Asia and Europe.[22] Supermarkets on the Broadway, the main street for leisure activities in the city centre of Tashkent, are 'Eurasian Shops' in the real sense of the word, where you will find all these famous 'Western products': Schwartau's jam, Granini juice, Kellogg's cornflakes, Bahlsen cookies, Langnese honey, Bavarian beer, CocaCola's soft drinks and Levis jeans – these often being produced in Asian countries. Competitors are the Uzbek–Turkish Mir-Burger supermarket, opened in January 1996, offering only Turkish products.

A Eurasian shop of another kind opened in association with a Turkish supermarket: this shop sells baby clothing and toys, as well as Moulinex electric appliances, jars and pots and tableware. All items in this shop have well-known brand names and are more expensive than the pots and glasses – usually made in China or Southeast Asian countries – offered in other shops in the vicinity of Tashkent. The cheaper items are familiar to us from Muslim-owned shops in Bielefeld or other European cities.

The interior décor in Eurasian-type shops differs profoundly from the far more simple Soviet-era stores. Generally speaking, the products, as well as the interior, appeal to a different clientele: they attract the 'New Russians', as well as the members of the nomenklatura, who now have the means to shop in these supermarkets. Women and men, expensively dressed, in fashionable Western outfits as well as modern Uzbek style or Muslim-like clothes, come to shop at stores offering more than locally produced items. They buy and hurry away in their expensive cars, speeding at 60–80 km per hour through the inner cities of the Central Asian capitals, turning the Soviet roads into dangerous highways. The BMW car, the nice suit and the attaché case are the insignia of the new businessmen.

As Fierman[23] asserts, the former aspirations of the Soviet youth in the Muslim republics can be lived out in the newly emerged Westernized youth culture in Tashkent, which is breaking with pre-Soviet and Soviet concepts, and the rules of the older generation and society found in other Asian societies. Music, discotheques (Asia), Lucky Strike bars and the Mir-Burger were the main media for this emerging youth culture. The Turkish amusement park (Aqua Park) is another site.

Music is very much a communal experience at in-house birthday parties and similar events. Cassettes and music videos spread as illegal copies. Mass concerts are shared events, such as when the pop group 'Boney M.' visited on tour. This group offered the chance for the audience to see the role model in person, in the flesh. Shared thoughts and feelings, and the relaxation experienced, create a sense of belonging to a Eurasian youth culture. The media play a key role in spreading Western culture and lifestyle. Indian soap operas are perceived as presenting the Western concepts of love and lifestyle. Television serials are shared experiences, and youngsters meet to have dinner and drink vodka whilst watching them.

To conclude, Asian goods with a Western accent can be seen as another dimension of a Eurasian integration. The specific links with Asia, combined with the attempted Westernization, creates a very specific and transnational Eurasian space. Generally, market traders conceal the Asian origin of Western-style goods. They laugh at anyone's stupidity if he or she is fooled by the French origin of a perfume or the Italian origin of a dress. Such knowledge may be termed a 'public secret' on the markets. None of the customers we spoke to admitted being fooled by the labels, and such labels were generally considered unimportant by both customers and traders.

The following statement derives from an interview in a marketplace in Tashkent, Uzbekistan:

> People who buy Reebok shoes in the Ippodrom market know that they are not *R* and for them it does not matter whether it says Reebok or Raabok or Ruubok. It makes no difference to the seller or to the buyer. They do not think about these things. For them it is not a reason ... If somebody finds a new article and it is labelled Reebok, and he thinks it will be a good article to sell, he will buy a batch and sell it, but not because of the name. It does not mean anything. I do not know why factories in China copy these names, because everybody knows that they are not true. I really do not know why those manufactures have these names sewn in (Marat, aged 42, Tatar, a trader in Tashkent, Uzbekistan).

Falsifications were legitimized by suggesting that there was no real distinction between a copied product and the Western equivalent, or that the copied product was of an even better quality than the original. Other discourses of legitimization exist.

> First it is necessary to ask what you mean by the term 'original'. For example, Adidas shoes are produced in Korea and sold in America, so are they original or not? All these companies like Nike and Puma manufacture goods in Korea and other Far Eastern countries because labour is cheaper there. Sometimes, when I buy something that says 'Made in Japan', I think I am buying the original article, but there are a lot of pirates producing very similar products. Sometimes they are very difficult to distinguish from the originals. Even the Japanese do not always distinguish between them (Oleg, aged 44, Russian, trader in Almaty, Kazakhstan).

In this case, Oleg is clearly connotating 'original' with 'Western'. The prestige of a given product derives, however, from its 'Westernness'. The high status enjoyed by Western clothes was apparently already prevalent in Soviet times. According to Shlapentokh[24], the West and Western items were not only very popular in the Soviet Union during the 1980s but were also copied by Soviet factories and sold as imported goods:

> The devotion to Western attire is so great that Soviet factories have begun to produce shirts, blouses and sweaters bearing various commercial logos printed in England, such as Marlboro, Mercedes Benz, or Levi-Strauss. The manufacturers attempt to pass them off as Western products. Given the ideological climate in the country in the 1980s, this action by factory directors is truly remarkable[25].

In addition, it is reported that in the second economy during Soviet times the illicit production of 'fake labels of origin' took place. Such goods were evaluated in terms of their ability to communicate a certain Western style.

On the other hand, especially in the recent years of economic transformation, transnational corporations have discovered the new local Central Asian markets among them Mercedes Benz and DAEWOO, representing Europe and Asia. In theory, everything is purchasable – due to partly liberalized import regulations – but not everything is affordable. For those, however, who can afford it, these new markets open up the possibility of creating what they perceive to be a European lifestyle.

The New Rich and the New Middle Classes

In ordinary language, nowadays, the concept 'New Russians', is applied all over the former Soviet Union to those who have quickly come into money and/or are in possession of necessary status through owning Western objects of prestige (for example, Western cars, a large apartment or house, buying in real stores, and so forth). 'New Russians' is a cliché referring to a non-Soviet and alien mentality, which is, according to Humphrey: 'rapacious, materialist and shockingly economically successful'.[26]

The 'New Russians' represent a different cultural group with new perceptions. They are different from the old Soviet nomenclatura, since they are more Western-oriented and found throughout the new states formed after the demise of the Soviet Union. They prefer a range of English-derived terms for themselves that express their cosmopolitanism. They refer to themselves as *professionaly* (professionals), *businessmeny* or *delovyye lyudy* (business people), *dilery* (dealers) and *menadzhery* (managers). This reveals unintended aspects of identity creation: 'these new people are understood not to be intrinsically other but indeed to have derived and spun away from "us", the unmarked mainstream, and furthermore it is felt that they may represent Russia's future'.[27]

The 'New Russians', the business elites, are rarely engaged in production, most of them involved in the export–import business or working as consultants, bankers, managers and related professions. Consumption is assumed to be very important in the lifestyling of the 'New Russians', not only in regard to the businessmen themselves, but also for the women surrounding them. The 'New Soviet Man' is accompanied by the 'New Soviet Woman': 'The New Russian [...] is pictured as man, with glamorous female dependants'.[28]

According to Humphrey, the identity of the 'New Russians' is increasingly constructed in a contradictory discourse. They do not have a shared history, or, at least, only a very short one. One kind of cultural work seems to be the new housing: the suburban villas or residential areas close to economically important places. Across the Ippodrom market in Tashkent such a residential area has developed recently. It is a place to show off one's own economic potential and position. To have well-equipped security staff is one sign. The newly emerged forms of housing construct their own world and a security guard controls the demarcations of middle-class living space.

The notion of 'New Russians' hints towards a comparison with recent work describing the New Rich[29] or New Middle Class[30] in East and Southeast Asia, and developments in the countries of the former Soviet Union and Eastern Europe. This body of research provides an important illustration of the rapid growth of the middle class, with attention to its ambivalence about the social consequences of economic change and about democracy. Asian and former socialist societies share an emphasis on collective, rather than individualistic, cultural values, making them different from the Euro-Atlantic experience. Balzer[31] (1997, p. 19) consequently asks if Asian values are now Eurasian values, or has Aziope replaced Eurasia. For Russia he argues that: 'An issue that emerges clearly from comparison with Asian cases pertains to Russian intolerance for income inequality enshrined in folktales, anecdotes and "national character".'[32]

Unsurprisingly, dislike of growing social disparities is a common theme in virtually all transition societies, including China. Robison and Goodman[33] state for the Chinese what could be equally true for Russians, Eastern Europeans and Central Asians. 'Many Chinese remain equivocal about the existence of the new rich, who are simultaneously admired and despised for their wealth ... Often an instinctive reaction is to attribute individual economic wealth solely to official corruption, or other illegal arrangements, rather than simply emphasising economic growth.'[34]

These social and cultural consequences are part of global transformation processes[35] characterizing both continents and making them one area.

Transport: Roads, Railways, Airways and Pipelines

Airways, roads and rails

The Eurasian transportation system being a mapable network of tracks and roads is metaphorically compared with the historical Silk Road in contemporary Central Asia. The drying up of the Silk Road was the opening of maritime trading routes between Asia and Europe, followed by the Iron Curtain. The Silk Road interchanged commodities, ideas, technologies and religions, cross-cutting the very different cultures and ethnic groups that used it. This imagination of the Silk Road, which was no single road but rather a fragile network of intercontinental caravan tracks, is used nowadays as a newly emerging Eurasian transport system connecting Europe and Asia once more. Another example of this is the extension of the railway, previously connecting Lanzhou to Urumchi, to the border with Kazakhstan, where, on 12 September 1990, it was finally joined to the former Soviet railway system, providing an important route to the new republics and beyond. Gladney states, in regard to the emerging Eurasian transport system, that:

> The Trans-Eurasian railway was completed in the autumn of 1990, far ahead of the 1992 schedule, and has already led to a jump in Sino–Soviet trade. While the 1988 trade was reported at 100 million Swiss Francs (an increase from 21 million in 1987), contracts for 200 million signed in 1988 have already largely been met.[36]

A Eurasian Continental Bridge, built to rival the Trans-Siberian Railway, has additionally been constructed from LianYunGang city in Jiangsu province (on the East China coast) to Rotterdam (via Bielefeld). The first phase of this development has already been completed, and the official opening of the railway was held on 1 December 1992. It already promises to be at least 20 per cent cheaper than the sea route, and, with its 11 000 kilometres, it is significantly shorter. From China, the route passes through Kazakhstan, Russia, Byelorussia and Poland, before reaching Germany and the Netherlands. The double tracking of the railway from Lanzhou to the border of the CIS has now been put high on the Chinese development priority list.

According to Gladney[37] the new transport infrastructure has enormously facilitated trans-Islamic travelling, especially among Muslims as Uighurs, Hui, Kazakhs and Kyrgyz in Central Asia and Xinjiang, China.

Pipelines

Another very central issue of the emerging Eurasian infrastructure is the development of the Caspian oil resources, raising the question of how the oil and natural gas should be transported to the consumption markets; especially to those in Europe and Asia.

> The calculations show that one of the best places to send the forthcoming oil and gas from the Caspian Sea Region would be through the Mediterranean to the European market, 'as oil demand over the next 10–15 years in Europe is expected to grow by little more than 1 million barrels per day'. However, there are even more promising regions – 'oil exports eastwards could serve Asian markets, where demand for oil is expected to grow by 10 million barrels per day over the next 10–15 years'. That's why one can mention two main possible directions of exports: to Western Europe and to East and Southeast Asia.[38]

This provides another evident link between Europe and (Southeast) Asia. Turkey, Russia, Iran, Pakistan and China are seeking to ensure that these pipelines are constructed across their territories.[39] These states would benefit economically from the royalty fees, transportation costs and the possible consumption of some of the oil and gas, while gaining political influence at the same time. On the other hand, Kazakhstan's long-term goal is to secure multiple oil-export routes to be more independent from Russia.[40] The short-term priority is to gain greater access to world markets via Russia to a terminal, via Novorossiysk, on the Black Sea coast. In addition to this Caspian Pipeline System, the Kazakh Kashagan and Tengiz oilfields will be connected through Samara, Russia, with the Baltic Pipeline System. A pipeline to link Kazakhstan and China by 2005 has already been agreed on as part of the sale of two big Kazakh oilfields to China. Pipelines linking up Iran and South Asia have also been discussed.[41]

The scenario is one of a regional power rivalry in world politics involving major global players. As regards the strategy of the United States, Shimizu and Yakushik summarize it as follows:

> The United States is pursuing a new strategy in the region, and with ever-growing impacts. One important strategic goal of the United States is to safeguard the 'independence' of the newly independent countries of the region, replacing Russia. Another strategic goal is to exclude Iran from participation in the production of Caspian oil and gas, and to prevent the development of transportation routes or pipelines that would lead from the Caspian region to either the Persian Gulf or the Indian Ocean via Iran. This second objective is not based on short-term economic considerations, but rather is closely linked to the United States' world strategy, especially its Middle East strategy. It is related to the ongoing dual containment

policy of the United States against Iran and Iraq, and the fact that Iran is to some
extent opposed to the American-led Middle East peace process, but it is also
anchored more deeply in the fundamental U. S. strategy in the Middle East, namely,
the strategy of not permitting the emergence of any dominant regional power
capable of influencing the oil market in the Persian Gulf.[42]

This new rivalry reminds one of the 'Great Game' when Britain and Russia
competed 'for the allegiances of the bejewelled satraps, khans and emirs who
ruled the Central Asian steppes in the 19th century'.[43] In those days, the independence of Afghanistan was considered in the same way as the independence
of Kazakhstan is viewed today: a matter of great importance for the welfare of
the USA, the European Union and the tranquillity of Asia. Thus Robbins[44],
rephrasing Mackinder, states, 'who controls the silk pipelines controls the
world'. The analogy with the old Silk Road is used to express economic
significance as well as to promote tourism.[45] In the end, a 'pipeline superhighway replaces the Silk Road'.[46] Oil and natural gas production and transportation is, however, only one, albeit important, aspect of economic integration.

Ethnicity and Religion

Travelling by train from Bielefeld to Beijing one crosses different cultural
zones. As one travels East, faces of fellow travellers, as well as the food items
sold on the platforms of the railway stations, become more Asian. Eating
pleasures include sweet cookies or beer, followed by Vodka and Soviet-type
sausages or dried fish, turning into Kumiz, melons and the Uzbek national dish
'plov', and so on.

   Eurasia as a whole, including Central Asia, is a region of great ethnic
diversity with far-flung migrant communities. The territories of ethnic co-
living overlap national boundaries and 'ethno-spaces' of other ethnic groups
(like concentric circles). Along this cross-continental axis, Kazakhstan,
located in the centre, shares not only a 7000 km border with Russia, but is
home to a Slavic minority comprising nearly 40 per cent of the population, and
also an Uighur minority in the south-west. China has been pressing territorial
claims on Kazakhstan, as the territory used to be considered 'Xi Yu'.[47]

   Recent works on migration suggest that migrant communities should be
viewed as transnational and translocal communities as a social reality beyond
the nation-state.[48] All these approaches capture migration as new multilocal
transnational social spaces developed between the region of departure and
arrival.[49] In this context, geographically separate places effectively become a
single community through the continuous circulation of people, goods, money
and information. Russians, Koreans and other ethnic groups in Central Asia
maintain their relationships with coethnics in the 'near abroad' (meaning other
Soviet successor states) and the 'far abroad'.[50]

According to official statistical data, 183 100 Koreans lived in Uzbekistan, and 103 300 in Kazakhstan in 1989. Most of them had been deported to Central Asia by Stalin.[51] In the city of Tashkent, Koreans make up 4.2 per cent of the population, according to the Statistical Office of Uzbekistan. Another 107 100 Koreans lived in Russia in 1989, providing the ethnic base for a vivid Asian multilocal space, bridging Asia, Central Asia and Europe. These are transmigrants according to the definition of Glick Schiller et al.: 'Trans-migrants develop and maintain multiple relations – familial, economic, social, organizational, religious, and political that span borders. Transmigrants take actions, make decisions, and feel concerns, and develop identities within social networks that connect them to two or more societies simultaneously.[52]

Russians, Koreans, Germans, Jews and others do not move between two bounded and separated worlds, but are present in different places in a single translocal community. They themselves and their culture are no longer tied to just one geographical location but their community is recreated trans-nationally. In this process, the place of migration, as well as the home community, are not static. Instead, as they become increasingly linked over the years, both are being transformed.

Taking this into consideration, one can describe a new kind of emerging population constituting Eurasia, composed of those whose networks, activities and patterns of life encompass both their host and home societies. Their lives cross-cut national boundaries and bring two societies – or more – into a single transnational social field.[53] Koreans in Uzbekistan call themselves Asian Russians, as the young generation speaks only Russian and reads Russian literature. Russians in Central Asia also refer to themselves as Asian Russians, being Russians with an Asian way of life.

Geocultural or macroethnic facts are important too in relation to the field of economics. Thus, the engagement of the German government in providing aid to Kazakhstan can partly be explained by Kazakh-Germans or Central Asian Jews being involved in development programmes within the region or migrated to Germany and assisted by special integration programmes in Germany. In the same way as the German-speaking minority provides a link to the European Union, Koreans play a similar role in the relations between Central Asia and the Korean peninsula. According to Shim[54], the relations between Korea and Central Asian countries are currently changing. During the Soviet era they had relations only with North Korea, due to ideological differences with the South, but now, as the Central Asian countries are much interested in the experiences of Korean economic development, South Korea has consolidated a relationship with Central Asian countries, centred on shared economic interest. Shim[55] speaks of the 'bridge role' of the Central Asian Koreans.

In 1993, South Korea was among the main donor countries of development aid. Its share in foreign trade with Kazakhstan was 4.5 per cent in 1996, matching that of Switzerland (5.3 per cent) and Turkey (4.5 per cent) (see Table 4.3).

Table 4.3   Foreign trade of Kazakhstan in 1996

Country	share in %
Germany	13.8
The Netherlands	10.5
China	8.0
USA	6.0
Italy	5.3
Switzerland	5.3
Turkey	4.5
South Korea	4.5
Hungary	3.7
Japan	3.6

Source: Institute of Developing Economies, Japan.

The importance of South Korea is even more evident looking at imports through joint ventures in Kazakhstan in 1996 (see Table 4.4).

Table 4.4   Imports of joint ventures with foreign participation in Kazakhstan in 1996

Country	volume, in US$000
South Korea	47 307
USA	43 321
China	41 950
Germany	40 920
Poland	37 642
Singapore	34 079
Austria	22 070
Turkey	15 949
Hungary	15 948
England	14 515

Source: Institute of Developing Economies, Japan.

Another ethnically based network exists among Russians, who have become, economically, the most important minority in the Central Asian republics. The Russian language is still the lingua franca here, supporting the flow of information between Europe and Central Asia.[56]

Ethnicity is only one resource for societal integration transgressing national borders. There is a flow of trans-Islam border-crossing movements, constituting a religious dimension to a Eurasia-in-the-making.[57] The former Soviet Union had the fifth largest Muslim population of any country in the world. 500 000 Muslims, out of 55 million, live in Moscow alone. According to Eickelman and Pasha[58], most Muscovite Muslims have remained closely linked with their communities of origin.

Muslims in St Petersburg, Moscow, Tashkent and Kuala Lumpur listen to Koran recitations or sermons among circles of friends or family members. Young Muslims acquire audiotapes of Koran and Sunna recitations by famous sheikhs. They originate from Saudi Arabia, the Middle East and Malaysia. Such audiotapes are crucial for the nourishment of a religious milieu in Muslim Eurasia. The latest exercise in religious politics for Malaysia has been in the new Central Asian republics of Kazakhstan, Tajikistan and, especially, Uzbekistan, where, according to Nagata,[59] there is a tempting vacuum. Before the Asian crisis, Malay officials negotiated to set up an institution of higher education in Tashkent. Nagata accounts the following:

> Political and trading overtures, followed by a prime ministerial visit to Uzbekistan mark this new alignment for the region's Muslim population and re-incorporation as members of the wider Muslim community. Also, in the name of the *ummah*, but outside the purview of the State, other Muslims, such as Dural Arqam, are forging their own independent connections with Central Asia, with emphasis on Uzbekistan. Whereas the Malaysian government treads carefully in religious matters, Arqam is the centre of a lively religious revitalisation in Uzbekistan, active in the restoration of mosques and resocializing of the youth, especially those in the university in Tashkent, in their ancestral faith. Arqam sweetens its overtures with offers of small-scale trade and investments, fruits of its own economic enterprises, and has already opened a Malay restaurant and invested in property in Tashkent.[60]

Turkish-speaking Muslim activists, based in Germany, have entered Uzbekistan and the other Central Asian republics as teachers of language and religion. They fund mosques, create religious study groups, and select promising Central Asian youth for further study and training in Germany.[61]

Krämer[62] depicted four women in Tashkent as being influential as 'cultural builders', offering religious advice in female circles based on their experiences in Mecca. She therefore acknowledges a change in Islamic practice and religious knowledge provided by such religious sojourners.[63] In the age of globalization, the media provide an additional source of ideas, concepts and messages.

Multilateral Associations

Six years after the independence of the Central Asian states a slight change
from bilateral agreements towards multilateral arrangements is observable as
neighbouring countries cooperate within the framework of ECO (Economic
Cooperation Organization) or CIS (Commonwealth of Independent States).
Similar examples of economic integration can be found in the West, with the
European Union, and in the East, with organizations in Southeast Asia such as
ASEAN, APEC, and EAEC (see Figure 4.1).

Figure 4.1   Economic integration, West and East

Notes: APEC – Asia-Pacific Economic Cooperation Conference; ASEAN – Association of
South East Asian Nations; BSECZ – Black Sea Economic Corporation Zone; CIS –
Commonwealth of Independent States; CSO – Caspian Sea Organization; EAEC – East
Asian Economic Caucus; EC – European Community; ECO – Economic Cooperation
Organisation.

Russian foreign policy is a good example. After an initial concentration on
internal issues and bilateral treaties, it is now aimed at a new multilaterality
within the CIS. However, in military cooperation there is a tendency towards
bilateral agreements as in the treaties on military aid and those between Russia
and the Central Asian states, such treaties envisage the stationing of border
troops in the various regions in question. Mongolia, for example, distanced

itself initially from Russia, after securing its independence, only later to sign bilateral agreements on security issues with Russia. In addition, Mongolia holds bilateral agreements with the USA, hoping for a warranty of security despite existing tensions.

Economic associations, however, are agreed on multilaterally. Only Turkmenistan denies itself multilateral agreements, despite its membership of ECO and its participation in the Turk summits. Thus, Turkmenistan refused to sign a follow-up agreement of the CIS charter at the Minsk summit in 1993, emphasizing instead its sovereignty. Turkey tends to seek multilateral cooperation within the framework of the Turk summits, while the hopes of Iran for cooperation within the framework of the ECO have, thus far, failed to materialize. According to Puri[64], India has enforced its pragmatic ties to the Central Asian states. All this gives evidence of the economic and political importance of the intercontinental axis, visible in trade statistics as well as in the development of economic regimes.

We have considered six dimensions of the integration process of Eurasia: trade, commodities, the development of a middle class, ethnicity, transport and international associations. They are all contributing towards a further integration of Eurasia. What is lacking so far is any epistemological construction of the concept. Eurasia has not yet become a powerful vision like Asia-Pacific. We shall, therefore, briefly look at the conceptualizing of Eurasia as it has been developed by various authors and politicians, recognizing that it has failed to gain global acceptance so far.

EURASIA: THE CONTESTED SPACE OF ASIA–EUROPE

The British geographer Sir Halford John Mackinder viewed geography as the science of distributions and thus campaigned for the study of regions. In a lecture delivered in 1904, Mackinder argued that Central Asia, as the 'Heartland of Eurasia', formed a geographical 'pivot of world politics'.[65] He noted a geopolitical antagonism between the Eurasian land power (that was, Russia) and the leading sea power (then Great Britain, subsequently the United States). His message was recently summarized by Robbins as follows: 'Whoever fully commanded and developed Eurasia's vast wealth would inevitably dominate the world'.[66]

In a short but significant monograph, André Gunder Frank[67] agreed on the 'centrality of Central Asia', simultaneously noting the unclear approaches by politicians and the scientific community towards the region, which has been cut off from the global economic and international political system by an artificial cross-continental border and a Soviet understanding of the role of the region.[68] However, recent studies on the spatial and societal formation of newly emerged Eurasia makes it evident that a comprehensive and systematic evaluation of the region is missing. One such book, *The Euro-Asian World*[69], establishes the concept of Euro-Asia as a means to discuss the European and Asian countries that are undergoing transformation. Dealing with security and economic aspects of the postcommunist transition over the last decade, the authors cover crucial elements of the transitional changes: conflicts and peacekeeping, geopolitical issues, economic realities. All of these points are addressed from a macro-perspective or from country studies limited in their perspective. Political advice and predictions are often based only on limited case or country studies, or on regionally concentrated ethnographies[70], and are highly speculative. There is a need to reflect further on the impact of the Soviet Union's demise and its impact on Europe and Asia.[71]

The core of the one area and the two continents is Central Asia, a region challenged by different corridorial claims. Mikhail Gorbachev referred to Eurasia in his book *Perestroika*, depicting the Soviet Union as a Eurasian state bridging Europe and the 'Asia-Pacific' region. His advisor, Igor Malashenko, argued that Russia was an ethnically and culturally unique country lying in Europe and Asia, a real Eurasian state, which was a source of attraction for other ethnic peoples around Russia.[72] Russia and the CIS (Commonwealth of Independent States) are seen by them as having a crucial role in shaping the region.

In contrast to such views, Huntington[73] named Turkey a 'torn country' in regard to an emerging geocultural Eurasia, unsure whether it belongs to Western civilization or not. He writes, 'having rejected Mecca, and then being rejected by Brussels, where does Turkey look? Tashkent may be the answer'.[74]

Overcoming national borders, Huntington speculates about a revitalized Turk civilization, covering a territory from Greece to China. Significantly, Suleyman Demirel, former Turkish Prime Minister, has often referred to the influential role Turkey is playing within Eurasia. It seems often that the expression 'Turkic world'[75], used to describe the area stretching from the Adriatic to the Great Wall of China, and Demirel's depiction of Eurasia are one and the same. The Istanbul-based British scholar, Winrow, states:

> Hence in a speech to the nationalist Turkish Clubs Association in Ankara in February 1993, Demirel declared that in Azerbaijan and in Central Asia a new community has evolved known as 'Eurasia' which was inhabited by Turks [...] The Turkish president noted that 'Turkey lies at the very epicentre of the vast geography and the new geopolitics of Eurasia'. This 'Eurasian reality' was inhabited by 200 million people spread from the Adriatic to the China Sea who shared common roots, language, religion, and culture.[76]

The spatial dimension of geocultural Eurasia, as shown, is not a very clear or agreed-on concept based on empirical evidence. Some stress the Persian,

Indian, or Chinese heritage and links, at the cost of others. It, therefore, should not come as a surprise that the Punjab University in Chandigarh, India, hosts a Centre for the Study of the Geopolitics of Central Asia, predominantly serving Indian needs.[77] The territorial notions of such conceptualizations of geographical space follow the line of argumentation put forward by Huntington[78] regarding the existence of confrontation between more or less homogeneous cultural circles or civilizations. This approach is based on the concept of cultural forms of integration beyond economic integration or competition of nations or regions. According to Wallerstein,[79] a civilization is a 'particular concatenation of worldview, customs, structures and culture [...] A civilisation refers to contemporary claims about the past in terms of its use, in the present to justify heritage, separateness, rights.[80] A deficit of such conceptualizations is that the division into relative homogeneous, culturally integrated, spatial formations reflects any empirical reality meaning that we are rather confronted with heterogenous, over-lapping habitats of various cultures, ethnic and religious groups of Asians and Europeans. Gladney,[81] for example, provides empirical evidence on the Islamization of Chinese geopolitics cross-cutting the supposed clashing civilisations of Islam and Confucianism and argues that trans-Islam is a relevant factor in Eurasia.

The macroethnic picture, as well as the distribution of those who believe in Eurasia, does not provide clear-cut evidence for territorial segmented civilizations. The cultural mixture varies along the cross-continental axis on the Eurasian landmass. The increase of geographical mobility, observed during recent years, has helped to strengthen regional integration despite greater emphasis on new national identities. By now it has become a commonplace to argue that globalization and localization are Janus-faced aspects of the same process, well expressed by Giddens in the following passage:

> Globalisation can thus be defined as the intensification of world-wide social relations which link distant localities in such a way that local happenings are shaped by events occurring many miles away and vice versa. This is a dialectical process because such local happenings may move in an observe direction from the very distanciated relations that shape them. Local transformation is as much part of globalisation as the lateral extension of social connections across time and space.[82]

Giddens' point that local transformations are part of the globalization process helps to explain why local nationalism and 'fundamentalisms' emerging in the 1980s and 1990s are not local counter-globalization developments or signs for clashing civilizations but are essential aspects of the global.

Furthermore, members of any 'we-group' are very likely to live in translocal, transnational or even transreligious neighbourhoods, which are in constant exchange with the absentees.[83] The fact is that translocal or transnational projects are very fragile, sequentially leading us to view them as opportunity structures rather than as constant entities calling for deterritorialized conceptions. It is the maintenance of such projects that we need to focus on. We propose to do this by using an actor-network approach that goes beyond national or other static formations.

CONCLUSION

As Said[84] has rightly asserted 'geographical and cultural entities ... are man-made'. Localities are not given, but socially constructed.[85] In contrast, one ought to focus on the processes of how locality is produced or constructed.[86] The production of local and translocal networks, neighbourhoods or lifeworlds is increasingly a struggle.[87] Different social actors are continuously involved in ongoing negotiations in the construction and production of 'locality' and 'networking'. In mastering space, discourse is more and more what counts.[88]

The reopening of the Silk Road is a newly emerged mode of globalization effected by actor-networks conducting small-scale trade. The transition may be interpreted as a movement from a locality to several global networks, leaving out nationality. The conditions of transitional society are especially mirrored in the Asian trade routes, and in the overall attempt to Westernize Asian merchandise. The economic activity of cross-border shuttle-traders is linking Europe and Asia. People, goods and knowledge are the essence of a sociocultural integration of this geocultural space. The prevalence of US dollars in the market, as well as the existence of fake Western commodities, therefore epitomize a discrepancy between the imagined 'Europe', the imagined 'West', and the actual Asian influences. A Eurasia beyond national borders appears to be in the making.

NOTES

1. Paper presented at the Asia–Europe Linkages Conference, University of Birmingham, 2–3 July 1999. The material was collected within the frame of the self-conceived project 'Development of a Eurasia Concept for Bilateral Cooperation between the Federal Republic of Germany and Central Asia' carried out by Markus Kaiser and initiated by Professor Hans-Dieter Evers. This project was part of the International Affairs Programme of the Robert Bosch Foundation.
2. Hans W. Haussig (1983), *Die Geschichte Zentralasiens und der Seidenstraße in vorislamischer Zeit*, Darmstadt; Hedin, Sven ([1938] 1994), *The Silk Road*, Delhi: South Asia Books.
3. David Anthony (1995), Horse, wagon, and chariot: Indo-European languages and archaeology, in *Archaeology* (March/April), 554–65.
4. I. M. Franck and D. Brownstone (1986), *The Silk Road: a History*, New York/Oxford: Facts on File, p. 1.
5. Calum MacLeod and Bradley Mayhew (1997), *Uzbekistan: the Golden Road to Samarkand*, Hong Kong Odyssey, p. 201.

6. Manabu Shimizu and Valentin M. Yakushik (1998), 'The Caspian Basin Oil and Its Impact on Eurasian Power Games: IDE Spot Survey, June 1998', Report, Tokyo: Institute of Developing Economies, p. 22.
7. Ibid.
8. Nigel Thrift (1996), *Spatial Formations*, London: Sage, p. 24.
9. Beng-Huat Chua (1992), 'Shopping for Women's Fashion in Singapore', in Rob Shields (ed.), *Life-style Shopping: The Subject of Consumption*, London: Routledge; Beng-Huat Chua (ed.) (2000), *Consuming Asians: Ideas and Issues*, London: Routledge.
10. EBRD is the abbreviation for European Bank for Reconstruction and Development.
11. We refer mainly to studies carried out at the Sociology of Development Research Centre, University of Bielefeld, as well as other research on related topics.
12. To cite one example: increasing small-scale cross-border trade within Southeast Asia indicated trends towards the economic integration of ASEAN.
13. Hans-Dieter Evers and Heiko Schrader (eds) (1994), *The Moral Economy of Trade: Ethnicity and Developing Markets*, London: Routledge; Markus Kaiser (1998a), 'Reopening of the Silk Road: International Informal Sector Trade in Post-Soviet Uzbekistan', Doctoral Dissertation, University of Bielefeld.
14. Kaiser (1998a).
15. Ui-Sup Shim (1997), *Transition to Market Economy in the Central Asian Republics: Korean Community and Market Economy*, Tokyo, Institute of Developing Studies, p. 198.
16. Kaiser (1998a).
17. Dru Gladney (1992), 'Transnational Islam and Uighur National Identity: Salman Rushdie, Sino-Muslim Missile Deals, and the Trans-Eurasian Railway', in *Central Asian Survey*, **11** (3), 6; Kaiser (1998a); Dale F. Eickelman and James P. Piscatori (1990), *Muslim Travellers: Pilgrimage, Migration and the Religious Imagination*, London: Routledge.
18. Judith Nagata (1994), 'How to be Islamic Without Being an Islamic State, in: Akbar S. Ahmed and Hastings Donnan: *Islam, Globalization, and Postmodernity*, London: Routledge, p. 83.
19. Ildikó Bellér-Hann (1998b), 'Transition, Entrepreneurship, and Religious Identity among the Uighurs in Xinjiang', lecture given at the Sociology of Development Research Centre, University of Bielefeld, on 29 April; also Ildikó Bellér-Hann (1998a), 'Temperamental Neighbours: Uighur-Han Relations in Xinjiang', Northwest China, unpublished paper, Berlin; Gladney (1992).
20. Evers and Schrader (1994); Hans-Dieter Evers (1988), 'Traditional trading networks of Southeast Asia', *Archipel*, 35, pp. 89–100.
21. Ministry for Foreign Economic Relations of the Republic of Uzbekistan (1998), *Uzbekistan: At the Doorstep of the Third Millennium. Investment Guide 1998-2000*, Tashkent, p. 74.
22. Chua (1992); Chua (2000).
23. William Fierman (1988), 'Western Popular Culture and Soviet Youth: a Case Study of the Muslim Regions', *Central Asian Survey*, **7** (1), 7–36.
24. Vladimir Shlapentokh (1989), *Public and Private Life of the Soviet People: Changing Values in Post-Stalin Russia*, New York and Oxford: Oxford University Press.
25. Ibid., p. 151.
26. Caroline Humphrey (1997), 'The villas of the "New Russians": a sketch of consumption and cultural identity in post-Soviet landscapes', *Focaal*, 30/31, 87; see also Caroline Humphrey (1998), 'The villas of the "New Russians": consumption and gender in suburbia', Paper presented at the research seminar of the Sociology of Development Research Centre, University of Bielefeld, 6.5.1998.
27. Humphrey (1997), p. 86.
28. Ibid.
29. Richard Robison and David S.G. Goodman (1996), *The New Rich in Asia: Mobile Phones, McDonalds and Middle-class Revolution*, London and New York: Routledge.
30. Solvay Gerke (2000), 'Global Lifestyles under Local Conditions: The New Indonesian Middle Class', in Beng-Huat Chua (ed.), *Consuming Asians*, London: Routledge.

31. Harley Balzer (1997), 'A Shadow Middle Class for a Shadow Economy', Paper presented at the XXIX Annual Convention of the AAASS, Seattle, Washington, 20–23 November, p. 19.
32. Ibid.
33. Robison and Goodman (1996).
34. Ibid., p. 227.
35. Hans-Dieter Evers (1996), 'Globale Märkte und soziale Transformation', in G. Mueller (ed.), *Weltsystem und kulturelles Erbe: Studien zur Sozialanthropologie*, Berlin: Reimer, pp. 165–173.
36. Gladney (1992), p. 5.
37. Ibid.
38. Shimizu and Yakushik (1998), p. 23.
39. Alvin Z. Rubinstein and Oles M. Smolansky (1995), *Regional Power Rivalries in the New Eurasia. Russia, Turkey and Iran*, New York: Armonk, London: M. E. Sharpe; Shimizu and Yakushik (1998).
40. *Financial Times* (1999), 'Kazakhstan. Annual Country Review III' (1 July), London.
41. Ibid.
42. Shimizu and Yakushik (1998), p. 30.
43. *Financial Times* (1999), I.
44. Gerald Robbins (1994), 'The Post-Soviet Heartland: Reconsidering Mackinder', *Eurasian Studies*, **1** (3), p. 43.
45. MacLeod and Mayhew (1997).
46. Stuart Parrot (1997), 'Pipeline Superhighway Replaces the Silk Road', in Radio Free Europe/Radio Liberty (RFU/RL), 19 November.
47. *Financial Times* (1999), I.
48. Katy Gardner (1995), *Global Migrants, Local Lives. Travel and Transformation in Rural Bangladesh*, Oxford: Clarendon Press; N. Glick Schiller, L. Basch and C. Blanc-Szanton (eds.) (1992), *Towards a Transnational Perspective on Migration: Race, Class, Ethnicity, and Nationalism Reconsidered*, New York: New York Academy of Sciences; Stuart Hall (1991), 'The Local and the Global: Globalization and Ethnicity', in Anthony King (ed.), *Culture, Globalization and the World-System*, Binghampton, NY: Department of Art and Art History, State University of New York; Ulf Hannerz (1996), *Transnational Connections: Culture, People, Places*, London: Routledge; Anja Peleikis (1998), 'Lebanese in Motion. The Making of a Gendered "Globalized Village"', unpublished dissertation, University of Bielefeld; Ludger Pries (1996), 'Transnationale Soziale Räume. Theoretisch-empirische Skizze am Beispiel der Arbeitswanderungen Mexiko-USA', *Zeitschrift für Soziologie*, **25** (6); Ludger Pries (1997), 'Transnational Spaces: the Example of Mexican-American Labour Migration', conference paper, 'Globalization of Communication and Intercultural Experiences', Berlin, 18–19 July, 456–72; 3.
49. Pries (1997).
50. Markus Kaiser (1998b), 'Russians as minority in Central Asia', *A European Journal of Migration and Ethnic Relations*, Special Displacement Issue, Migration, No. 31, Berlin; Markus Kaiser (2000), 'Translokale Zivilgesellschaft im postsowjetischen Vergesellschaftungsraum', in Dimitri Gavra, Manfred Glagow, Michael Kleineberg and Heiko Schrader (eds) *Zivilgesellschaft in Russland*, Hamburg: LIT Verlag.
51. Shim (1997), p. 182.
52. Glick Schiller et al. (1992), p. 2.
53. Ibid., p. 4.
54. Shim (1997), p. 203.
55. Ibid.
56. Kaiser (2000).
57. James P. Piscatori (1987), 'Asian Islam: International Linkages and Their Impact on International Relations', in John L. Esposito (ed.), *Islam in Asia*, New York: Oxford University Press; Ro'i Yaacov (1995), *Muslim Eurasia: Conflicting Legacies*, London: Frank Cass.

58. Dale Eickelman and Kamran Pasha (1991), 'Muslim societies and politics: Soviet and US approaches – a conference report, *Middle East Journal*, **45** (4), 632.
59. Nagata (1994) p. 83.
60. Ibid.
61. Dale Eickelman (1997), 'Trans-State Islam and Security', in: Susanne Hoeber Rudolph and James Piscatori (eds), *Transnational Religion and Fading States*, Boulder, Colo. Oxford: Westview, p. 33.
62. Annette Krämer (1998), 'Religiosität im Wandel – otinoji und khalfa in Usbekistan', paper presented at the 'Junges Forschungsforum Zentralasien', (4/5 April), Bamberg.
63. Sergei P. Poliakov (1992), 'Everyday Islam. Religion and Tradition in Rural Central Asia', New York: Armonk, London: M. E. Sharpe; Ludmila Polonskaya and Alexei Malashenko (1994), 'Islam in Central Asia', Reading: Ithaca Press.
64. Madan Mohan Puri (1995), 'India and Central Asia, Geopolitical Stakes and Strivings', paper presented at the international seminar 'Central Asian Geopolitics, Tendencies and Transformation', held at the Panjab University, Chandigarh, 3–10 December.
65. H. Mackinder (1904), 'The geographical pivot of history', *Geographical Journal*, **XXII** (4), 421.
66. Robbins (1994), p. 34.
67. André Gunder Frank (1992)' 'The centrality of Central Asia', *Comparative Asian Studies*, **8**, 50–74.
68. Martha B. Olcott (1982), 'Soviet Islam and world revolution', *World Politics*, **34** (4); Martha B. Olcott (1992), 'Central Asian independence', *Foreign Policy*, **71** (3).
69. Yelena Kalyuzhnova and Dov Lynch (eds) (2000), *The Euro-Asian World. A Period of Transition*, Basingstoke: Macmillan.
70. Jack Goody (1990), *The Oriental, the Ancient and the Primitive. Systems of Marriage and the Family in the Preindustrial Societies of Eurasia*, Cambridge: Cambridge University Press; Mehrdad Haghayeghi (1995), *Islam and Politics in Central Asia*, New York: St Martin's Press; J.S. Schoeberlein-Engel (1994), 'Identity in Central Asia: Construction and Contention in the Conceptions of "Özbek", "Tâjik", "Muslim", "Samarqandi" and Other Groups', PhD Dissertation, Harvard.
71. Many experts in Europe and Asia analyse the Caspian Sea region and its land-locked states on the basis of two notions: 'a "corridor" and a "route"' (Shimizu and Yakushik, 1998, p. 22). Following Shimizu and Yakushik, a corridor may be defined as a spatial system of geopolitical, geoeconomic, geocultural and other interests. Those are, or are claimed to be, based on trading relations, and historic, cultural or ethnic links, on a global or regional level, as the Trans-Atlantic (Western Europe–Northern America), Asia-Pacific (Northern America–Southeast Asia), Pan-American (Northern–Southern America) and Ibero-American corridors exemplify.
72. Milan L. Hauner (1994), 'The Disintegration of the Soviet Eurasian Empire: the Ongoing Debate', in Mohiaddin Mesbahi (ed.), *Central Asia and the Caucasus after the Soviet Union: Domestic and International Dynamics*, Gainesville: University Press of Florida, p. 229.
73. Samuel Huntington (1993), 'Clash of Civilizations?', in *Foreign Affairs*, **72**, pp. 22–49.
74. Ibid., p. 42.
75. Gareth M. Winrow (1995a), 'Turkey and Former Soviet Central Asia: A Turkic Culture Area in the Making?', in K. Warikoo, *Central Asia: Emerging New Order*, New Delhi: Har-Anand Publishers.
76. Gareth M. Winrow (1995b), 'Geopolitics and Geoculture: Turkey and Central Asia', Paper presented at the international seminar 'Central Asian Geopolitics, Tendencies and Transformation' held at the Panjab University, Chandigarh, p. 15.
77. Puri (1995).
78. Huntington (1993); Samuel Huntington (1996), *Clash of Civilizations and the Remaking of World Order*, London: Simon & Schuster.
79. Immanuel Wallerstein (1990), 'Culture as the Ideological Battleground of the Modern World-System', in M. Featherstone (ed.), *Global Culture*, London: Sage, pp. 31–55; Immanuel Wallerstein (1991), *Geopolitics and Geoculture: Essays on the Changing World-System*, Cambridge, UK and USA: Cambridge University Press.

80. Wallerstein (1991), pp. 187, 215, 235–6.
81. Gladney (1992).
82. Anthony Giddens (1990), *Consequences of Modernity*, Stanford: Stanford University Press, p. 64.
83. Peleikis (2000), 'The Emergence of a Translocal Community, the Case of a South Lebanese Village and its Migrant Connections to Ivory Coast', CEMOTI, Cahier d'études sur la Méditerranée Orientale et le monde turco-iranien, (30), Juin-Décembre, pp. 297–317. In Richard Fardon (ed.), *Counterworks. Managing the Diversity of Knowledge*, London: Routledge; Pries (1996), (1997); Kaiser (1998b).
84. Edward W. Said (1995), *Orientalism: Western Conceptions of the Orient*, London: Penguin, p. 5.
85. Appadurai (1995).
86. Peter L. Berger and Thomas Luckmann (1969), *Die gesellschaftliche Konstruktion der Wirklichkeit. Eine Theorie der Wissenssoziologie*, Frankfurt: Suhrkamp.
87. Peleikis (1998).
88. John Agnew and Stuart Corbridge (1995), *Mastering Space. Hegemony, Territory and International Political Economy*, London and New York: Routledge, p. 227.

5. The unfolding Asia–Europe Meeting (ASEM) process[1]

Paul Lim[2]

INTRODUCTION: ASEM IN CONTEXT

European Union–Asia relations have been characterized by bilateral relations with selected countries of Asia, particularly with the North-East Asian and South Asian countries, and with the members of the South Asian Association for Regional Cooperation (SAARC). With South East Asia, it has been a bloc-to-bloc relationship grounded in the EEC–ASEAN Cooperation Agreement of 1980. The EU had little relationship with the Indo-Chinese states until recent years, culminating with bilateral agreements with them. There was a limited and low key relationship with Burma but, in response to the student demonstrations of March to August 1988 and the May 1990 elections, Burma became an issue in relationships between the EU and ASEAN.

In July 1994, Europe–Asia relations got a boost when the European Commission produced its Communication entitled, 'Towards a New Asia Strategy' (TNAS).[3] This was followed by the Prime Minister of Singapore proposing a meeting of European and Asian leaders to his French counterpart; a proposal that was accepted. Prime Minister Goh spoke of the missing link in the triangular relationship between Asia, the USA and the EU. ASEM was endorsed and adopted by ASEAN. Consequently, the first ASEM was held in Bangkok in 1996, the second in London in April 1998, and the third in October 2000 in Seoul, Korea.

Some say ASEM was, in a way, a consolation prize to the EU, which had been excluded from the Asia Pacific Economic Cooperation (APEC). The EU felt isolated by APEC. ASEM gave the EU a special relationship with Asia, similar to that the Americans had via APEC. The EU realized that it should not be left behind by the USA and Japan in having a stake in the Asian economic boom.

This chapter begins by offering a descriptive analysis of the ASEM process and the issues addressed at the ASEM II in London. On the basis of this, the prospects for the ASEM process are assessed, focusing on issues of membership, the involvement of civil society in the ASEM process, the relationship between ASEM and EU–ASEAN countries, and the scope for more active cooperation between Northeast Asian and Southeast Asian leaders within the ASEM process. These issues are explored under three headings: (i) What is ASEM?; (ii) What did the London ASEM II discuss?; and (iii) What are the issues to be settled?

WHAT IS ASEM?

The ASEM Players

The ASEM players are the heads of state/government from ten Asian countries and from the 15 Member States of the European Union, together with the President of the European Commission. These are the summit participants. Apart from them there are the foreign ministers and the two European Commissioners responsible for external relations (including Asia), who do not join the summiteers but meet between themselves. They are joined by scores of top civil servants and ambassadors.

However, a closer look will reveal that, among the EU member states, it is only certain ones who have a major stake in ASEM. These are the UK, Germany, the Netherlands and France, in that order, in view of their major economic interests in Asia in terms of investments and markets. Even in political and security terms, few of the EU member states would see any role for themselves in Asia. Although Burma, Cambodia and East Timor are, in theory, political issues for all member states, in reality they concern only a few, the rest following the leaders. The Korean peninsula and the Korean Peninsular Energy Development Organization (KEDO) are other EU concerns (as also are the USA, Japan, South and North Korea) but the EU is excluded from the inter-Korean four-party talks. Funding KEDO is principally the project of the European Commission. The European Parliament's endorsement started with reservations on consultative procedures related to the Euratom Treaty.

Agence Europe noted, on 21 August 1997, the European Commission's wish that the 15 member states present a united front to Asian countries but this attitude is not shared by all states. Some among them seek a high degree of national autonomy in relations with the Asian continent. This clearly demonstrates that the EU is not a superstate but merely a community of common interests. Nation-states continue jealously to guard their national interests and sovereignty.

On the Asian side, it appears that there is much interest in ASEM in terms of drawing potential investors from Europe to Asia, and also in exploiting Europe as a market and source of technology.[4] There are, however, concerns about how EU enlargement and the introduction of the euro might affect them. There are also security concerns on the Asian side. Only Malaysia and Japan have concrete interest in Bosnia, the former having troops there and, as a gesture of Muslim solidarity, taking in Bosnian refugees on its soil, while the latter contributes in funding Bosnia's reconstruction. Neither would wish Burma, East Timor or human rights in general to cloud their relations with the EU. They have appealed to the EU not to allow these sore issues to block relations but to look at the wider picture of relationships, which intrinsically includes the economic benefits of relationship with Asia.

The Activities of ASEM and the Question of Institutionalization

European Union spokepersons describe ASEM as informal, non-institutional and not an organ for negotiations. However, summit meetings are the culmination of working meetings that took place at the level of foreign, finance and economic Ministers plus meetings of civil servants at the levels of the Senior Officials Meeting (SOM), the Senior Officials Meeting on Trade and Investment (SOMTI) and the financial deputies. Is this not institutionalization? ASEM has set in motion, through such meetings, the process of institutionalization that is unavoidable when human social actors get together, if something is to be achieved. At such meetings, negotiations take place and decisions are taken producing common plans, activities, projects and agendas. Although the Chairman's Statements of ASEM I and II reiterate that there will be no institutionalization, and although there is no ASEM Secretariat such as APEC has, ASEM is nonetheless being institutionalized, for otherwise it simply cannot function. It is, therefore, not quite as informal as the Chairman's Statements of both ASEM I and II claim. It is only informal in the sense that the heads of state and governments, and the President of the European Commission, meet in a relatively informal atmosphere. That institutionalization has begun is evident from the Chairman's Statements of both ASEM I and II, which lay out the programme of activities till the next ASEM. Let us look at the programme of activities of ASEM II, taking into account that of ASEM I.

ASEM I's activities consisted of the following: the Asia–Europe Business Forum (AEBF), the Asia–Europe Business Conference (AEBC), a study of the Trans-Asian railway network by Malaysia, the Asia–Europe Environmental Technology Centre (AEETC), the Asia–Europe Foundation (ASEF), the Asia–Europe University Programme (AEUP), intellectual exchanges and networking between think-tanks, economic synergy between Asia and Europe, youth exchange programmes of the 'Davos' type, ministerial meetings, SOMTI, WGIP involving governments and private sectors, the Asia–Europe Cooperation Framework (AECF), a study group on enhancing technological exchanges and cooperation, customs cooperation on procedures and preventing the illicit drug trade, and cooperation in the development of the Mekong River Basin.

ASEM II came up with more new projects while noting, welcoming and adopting those of ASEM I. The AECF was adopted. The Trade Facilitation Action Plan (TFAP) and Investment Promotion Action Plan (IPAP), which includes the Investment Experts Group (IEG), were also adopted. The AEETC was launched. The Asia–Europe Young Leaders Symposia (AEYLS), which already had a calendar of meetings and venues, was welcomed, as was the establishment of the Asia–Europe Centre at the University of Malaya in Malaysia, which will ultimately be upgraded to the Asia–Europe University. A report of the Trans-Asian railway network coordinated by Malaysia was noted. New AEBF, with specific dates and venues, were welcomed. Continued work on developing policies, and measures of cooperation in other fields like infrastructure development, energy and the environmental sector, were emphasized. The new projects are:

- an Asia–Europe Vision Group (AEVG), which met for the first time in Cambridge on 6–7 April 1998;
- an Asia–Europe Small and Medium Size Entreprises (SMEs) Conference in Naples;
- an ASEMConnect electronic resource network for SMEs;
- a meeting of experts on the promotion of the welfare of children and combating illicit drugs, which seems to be a follow-up to discussions on the same matter in ASEM I;
- enhancing and expanding educational links between young people;
- strengthening cooperation on environmental issues: fresh water, forestry, climate change and sustainable development, the Rio Agreements, Agenda 21, the Conventions on Biodiversity and Climate Change, the follow-up to Kyoto and the Statement of Principles on Forests;
- cooperation on environmental disaster preparedness and management capacities via programmes like the Disaster Preparedness Programme of the European Community Humanitarian Office (DIPECHO);
- protecting and promoting ASEM cultural heritage, a subject which had come up in ASEM I but about which nothing apparently was done;
- 'State and Market' seminar in Copenhagen, held before the Foreign Ministers' Meeting in 1999;
- setting up the Asia–Europe Information Technology and Telecommunications Programme (AEITTP), to be coordinated by Thailand;
- in the field of community healthcare, a meeting of experts on combining traditional and modern medicine;

- network of megacities of ASEM countries, with the first Asia–Europe Forum of Governors of Cities (AEFGC) in Thailand in 1999;
- ASEM education hubs for student exchange between Asian and European universities;
- an Asian–Europe Agricultural Forum (AEAF);
- SME centres;
- an Asia–Europe Management (AEM) programme at the Asian Institute of Management (AIM);
- a seminar on labour relations and a seminar on peace and society building.

Looking at all these projects, is this not an institutionalization process? Legally speaking, one may argue that it is not institutionalization because what is agreed at ASEM is not legally binding, unlike the EEC–ASEAN Cooperation Agreement or any other bilateral agreement, which is a formal, binding commitment. In the case of ASEM, the fulfilment of projects, plans and so on is based upon peer pressure or obligation. However, from a sociological perspective the process of institutionalization is the outcome of human activity, especially when that activity is conducted in an organized and planned way. Institutionalization in the sociological sense is not dependent upon whether or not there is a signed binding agreement. It is a process independent of the social actor's perception or belief that ASEM is informal, non-institutional and non-binding.

Some hold the view that the informality of ASEM has to be internalized rather than institutionalized. The Asian side has a difficulty with this, because they have APEC as a point of reference. Both sides, the European and Asian, perceive ASEM as consultative and, hence, not an organ of negotiations leading to legally binding agreements, as is the case, for example, with the WTO. Hence, the ASEM social actors prefer to speak of discussions leading to agreed projects and plans whose fulfilment depend upon peer pressure.

Reflecting on this 'legalistic' definition of institutionalization and negotiations, one may perceive a European approach which differs from the Asian one. The Asian approach is the gentleman's agreement based on trust and confidence in your interlocutor. The European legalistic approach is based on impersonality and distrust *a priori*, hence requiring a written contractual relationship. ASEM clearly follows the Asian way and this suits the EU side since it is legally non-binding, hence no negotiations and no institutionalization. The Asians also fear a binding ASEM commitment. If the Asians had their way, they would not want other legally binding international instruments like that of the WTO. This is not simply because it goes against the Asian way of doing things, but because they do not want to be bound by international agreements. Gentleman's agreements can be broken and the only sanction is loss of face and/or group exclusion.

WHAT DID THE LONDON ASEM II DISCUSS?

EU-ASEAN and Burma

ASEM is about political dialogue, and in London several thorny political issues were discussed. Among these were EU–ASEAN relations, and the relations of both with Burma. The ASEAN side took the line that the EU position on its relations with ASEAN was inconsistent with an ongoing dialogue at ministerial level on the one hand and the suspension of the Joint Cooperation Committee (JCC) on the other. ASEAN asked for a compromise solution with regard to the JCC. The message conveyed was that there were signs that the Burmese regime was listening to ASEAN overtures. The best way forward was dialogue instead of confrontation. Cutting off contacts with Burma would not help. In ASEAN's Regional Forum (ARF), Burma had been allowed to attend as an observer and this had been helpful. The same, they argued, should apply in terms of EU–ASEAN dialogue: the EU needed to show more flexibility.

The EU side made clear the difference between EU–ASEAN political dialogue and the EC–ASEAN relationship in general. The latter was based on a specific agreement that could only be changed with parliamentary approval. The EU hoped that ASEAN's efforts with regard to Burma would be successful. It noted, however, that Burma was one of the biggest drug-exporting countries. ASEAN leaders noted in turn that even the USA was now releasing funds for anti-drug programmes in Burma and that the EU had, in the past, dealt with autocratic regimes. The discussion ended by calling for efforts to overcome the impasse and to do justice to the oldest dialogue relationship that ASEAN had been involved with. That EU–ASEAN relations were made a special item on the ASEM II agenda, points definitely to the crucial place of ASEAN in the ASEM process. EU–ASEAN and ASEM cannot be divorced. They are fora where the same issues are discussed. The ASEAN Post-Ministerial Conference (PMC) is another.

Human Rights in ASEM

Unlike ASEM I, human rights was absent from the Chairman's Statement of ASEM II. Why should this have been? Observers say that there was no need to repeat what had already been said in the ASEM I Statement. At the press conference, the UK Prime Minister, Tony Blair, stated that fundamental rights had been discussed. Mr Blair confirmed that Portugal raised the issue of East Timor.[5] Human rights, along with civil society, was described by Agence Europe[6] as being on short allowance, but Mr Blair assured the press that human rights were discussed. The Asia–Europe People's Forum (AEPF)[7] expressed deep concern that the issues of democracy and human rights were not centre-stage in discussions at ASEM II.[8] The impression one gets of ASEM II is that there was an avoidance of anything conflictual.[9] Why? The Singapore prime minister stated that human rights was not a burning issue for this meeting, which was centred instead on the economic crisis prevailing at the time. Given that crisis, important rights were simply to be able to have a roof over one's head and eat, said the Malaysian Prime Minister and the Chinese foreign minister.[10] Agence Europe[11] reported that, during the Luxembourg presidency, a Japanese compromise was accepted on the matter which did not put human rights in the first list of discussion topics but promised it would eventually be included. The Europeans wished human rights to be included in the list but the Asians only included general subjects of international politics like UN reform, nuclear non-proliferation, drugs and regional integration. Discussion of human rights, it seems, was left to chance.

The informal nature of summits is designed to create an atmosphere conducive to good relations. One cannot discuss the human rights' record of a country in a plenary of heads of state and government. If there was any discussion on human rights, it would be in bilaterals between leaders, foreign ministers, economic ministers or finance ministers. China, in particular, does not tolerate public criticism of its human rights' record although it is willing to engage in dialogue privately. At the press conference after ASEM II, Mr Blair, in reply to a question, noted 'a great deal of support for the very welcome progress that has been made in the EU/China summit on the issue of human rights dialogue'.[12] In this way the atmosphere of camaraderie was maintained.

Other issues of political dialogue were also discussed at ASEM II, such as the Korean peninsula, Bosnia and Kosovo, and Cambodia. Asian countries were happy to have a frank discussion of sensitive issues in Europe such as Kosovo, a fact which is unsurprising given that it did not concern their countries directly. Apparently the reference to racism and xenophobia in the Chairman's Statement came out of this Kosovo discussion. The euro was also discussed. It was stated that the euro would become an important currency and would influence the present role of the US dollar. 'Fortress Europe' was also talked about. It was said that the European house would never turn into a fortress. It was stated that the EU would not and cannot close. One question was whether the EU would turn inward as a result of enlargement. EU enlargement would attract even more imports than at present. There was no question of protectionism.

Finally, the UN reform was discussed with particular reference to the Secretary General's Track II reform package, but nothing was said about new permanent members of the Security Council (Germany and Japan) as had been mooted in ASEM I. Issues discussed included arms control, disarmament and non-proliferation, a Chemical Weapons Convention, the Comprehensive Test Ban Treaty (CTBT), and a Biological and Toxin Weapons Convention. However, ASEAN's Southeast Asia Nuclear Weapons-Free Zone Treaty (SEANWFZ) was left out of discussion, unlike in ASEM I. Perhaps ASEAN did not want to push it because the EU member states had been unwilling to go along with it at ASEM I.

Economic Cooperation

On this matter, there does not seem to be any disagreement over strengthening the WTO as the main forum of negotiation, or over strengthening this organization through full participation by ASEM partners. There seems to be general accord on international rules, global liberalization of trade, and the full implemention of all existing WTO commitments, including the built-in agenda according to agreed timetables and cooperation at the next WTO Ministerial. On WTO membership, with an eye to China, the Chairman's Statement stated that, in a highly integrated world economy, it was essential that all trading nations were members of WTO. It undertook to step up efforts to obtain an early accession of such nations to the WTO, on the basis of congruous market-access commitments and adherence to the WTO rules.

In the context of the financial crisis, the leaders agreed that, to enlarge the understanding of the consequences of the present crisis, a high-level business mission be sent to the region for the purpose of encouraging investment. They underlined the importance of generating global confidence in the future of Asia's economies.

Issues like anti-dumping and the GSP, which one would have thought ought to have been discussed in such a gathering, taking advantage of the presence of all leaders, appeared not to have figured. Once again, the atmosphere had to be friendly and non-confrontational.

Statement on the Financial and Economic Situation in Asia

Confidence was the first message conveyed in the ASEM II Financial Statement on 'The Financial and Economic Situation in Asia', a separate statement from the Chairman's Statement dealt with above. This was to come through fulfilling the programmes of reform agreed with the IMF, the World Bank and the Asian Development Bank, aimed at restoring confidence in the Asian economies and financial markets. Leaders welcomed the reforms being undertaken and expressed appreciation and encouragement over the adjustment efforts being made towards financial and economic stability in the Asian countries concerned. Leaders noted Europe's deep interest in the resolution of Asia's financial difficulties, and also its full participation in multilateral and bilateral efforts to overcome the problems being faced. They also took note of the significant financial and economic support provided by Asian partners.

Technical cooperation initiatives, where the EU concretely contributes, were the ASEM Trust Fund at the World Bank and the creation of a European network of expertise. The former was to help finance technical assistance and advice, both on restructuring the financial sector and on finding effective ways to redress poverty, drawing on European and Asian expertise. The latter was to work with Asian expertise, for increasing the quality and quantity of technical advice in reforming the financial sector. The network was also to encourage financial supervisors to increase cooperation amongst Asian financial institutions.

In reducing the social impact of the crisis, it was stated that, in implementing comprehensive reform programmes, it would be important to protect social expenditure wherever possible, and to develop well-designed and affordable social safety nets to safeguard the poor. It was agreed to adopt a balanced approach in addressing the socioeconomic impact of reform programmes. The statement supported the efforts of the World Bank and the Asian Development Bank in this respect, and welcomed the poverty focus of the new and existing trust funds at these institutions.

On the impact of the Asian financial crisis on the world economy, it was noted that, with continued implementation of sound economic and financial policies, the overall impact on the world economy was likely to be significant but manageable. There were already signs of substantial improvements in the external account of some Asian countries. Appropriate measures were needed to strengthen consumer and business confidence in order to overcome the crisis. It was also more important than ever, in terms of global economic stability, for the European countries to keep their own economies in good order.

Protectionism could be triggered as a result of shifts in trade and investment flows or of requirements for adjustments. The leaders expressed their resolve to resist any protectionist pressures and to at least maintain the current level of market access while pursuing multilateral liberalization, which was recognized as the most effective means of overcoming protectionist pressures and helping to alleviate the crisis. They undertook not to adopt any restrictive measures in the legitimate exercise of their WTO rights that would go beyond that which is necessary to remedy specific situations, as provided for in WTO rules. The leaders acknowledged the vital contribution of economic reforms programmes, including reforms in the financial sector in Asia, to global efforts to resist protectionism, stimulate investment and strengthen the international trading system. They noted that developments in Asian markets could lead to a drop in investments in both directions and pledged to do their best to facilitate the maintenance and expansion of foreign direct investment. They urged full and rapid implementation by all ASEM partners of the Trade Facilitation Action Plan (TFAP) and the Investment Promotion Action Plan (IPAP) in order to further open up trade and expand investment between Asia and Europe.

Noteworthy is the position of the Asia–Europe People's Forum (AEPF) which expressed deep concern over the lack of serious discussion at ASEM II on the social impact of the International Monetary Fund (IMF) loan packages in East Asian countries. It maintained that IMF policies have intensified poverty and increased hardship for ordinary people. It urged the EU to take a lead on radical reform of the IMF. It asked EU governments to use their 29 per cent share of voting power within the IMF, and their influence on the IMF Executive Board, to press for a review and restructuring of the organization in order to make it more transparent, accountable and democratic. It opposed the proposed revision of the IMF's Article of Association to include capital account liberalization until after the results of the review stated previously. It called for a reversal of the contradictory stabilization programmes being imposed by the IMF on East Asian economies. IMF reform, it argued, must be accompanied by democracy and transparency. According to the AEPF, the ASEM fund is a contradiction. However, while the financial rescue packages of the IMF, endorsed by the UK and the EU, have intensified the poverty caused by the crisis, money is being given to the ASEM fund to study that poverty. Detailed information on the human impact of the crisis has already been collected by civil society groups and NGOs working in the region.[13]

WHAT ARE THE ISSUES TO BE SETTLED?

The Question of Membership

Membership, a point of dispute prior to ASEM II, was not discussed and hence Burma and other potential new members of the club were off the agenda. The Asians were not able to reach a consensus on this matter. According to Agence Europe[14], the Asian countries since the first summit had given the impression that they did not wish to enlarge the cooperation framework to the Indian subcontinent. They estimated that the problems of India and Pakistan were of a different nature to their own. *Straits Times*[15], in its editorial, raised the question of the Indian subcontinent in ASEM, maintaining that India is an integral part of the Asian economic organism; a statement the logic of which ASEM's current members will find hard to deny. It quoted the Indian Ambassador to the EU asking whether ASEM is incomplete without the participation of India, the second largest country in the world. So, what is the future of ASEM if the Asian countries cannot agree among themselves? For the EU, membership of an Asian country in ASEAN did not imply automatic participation in ASEM, for certain political conditions had to be fulfilled to participate in the dialogue. Burma and Cambodia are referred to.[16] The Chairman's statement simply states that enlargement should be conducted on the basis of consensus by the heads of state and government. While each side proposes future members of the club from their continent, admittance will be by consensus of such heads of state and government.[17] The British chair stated that the question should therefore be gone into more thoroughly by foreign ministers between that meeting and the Seoul Summit in 2000. There is no consensus on the applicant countries at the present time.[18] Agence Europe reported that the delegations stated that ASEM must first be consolidated.[19]

The Involvement of Civil Society Actors in the ASEM Process

The Chairman's Statement does not mention the non-governmental organizations (NGOs) or, more specifically, the non-profit sector upholding human rights, working in the fields of development and the environment, or women's groups, indigenous peoples' groups and groups working with these. Nothing about people's organizations, the basic communities, is mentioned either. Is this due to the objection of certain Asian governments? There is no reference to such NGOs and groups, but AEYLS and the AEBF are specifically mentioned. Is it enough to finance the Asia-Europe People's Forum (AEPF) in London to keep them happy? Does not civil society at large have a right to have an input into the discussions of the intergovernmental ASEM and to shape any vision of Europe-Asia relations? In contrast, the AEBF provided inputs to the Chairman's Statement of ASEM II.

There is no mention of the role of parliamentarians and parliaments in the Chairman's Statement of both ASEM I and II. There was never any parliamentary delegation received by ASEM I or II. Is it enough that British members of the European Parliament and members of parliament are invited to the opening and closing ceremonies of ASEM II? One asks whether national parliaments were involved in discussions over ASEM. The European Parliament is left to its own devices to organize the Asia–Europe Parliamentary Partnership (ASEP) which has no input into ASEM. The European Parliament, like other national parliaments, is marginal to the ASEM process.

The situation raises the problem of democratic deficit when neither NGOs nor parliaments participate in the ASEM process. In London, the AEBF, which had its conference just before ASEM, met with ASEM leaders in reading the Chairman's Statement and had its views delivered by the President of the British Board of Trade. The Director of ASEF gave his report to ASEM leaders. The NGOs, on their own initiative, asked for meetings with the British Presidency, though without success[20] but they did manage to meet senior officials of the European Commission.

Jacques Santer, President of the Commission, in his speech at the opening of ASEM, called for the broadening and multiplying of the network of contacts linking civil society in the two regions. He stated,

> Our Parliaments will certainly wish to enhance their existing contacts, as will our local authorities, academics and researchers, trade unions and non-governmental organisations, artists and intellectuals. We must encourage civil society in these efforts, and help ensure that the ASEM process has a human dimension, which will meet the expectations of our citizens. (Opening ceremony of ASEM II.)

The AEPF welcomed President Santer's statement but expressed concern that governments were paying lip service to the role of civil society in the run up to and during the London ASEM. It stated that ASEM must not be an elitist and exclusive club. The ASEM process should become consultative and participatory. It called for mechanisms to be put in place to enable civil society groups to have a say in all aspects of the ASEM process, including the heads of government meeting itself. It called for the development of space within the ASEM process to enable the participation of civil society groups such as women's organizations, farmers, workers and groups working with the urban poor. The forum believe that the AEBF and ASEF have shown that non-governmental involvement in the process does work. As NGOs, they have opened the door for other NGOs to be involved in the ASEM process.[21]

It has to be said that one group of civil society welcomed by both ASEM I and II are the think-tanks and the universities. The introduction to the Chairman's Statement of ASEM II explicitly referred to research groups. Under this rubric of research groups, the AEPF, in which various papers are presented, was included. However, the forum is a gathering of European and Asian NGOs aimed at input into the ASEM process. It is not a gathering of academic researchers.

It is to be noted too that, in the AEVG, members include academics. The Portuguese representative, for example, was a professor. Parliamentarians and NGOs are excluded from shaping the future of Asia–Europe relations. The AEPF stated that it looked forward to having an ongoing input into the work of the Vision Group. It hoped that the group would fully discuss the views and recommendations of the countless thousands of networks and organizations, representing millions of ordinary people across Asia and Europe, whose own vision of Asia–Europe relations was expressed in the People's Vision.[22]

The Possible Overshadowing, Overlapping or Replacement of the EEC–ASEAN Cooperation Agreement by ASEM and Its Activities

Having looked at ASEM and its activities, one could ask whether there might be an overshadowing, overlap or indeed replacement of the existing EEC–ASEAN Cooperation Agreement or the bilateral agreements with the Northeast Asian countries. Acknowledging that it is too early to make any judgements after what is, after all, only the second ASEM, one cannot help questioning the complementarities between ASEM and the earlier EU–ASEAN cooperation.

Concern has been expressed about a possible overlap between ASEM and EU–ASEAN relations. ASEM will be a way of going around the problematic EU–ASEAN relationship, dogged as the latter is by issues of East Timor and Burma. From the EU it is reaffirmed that there is no intention of allowing ASEM to dilute EU–ASEAN relations. While ASEM has an informal intergovernmental character, EU–ASEAN relations remains the cornerstone of the Towards a New Asia Strategy (TNAS). ASEM and EU–ASEAN are two different tracks of relationships. ASEM will not overshadow or replace EU–ASEAN relations. Mr Jacques Poos, as President of the Council at an ASEAN–EU Ministerial Meeting (AEMM) in July 1997, reaffirmed that ASEM must remain complementary to EU–ASEAN dialogue and not replace it.[23]

However, there are areas which overlap with activities in bilateral agreements with Northeast Asian countries and the EEC–ASEAN Cooperation Agreement. Examples include: cooperation over illicit drugs; the AEETC, and the Regional Institute for Environmental Technology (RIET); the existing work of the Commission with SMEs (European Business Information Centres (EBICs)[24], BC-NET[25], EC NET[26], Asia Invest) and with the proposed SMEs Centre and SMEConnect[27], university exchanges; European Studies Programmes; the AEM programme at the AIM with that of the EC–ASEAN Management Centre; the AEBF with EU/Japan, EU/China, EU/ASEAN Business Forums and Industrial Roundtables. Jacques Poos, in Kuala Lumpur at the meeting of EU and ASEAN Ministers, the AEMM, recognized the risk of overlap and stated that it must be explored to avoid this.[28]

Here there is definitely a role for the European Parliament in monitoring expenditure on ASEM activities and questioning whether they overlap with activities in bilateral agreements with Northeast Asia and the EEC–ASEAN Cooperation Agreement.

The more fundamental question is whether there is a move in the direction of ASEM being a privileged set of relations with Asia over and above the existing EU–ASEAN relations and bilaterals with Northeast Asian countries. It is easy to speak of complementary relations and to claim that there will be no dilution of existing relationships. However, relationships can take on a momentum of their own, especially if, in another set of relationships, difficult issues are in the way. What is the direction of relations with Asia? Over time, ASEM may become the primary forum of dialogue of relationships. It has still to be seen how the European Council and Commission will stick to complementarity of relations while each member state still fashions their priorities in their relationships with ASEM countries. Since it takes at least two to tango, the Asian ASEM countries also have to decide which set of relations is most important to them. As it is, for ASEAN the EU–ASEAN relationship remains a priority over ASEM. What one does note, however, is the proliferation of international meetings, where the same leaders, ministers and civil servants meet and discuss almost the same or similar issues.

AN UNINTENDED OUTCOME: THE EAST ASIA ECONOMIC CAUCUS

The ASEM process has brought into practice the EAEC of Prime Minister Mahathir because ministers of Southeast Asian and East Asian countries meet in an attempt to formulate common positions for ASEM meetings, although formally the EAEC does not exist. ASEM too is instrumental in bringing the three Northeastern Asian countries into some kind of cooperative relationship. December 1997 saw China, Japan and South Korea meet up with ASEAN leaders for the first time when they met for the ASEAN summit, contributing to closer dialogue and cooperation within the region.[29] Is this not a functioning EAEC? It should be noted that Asian countries have always had difficulties working together. ASEAN is an attempt by South East Asian countries to cooperate together while North East Asia does not have an equivalent regional organization which can forge closer cooperation.

CONCLUSIONS

It still early to say what ASEM as a process has achieved but ASEM II has reaffirmed a framework for continuing dialogue and cooperation. While ASEM actors speak of its informal character, at least the seeds of institutionalization have been sown and it is only a matter of time before these come to fruition.

The second summit was a success in coming up with measures (trust fund and network) to deal with the financial crisis, noting that the Asian ASEM countries felt that the EU was not doing enough. Apparently, a substantive political dialogue took place leading to improved understanding among leaders. A whole series of initiatives suggested in Bangkok was completed as a result. A future set of priorities and new initiatives for the coming two years was also laid out. ASEM IV will meet in Europe in 2002.

The success of ASEM depends upon what it can achieve on the ground with its projects, at least for interested parties and for the business community in particular (politics is about business), but it will be a real success only if it means something to the general public. Here, civil society actors come in. The reality, however, is that interest in ASEM remains reserved for certain interested actors. Governments can do so much, but the rest will always be up to non-state actors in society.

What remains to be achieved is progress on the enlargement question. The Asian side could not reach a consensus among themselves on this issue. It was also said that the Asian side could not accept giving recognition to Thailand and South Korea for the reforms which they had started. There was also no agreement on showing solidarity with Indonesia.

The sustainability of the ASEM process also hinges on whether enthusiasm will be whittled away by fatigue. Rounds of meetings and activities could do just that. This is the human, psychological side.

On the future of ASEM, apparently the idea of a 'tripolar' world was dismissed by Europeans in favour of a multipolar world. Latin America and Africa are the two other poles. What all this means is that the importance of ASEM to the EU and its member states depends upon their perception of how important Asia is in relation to these other continents. Asian countries, on the other hand, do not have as strong a relationship with these continents despite the non-aligned movement, the Third World movement, G15, G77 and whatever else promotes South–South cooperation in the context of international relations that, at present, are more North–South than South–South. The Asian countries have less cards to play with. The privileged triangular relationship has been put to rest. The transatlantic partnership and market also poses a question mark for ASEM. For the EU, is not its relationship with the USA more important than ASEM? Does not the USA similarly view its relationship with the EU as being more important than that with APEC? What place has ASEM and APEC in American and European eyes? The Asian countries have to formulate a position *vis-à-vis* EU–USA relations. To what extent is ASEM a counterweight to APEC?[30] Other scenarios are the older Japan–USA relations and Japan–USA–EU relations, which these other Asian countries have to enter into their calculation. APEC does not also replace Japan–USA relations.

In a wider perspective, the EU–Asia, EU–ASEAN, EU–East Asia relations are not intergovernmental relations. They include many other elements. ASEM speaks of Track II activities, one of which is people-to-people relations. This has to be promoted if relations are to take root and be substantial and solid. However, Track II activities already exist. Civil societies' actors of both continents have been communicating and meeting with one another. Inter-university exchanges are not new. Development, human rights and environmental NGOs meet, as do trade unions and workers of both continents. Women and indigenous peoples' group meet. Travel and tourism have brought people together. Interest in Asian philosophies and religions has brought Europeans to Asia. The Internet is the newest way of communicating. Perhaps it is these other fora for cross-continental relations which will build substantial and solid relations between the peoples of Europe and Asia. ASEM offers another framework of opportunities to meet. However, up to now, it is aimed at the elites or the future elites of ASEM countries.

Mutual understanding is said to be one way to bring Europe and Asia closer together but when one looks at what happens when the leaders meet, or even when NGOs meet, little or nothing is discussed about each other's culture, about ways of behaviour and about ways of thinking. Problems of comprehension in disputes are often due not to different values but to behavioural patterns and different ways of thinking. In the activities of ASEM this issue of poor understanding does not figure prominently.

Much stress is placed on equal partnership in ASEM and EU–ASEAN but one can ask what is behind it? Against a past colonial background, which certain ASEAN leaders have personally experienced, to be treated now as an equal partner shows welcome respect. The push for equal partnership took place at the time when Asian economies were on a rapid growth path. Economic strength underpins political strength and position. However, with the recent financial crisis, where does this leave them? They are in the position of appealing for help. The crisis highlights the fact that they are economically weak. EU member states, with their history of industrial and technological development, are economically stronger. Asian countries know their weaker position, which explains why, during their growth period, they attempted to build their industrial and technological capacities. However, the financial crisis has seriously jeopardized their ambitions. Apart from Japan, they were and still are on a learning curve. At the economic level, these Asian countries are clearly not equal to European countries. On the other hand, they do not want to be classified as developed countries because in doing so they would also lose trade preferences from the developed countries.

Another thing that is striking, whether in the EU–ASEAN context or that of ASEM, is the role of the state (and the European Commission) in facilitating trade and investment towards Asia when the creed is that of the free market.

What is the role of the state in a free market? What are the parameters of state activity and what are those of the market? Is the liberal state of competitive capitalism back on stage? Do economic operators bother whether their capital and technology comes from Europe, the USA or Japan? What they want is the best deal they can get in the free market. It is only governments that are concerned about economic and political ties.

It must also be said that other activities in the cultural field, university exchanges and non-economic activities all foster ties between the EU and Asia, which in turn help to strengthen economic ties. State intervention is not just economic but in fields which are not directly related. It must not be forgotten that interest in the cultural field was apparently first raised by the business community in a conference in Essen, when the ASEAN–EU AEMM met in Karlsruhe in September 1994. This started the emphasis on cultural activities.

Despite critiques one may make of ASEM, and the present author holds the view that it is too early to make these, ASEM remains a positive mechanism which can contribute to world peace in a wider context, to stability and prosperity, and to bringing ASEM peoples together, provided that it is not carved out purely to serve business interests.

NOTES

1. This chapter has benefited substantially from discussions with EU officials, Members of the European Parliament and diplomats of ASEM missions in Brussels.
2. The author is presently Senior Research Fellow at the European Institute for Asian Studies.
3. The TNAS was the policy statement emphasizing renewed attention of the EU to Asia, and aimed at strengthening ties to Asia. It provided a basis for engaging with Asia. It is a basic document guiding actions towards Asia. It aims at a coherent policy and strategy towards Asia.
4. See *Far Eastern Economic Review* (FEER), 13 February 1997, p. 21.
5. Full text of press conference available on ASEM website.
6. Agence Europe, 6/7 April 1998.
7. The AEPF is a gathering of European and Asian NGOs, which met at ASEM I and II to put out its message to ASEM leaders for them to take into consideration. It gathers around a conference which lasts for approximately the same duration as ASEM.
8. ASEM Watch newsheet no. 31.
9. At the international press conference following the ASEM Foreign Ministers' Meeting, the Singapore foreign minister outlined five principles for the conduct of political dialogue, which *Kompass*, the Indonesian newspaper, described as totally non-confrontational. These five principles are 1) reciprocal respect for the members, 2) political dialogue held in a positive spirit to understand each other and learn from each other, 3) that members shall not accuse each other, 4) to avoid efforts to accommodate pressures from lobbies in each country and 5) to avoid pressures from the agenda of international news media (source: ASEM Watch 11). According to the Indonesian foreign minister, Mr. Ali Alatas, political dialogue focuses, and tries to develop, matters which are agreed together with the aim of increasing mutual understanding and friendship, and to increase cooperation. These are wise selections that conform to the wishes of the heads of state/governments. The advice is essentially do not discuss problems which are not relevant and which do not contribute to

settlements because it has already been negotiated in another forum. Is he referring here to the problem of East Timor? The London meeting seems to conform with the five principles propounded by the Singapore foreign minister, and the EU seems to accept these principles. So, the human rights, social, environmental and development lobbies should not be listened to. According to the FEER (27 February 1997, p. 22), a European diplomat, reacting to this, quipped, 'All that's left to talk about is the colour of the wallpaper.'

10.   Agence Europe, 6/7 April 1998.
11.   5 November 1997.
12.   See note 9. The press conference is available on the ASEM II website.
13.   ASEM Watch newsheet nos 31 and 32.
14.   21 August 1997.
15.   Of 10 April 1998.
16.   Agence Europe, 21 August 1997.
17.   Explanation in the same vein in Agence Europe, 3 September 1997.
18.   Agence Europe, 6/7 April 1998.
19.   Agence Europe, 4 April 1998.
20.   ASEM Watch newsheet no. 33.
21.   ASEM Watch newsheet no. 33 and ASEM Watch newsheet no. 31.
22.   ASEM Watch newsheet no. 31. A list of members of the AEVG is available on the ASEM II website.
23.   This is reported in Agence Europe, 28–9 July 1997, p. 2.
24.   European Business Information Centre.
25.   Business Cooperation Network.
26.   Economic Cooperation Network.
27.   From Agence Europe, 24-5 November 1997, p. 12, one sees also that the member states of the EU, plus a few of the Asian countries, have their own Internet system too, or facilities facilitating SMEs.
28.   As reported in Agence Europe, 28–9 July 1997, p. 2.
29.   ASEM II's Chairman's Statement.
30.   In FEER, 25 September 1997, p. 29, Rolf Langhammer posits the position that ASEM is a counterweight to APEC.

6. Europe–Asia: the formal politics of mutual definition

Julie A. Gilson

INTRODUCTION

The Asia–Europe Meeting (ASEM) presents a new kind of partnership between novel partners. Its purpose, as the European Commission restated in April 2000, is to 'establish a new relationship between the two regions' and 'build a comprehensive partnership among equal partners'.[1] Since it began in 1996, ASEM has been criticized for its inability to be more than a mere talk shop[2], whilst simultaneously fears over greater 'institutionalization' have been voiced from both groups of participants. Ostensibly, then, ASEM is a no-win arrangement for its participants, for either it continues to function as a casual clubhouse and takes no major decisions or else it deepens its institutional roots, to threaten vested interests already existing within each region. In fact, ASEM raises several interesting questions about the nature and purpose of institutionalized relations and needs to be examined in its own right. It conducts its affairs as an explicitly region-to-region grouping, whilst at the same time (to date, at least) dispensing an 'Asian way with western agenda', thus accommodating within its own framework apparently contradictory modes of decision making and failing to problematize the difficult issues which the discussion of such modes of behaviour should provoke.

ASEM began life as an informal channel of communication between the heads of state or government of its 25 participating countries (plus the president of the European Commission), and a host of practitioners involved at other levels of activity.[3] Designated from the beginning as an informal armchair dialogue that was not to be utilized as a negotiating body, it nevertheless built upon a range of existing formal agreements which were officially acknowledged in its first Chairman's Statement. These include the EU–ASEAN summit, the ASEAN Regional Forum (ARF), as well as various EU agreements with individual countries such as Japan, South Korea and (later) China. At the same time, it also offered a counterbalance to APEC (using it both as a model and counter-model) and drew upon the agenda and language of global fora, notably the United Nations (UN) and the World Trade

Organization (WTO). Other highly institutionalized arrangements (in the most formal sense) were therefore used either as a template for, or background to, ASEM's development. In spite of this, it was made clear from the start that the process of dialogue would be conducted the 'Asian way'. However this may be defined, its most frequent iteration includes the assertions that 'consensus is more important than breakthrough, camaraderie than formality and process than substance'.[4] This informal approach was in many ways necessitated by the fact that 'Asia' itself (notwithstanding attempts by Malaysian Prime Minister Mahathir to create the East Asian Economic Grouping, which later became a caucus within APEC) was not an institutionalized collective in the same manner as the European Union (EU), its dialogue partner in this process. In essence, then, ASEM created a pragmatic framework in which to situate the EU's political, economic and legal personality alongside a disparate collection of national interests within Asia. By conventional standards, therefore, ASEM is held together by only the flimsiest of institutional tissue. This chapter aims to recast the debate over the nature of interregional cooperation in the ASEM context and to show how, in fact, ASEM is amenable to different kinds of institutional behaviour and needs to be removed from the intellectual straitjacket imposed upon it by both scholars and practitioners.

TYPES OF INSTITUTION AND ASEM

Cooperation between international actors is assessed in various ways by scholars from differing theoretical perspectives, as well as by practitioners with differing agenda. For some observers, the process of mutual interaction denotes expeditious instances of independent interest convergence: for others, it represents a moral and value-laden exercise. Whether or not subjective inferences are made, and irrespective of whether the term is premised upon a shared set of values or internalized norms, many forms of cooperation in modern international life now preoccupy a large number of scholars.[5] This large body of literature examines institutional behaviour from a range of perspectives: from an emphasis on the locus of interaction at the level of state-to-state convergence to insights which illustrate the impact of the institution itself upon any given relations.[6] The term 'institution' itself may signify associations, 'programmed actions' or 'common responses to situations'.[7]

In its broadest scope, literature that deals with institutions can be found in the writings on multilateralism and international organizations, but it also includes critical theory, post-structuralist and post-modernist interpretations of interaction. These writings share the tendency to conceptualize the term 'institution' as 'some sort of establishment of relative permanence of a distinctly social sort', a feature that distinguishes this broad perspective from that which focuses upon state unit interest uniquely.[8] Given the presence of the European Commission within the process, the multiple levels of non-governmental activity, and differences between the two supposed interlocutors of ASEM, an institutional approach offers one broad framework within which to set the debate.

For the purpose of our analysis, it is instructive to separate this literature into two categories: functional institutionalization, which places an emphasis on the practical and normative services that an institution provides for its participants; and cognitive institutionalization, which stresses the underlying cultural, social and linguistic associations that come to be inextricably linked with that institution and which inform subsequent behavioural patterns of that institution, as well as those of its constituent participants.[9] It is generally assumed that ASEM acts only as a loose functional institution, by providing a regular venue for various representatives to meet and by enabling participants to address mutually significant contemporary concerns. Similarly, questions regarding the desirability and feasibility of creating a secretariat, and the future membership of the forum, ensure that current concerns remain fixed upon this practical level of managing interaction. This chapter contends, however, that discussions over institutionalized behaviour between Asia and Europe need to take into account the cognitive dimension of institutional relations. While the formalized informality of ASEM proscribes further rule-based developments within the forum, the impact of ASEM activities is, nevertheless, likely to be felt in the domain of mutual recognition, intra-Asian community building, and possibly even Common Foreign and Security Policy modelling within the EU, regardless of whether a secretariat sits in Singapore or elsewhere. The apparently functional idea espoused at ASEM 1 of establishing 'an equal basis between Asia and Europe in a spirit of cooperation and the sharing of perceptions on a wide range of issues' may indeed turn out to be felt more keenly at the level of deeper, cognitive institutionalization.[10] The following sections propose some of the mechanisms through which such institutionalization might take place.

FUNCTIONAL AND COGNITIVE INSTITUTIONS

A functional emphasis focuses on how participation in an institutional arrangement can 'reduce the transaction costs of bargaining, provide opportunities for linking issues ... and mitigate fears of uncoordinated or exploitive strategies by stabilizing expectations about future state behavior'.[11] Such reasoning was evident during the World Economic Forum Business Conference in Singapore in September 1994 where the idea for ASEM was first mooted in response to the growing salience of economic issues of a global

and regional scale.[12] In terms of political dialogue, too, both ASEAN as a
group and the European Commission recognized the need to promote closer
relations, particularly since the ASEAN–EU dialogue had stalled over the
problematic question of Burma. In addition, the supplementary membership of
Japan, China and South Korea offered ASEAN a level of political authority
which it could not muster alone.

By the time of the first summit, Asia itself constituted (depending upon
one's definition) up to half of the world's population and one quarter of its
production, and had provided the EU since 1994 with a larger exchange of
trade than that between Asia and the USA. Moreover, between 1993 and 1995,
the European Investment Bank (EIB) undertook to commit 100 million ECU
per year to Asia, in the form of investment rather than assistance. The EU, for
its part, aimed to strengthen its weak position in Asia after being refused
association status to APEC and in order to advance the pledges made in its
1995 document, *Towards a New Asia Strategy*.[13] In addition, key member
states such as Germany, France and the UK supported the initiative.[14] From an
Asian perspective, too, the need to attract European investment provided
members with the stimulus to participate as a functionally specific grouping,
while concerns over Eurocentrism within the Union fuelled further efforts.

Institutions are also the product of their historically contingent
environment, which makes certain conditions salient.[15] ASEM was born in a
post-cold war climate, in recognition, among other issues, of the changing
regional roles of Japan and the USA, and the simultaneous rise of China.[16] In
an era of globalized markets and shared security concerns that reach beyond
the cold war imperatives of nuclear bilateral stand-off, there are greater
international incentives for multiple levels of cooperation, and region-to-
region activities form part of a complex mosaic of intercourse. This context
has both a positive and a negative impact on Asia–Europe relations. On the
one hand, the USA has pushed its European and Asian allies to play a greater
part in global burden sharing, particularly by addressing concerns within their
respective regions. It has done so by promoting multilateral coordination, most
notably in fora in which it takes a leading role, such as APEC or the
International Monetary Fund (IMF). Whilst American hostility to the intra-
Asian Monetary Fund (AMF) of 1997 demonstrated a desire to retain the
hegemonic balance in the region, Japan's own position in its region remains
historically contingent and fragile. Not only does this environment determine
the degree to which Asia–Europe cooperation is possible; it also provides the
nature of the agenda and means of implementing this, by forming the models
upon which Asia–Europe relations are based. Thus, IMF packages are actively
supported at ASEM level, even as the Asian membership of ASEM contests
them and the Europeans attempt to question their value. This external force
has been particularly salient in the promotion of Asia–Europe linkages. Other

reasons for which institutions are functionally desirable or necessary include: the need to offset asymmetries of power held by constituent members (ASEM is arguably an important forum for ASEAN visibility, as well as a means of embracing China within the region and offering Japan a new, benign, role there); the possibility they hold for 'diffuse reciprocity' to occur (buy now, pay later); the opportunity to balance other existing institutions (as with the case of APEC or the role of the USA more generally).[17] Institutional literature also recognizes the potential importance of establishing repeated habits of behaviour, in such a way that previous actions taken by participants then become the basis for future ones.[18] In the case of ASEM, the fact that the meeting was held at all (a genuine surprise to some observers) introduced a channel for such habits to develop, and provided the opportunity for norms to become associated specifically with this forum over time.[19]

A more advanced form of such functional behaviour is presented by scholars who demonstrate how institutional frameworks come to shape a participant's activities and affect the implementation of decisions, by acting as a buffer between 'processes of thought and decision [and] processes of action'.[20] Jepperson outlines how such institutional 'structuration' takes place, by: increasing the extent of interaction amongst participants; defining and developing patterns of structure and coalition; increasing the information load among participants; and developing mutual awareness regarding their involvement in a common enterprise.[21] By the time of ASEM 2, and in spite of the different problems presented at that summit, the notion that 'Asia' and 'Europe' were meeting had become a common and unchallenged frame of reference.

The works of Young, Puchala and Hopkins bridge some of the conceptual gaps between functional and cognitive forms of institutionalization, by focusing more closely upon the shared expectations that may result from a pattern of institutionalized behaviour and upon the subjective definition of what constitutes an institutionalized arrangement in the first place.[22] Young begins with the definition of institutions as 'recognized practices consisting of easily identifiable roles, coupled with collections of rules or conventions governing relations among the occupants of these roles', but goes on to note that these practices may lead to the creation of 'identifiable social conventions' that are established as practices become encoded in an institutional framework.[23] These definitions allow the observer, in the absence of formalized rules and procedures, to interpret some of the alternative institutional parameters of non-conventional bodies such as ASEM. Nevertheless, while accepting that roles create an institution, Young does not allow that those role performances or the institution may be constitutive of individual participants. For Hopkins and Puchala, such patterned routinized behaviour leads to shared expectations which can then become infused with normative meaning.[24] For these writers in particular, then, institutions are seen to be 'patterns around which expectations converge', and are social structures with their own 'widely accepted social conventions', rather than merely the instruments through which convergent interests are channelled.[25] After only two summit encounters, it is difficult to see evidence of such 'social conventions' within ASEM, but the parameters of interaction are clearly becoming standardized to create an ASEM *modus operandi*, as can be seen by the most recent Chairman's Statement, at ASEM 3.

While functional institutionalization is premised upon the need to resolve collective action problems, cognitive forms accept that the very creation of the 'sense of self' of a participant may derive in part from the formation and development of institutional activities. Put simply, this deeper form of institutionalization goes beyond formal rules and structures to acknowledge institutions as social phenomena, with the result that their physical qualities are subordinate to the practices occurring within them. Cognitive institutionalization thus delineates the margins of the social script through which institutional participants communicate, and provides the basis upon which fixed and readily identifiable idea-sets for an institution's practices are founded.[26] In the case of ASEM, these practices are already taking shape in the formation of an 'Asian' identity within the forum (indeed, the Asian Ten meet as a group prior to ASEM meetings, in order to coordinate their positions), as well as through the formulation of a certain 'ASEM' way of doing business. These factors are examined below. In addition to these influences of cognitive institutionalization, an institution can also learn, based on its own memory, and can come to reflect more than the initial convergence of the interests of its constituent parties.[27] Similarly, conventions or rules may also create collective meanings which in turn influence actor identities.[28]

Closely associated with cognitive approaches is an emphasis on ideas and language, in the sense that ideas 'serve the purpose of guiding behavior under conditions of uncertainty'.[29] In such a way, a cognitive approach is able to show that collective understandings of the meanings of explicit rules, and not so much the norms themselves, have causal consequences for interaction patterns between allies, by effectively locking the participants into an institutional discourse.[30] Institutions, then, come to be dominated by one discourse from among those available to them, since 'once particular arguments and phraseology have been deployed, a "rhetorical momentum" is generated which operates independently to affect policies'.[31] Importantly, in the case of ASEM, its discursive patterns are drawn from existing, but qualitatively different forms of institutions. This means that most participants are already parties to a familiar dialogue. In addition, ASEM is sustained by the rhetoric of the triangle, whilst its development further strengthens the notion of the triangle. This aspect of ASEM is also explored below. At the same time, this momentum within ASEM derives, as argued below, from Western discourses which have become cloaked in an 'Asian' style.

ASEM AND INSTITUTIONALIZATION

It has already been noted above that the form of institutionalization it adopts will affect the development of ASEM. For this reason, it is important to locate the type of institution constituted by ASEM's origins, before suggesting its potential impact on Asia–Europe relations. At a first glance, ASEM represents a clear example of early functional institutionalization, accommodating as it does representatives of 25 constituent states in a non-confrontational, non-negotiating forum which is driven by specific national concerns (and hence is able to avoid 'contentious' issues, such as human rights). As far as cognitive institutionalization is concerned, ASEM apparently has little to offer: its agenda is drawn from issues and discourses found in fora such as the UN, WTO and APEC; and within Asia, let alone between Asia and Europe, there exists no common conceptualization of collective engagement. The remainder of this chapter aims to show that, in fact, the informality of the process is most amenable to a cognitive form of institutionalization.

ASEM AS A FUNCTIONAL RESPONSE

As a functional entity, despite its apparent institutional lacunae, the five-year-old arrangement already has much to show for itself: and its activities to date include the following: government and private working groups on investment promotion; Senior Officials Meetings on Trade and Investment (SOMTI); an Asia–Europe Business Forum (AEBF); foreign ministers' meetings; economic ministers' meetings; meetings of finance ministers; an environmental technology centre; the Asia–Europe Foundation (ASEF); an Asia–Europe university programme; and youth exchange programmes.[32] High-level trade discussions have also resulted in concrete initiatives such as the Trade Facilitation Action Plan (TFAP) to reduce trade barriers, and the Investment Promotion Action Plan (IPAP), as well as the drafting of a separate statement at ASEM 2 to pledge support towards the resolution of the financial crisis and to establish a Trust Fund towards the same end.

More importantly, perhaps, is the fact that this new institutional basis confers an element of international legitimacy upon what would otherwise be random, ad hoc encounters. It does so in three ways: namely, by being associated with, or compared to, other existing institutions (such as the UN upon which much of the ASEM is based, or APEC, with which it is compared); by collecting within an umbrella framework a host of disparate activities (so that ASEF, TFAP and the AEBF are all 'ASEM' activities); and by using past encounters as the basis for present and future legitimacy (thus, the Bangkok Statement becomes the foundation for subsequent actions). In so doing, ASEM facilitates the reduction of transaction costs, the provision of greater information, the promotion of mutual transparency and the monitoring of participants' behaviour.

ASEM AS A COGNITIVE RESPONSE

That ASEM also holds cognitive implications for its members is not initially evident. However, there are a number of ways in which an 'ASEM' mode of conducting relations has come into being. First, ASEM is, to a large extent, a product of its environment or 'order'.[33] This denotes those 'cultural rules giving collective meaning and value to particular entities and activities, integrating them into the larger schemes'[34], and includes those ideas, values, concepts and linguistic frames within which specific institutional arrangements are situated for a given issue-area at a given time. An analysis of the conceptual order indicates the derivation of possible dominant discourses for an institution, and in this way explores the possible sources of those cognitive factors noted above. It is particularly important to understand these for ASEM, which takes its place alongside a multitude of existing groupings and which takes not only its discursive patterns from them but also the agenda items it addresses. A brief glance at the Bangkok Chairman's Statement demonstrates ASEM's adherence to the United Nations Charter, the Universal Declaration on Human Rights, the 1992 Rio Declaration on the Environment, other UN conferences, the Nuclear Non-Proliferation Treaty (NPT) and the WTO, as well as to regionally based fora such as the ASEAN Regional Forum and its Post-Ministerial Conference (PMC). Previous experience by participants of ASEM in these other fora provides a guide for the type of behaviour and even language adopted within ASEM itself. This well-established 'order' is also important for conferring legitimacy on the ASEM process: for, if UN and WTO agenda are followed, and APEC used as a regional model, they cumulatively provide an institutional history for this new forum and serve to 'map the complexity of environmental elements into their own structures'.[35] The principal significance of this notional linkage with an external order is that it provides an externally-originated mythified *raison d'être*, which is used to sustain the existence of the institution, so that arrangements 'which incorporate institutionalized myths are more legitimate, successful, and likely to survive'.[36] The ASEM framework serves, in this way, to offer Asian or Asia–Europe responses to global questions. Most important in this context is the use of the triangle in legitimating ASEM's existence.

Viewed from the start as the 'missing link' in a (variously defined) triangle of (primarily economic) relations between the EU/Europe, Japan/East Asia, and the USA/North America[37], this abstract notion has become the concrete rationale for Asia-Europe developments. Thus, the 'tripolarization' of the global economy becomes the mantra of ASEM's advancement, with the resulting reasoning that if ASEM did not exist, it would have to be invented.[38] The inherent contradictions in this label, however, mean that on the one hand, tripolarity serves as a legitimation *tout court* for Asia-Europe communication, while on the other it also causes Asian and European interaction inevitably to be seen as the 'weak side of the triangle'.[39]

EMBEDDING REGIONAL IDENTITIES

At a first glance, it is clear that the process of the Asia-Europe Meeting was never designed to match like with like: for, whilst the EU is neither a supra-state nor straightforward interstate forum[40], notions of 'Asia' are still more difficult to pin down. ASEM itself, then, on one level facilitates the very definition of its own participants in a purely functional way, to the extent that each 'side' represents a defined membership so that each may be seen as a 'collectivity' within the ASEM context.[41] However, in cognitive terms, too, and in the case of the ten Asian participants in particular, this factor is also important in creating a sense of identity amongst a group which previously had no such group formation. Drawing on the fact that the membership of the East Asian Economic Caucus (EAEC) is also embedded within ASEM, references to the 'Asian way' of decision making within ASEM are also used to distinguish Asian from non-Asian (European) modes of behaviour. Such group identities may or may not cause the same collectivity to form in other circumstances[42], but they are important, nevertheless, in consolidating one form of 'Asianness' in the face of a verifiable external other.

ASEM's discursive patterns have also come to deproblematize the identity of the regions *per se*, by embedding the notion of region-to-region dialogue. Thus, instances of 'regional problems', 'regional crises', 'regional meetings' and 'regional networks' are evoked interchangeably, and within that dialogue the growing notions of both 'Europe' and 'Asia' continue to flourish, while the networks created between them are premised on existing discourses to locate a dialogue of equals between Asia and Europe. In addition, within the ASEM process itself, participation has become associated with a three-pillared structure of political dialogue, the reinforcement of economic cooperation and the promotion of cooperation in a range of other issue areas, particularly in the sociocultural domain. In these ways, and supported by the foundations established at Bangkok, ASEM is already beginning to carve out its own cognitive route-map.

NEW DISCOURSE?

Sustained institutionalized activity in the context of the ASEM structure offers the possibility of engendering new norms of collective behaviour which, through the process of interaction itself, are able to 'alter preferences, create feelings of shared identity, stimulate the development of norms and encourage cooperative behaviour'.[43] As such, the institutionalization of relations through ASEM offers a means of locking participants into a particular institutional discourse and creating a new understanding of interests and identities.[44] In terms of its own discourse to date, ASEM has no APEC-like 'open regionalism' and is instead dependent upon Western-style international diplomacy, in spite of the ways in which activities are conducted through ostensibly 'Asian' means. The initial reluctance of the Asian participants to entertain political dialogue is testament to the driving force of the Commission's discursive dominance in the formation of their interregional agenda: to date, the types of discourse available to ASEM's participants have been drawn from existing Western-originated groupings. In the case of APEC, its structure has come to be associated with ideas of market-led integration through a process of open regionalism and multilateral dialogue. This process has come about both through an awareness by policy elites of the need to utilize the regional or institutional discourse for achieving certain goals, and through the driving force of a US foreign policy agenda. Over time, this has allowed the development within APEC of a level of 'consensual knowledge', which allows participants to, as it were, speak the same language; a tendency which has begun already within ASEM.[45]

CONCLUSION

Practical experience has rendered ASEM functionally useful, by facilitating the creation of enterprises such as ASEF and the Environmental Technology Centre. More fundamentally, however, participants within the ASEM forum have begun to engage in an (often frustratingly slow) process of mutual identity formation. Indeed, the momentum of interregional discourse had assumed a taken-for-grantedness by ASEM 2, and the 'self', in terms of the Asian contingent at least, had begun to assume a certain 'ASEMness' in its collective identity.[46] The difficulties with ASEM, therefore, are not based upon its inability to overcome great intercultural and intersubjective barriers, but instead derive from a constant focus upon the need to expand the formal institutional parameters (such as a secretariat) of the forum. As a result, cognitive misconceptions or 'disperceptions' become appropriated at the functional level, to render issues such as human rights and future membership *hors de combat*. Mutual understanding (and self-understanding) will be advanced by an ability to speak more fluently the same (cognitive) language; not by building a secretariat. Thus, cognitive linkages make possible the private meeting of the Portuguese and Indonesian leaders to discuss East Timor on the periphery of ASEM, where functional institutions get in the way. ASEM, therefore, needs greater cognitive institutionalization, rather than being overly concerned about its structural façade.

To date, the slow development of regional identity is taking root at the cognitive core of ASEM, while European discursive dominance in the framing of the ASEM agenda is ensured by its continued location on the functional level.

In the absence of common understandings and ideas, Asia–Europe relations within ASEM will continue to be hindered from achieving deeper development. By resting on increasingly entrenched sets of stereotypes and ignoring the cognitive roots of functional actions, representatives of ASEM may lose the opportunity to develop a genuine dialogue of equals equipped to negotiate the interregional issues of the 21st century.

NOTES

1. European Commission (2000), *Perspectives and Priorities for the ASEM Process (Asia–Europe Meeting) into the New Decade*, Brussels: COM 2000 (241), 18 April.
2. Davis A. Bobrow (1998), 'The US and ASEM: why the hegemon didn't bark', *The Pacific Review*, **12** (1), 103–28.
3. See David Camroux and Christian Lechervy (1996), '"Close encounter of a third kind?": The inaugural Asia–Europe Meeting of March 1996', *The Pacific Review*, **9** (3), 441–52.
4. Victor Pou Serradell (1996), 'The Asia–Europe Meeting (ASEM): a historical turning point in relations between the two regions', *European Foreign Affairs Review*, **1** (2), 196.
5. Peter Haas (1992), 'Introduction: epistemic communities and international policy coordination', *International Organization*, **46** (1), 1–35; Stephen D. Krasner (ed.) (1983), *International Regimes*, Ithaca: Cornell University Press.
6. Albert S. Yee (1996), 'The causal effects of ideas on policies', *International Organization*, **50** (1), 69–108.
7. Ronald L. Jepperson (1991), 'Institutions, Institutional Effects, and Institutionalism', in Walter Powell and Paul DiMaggio (eds), *The New Institutionalism in Organizational Analysis*, Chicago: University of Chicago Press, pp. 143, 147.
8. Lynne G. Zucker (1991), 'The Role of Institutionalization in Cultural Persistence', in Powell and DiMaggio, *The New Institutionalism*, p. 83; Michael Smith (1996), 'The European Union and a changing Europe: establishing the boundaries of order', *Journal of Common Market Studies*, **34** (1), 6.
9. See Robert O. Keohane (1988), 'International institutions: two approaches', *International Studies Quarterly*, **32** (4), 381–2.

10. Jacques Pelkmans and Hiroko Shinkai (eds) (1997), *ASEM: How Promising a Partnership?*, Brussels: European Institute for Asian Studies, Appendix 4.
11. Robert O. Keohane, Joseph S. Nye and Stanley Hoffmann (eds) (1993), *After the Cold War: International Institutions and State Strategies in Europe, 1989-1991*, Cambridge, USA: Harvard University Press; 175.
12. Serradell, 'The Asia–Europe Meeting', p. 185.
13. Christopher M. Dent (1997/8), 'The ASEM: managing the new framework of the EU's economic relations with East Asia', *Pacific Affairs*, **70**, p. 495.
14. Serradell, 'The Asia–Europe Meeting', p. 185.
15. Robert Axelrod and Robert O. Keohane (1985), 'Achieving cooperation under anarchy', *World Politics*, **38** (1), 226-54; Michael Taylor (1987), *The Possibility of Cooperation*, Cambridge, UK: Cambridge University Press, p. 179.
16. See Camroux and Lechervy, 'Close encounter of a third kind?'.
17. See Robert O. Keohane (1986), 'Reciprocity in international relations', *International Organization*, **40** (1), 2.
18. Thomas Risse-Kappen (1996), 'Exploring the nature of the beast: international relations theory and comparative policy analysis meet the European Union', *Journal of Common Market Studies*, **34** (1), 69.
19. See Krasner, *International Regimes*, p. viii; James G. March and Johan P. Olsen (1989), *Rediscovering Institutions*, New York: The Free Press, p. 168.
20. March and Olsen, *Rediscovering Institutions*, p. 11.
21. Jepperson, 'Institutions, Institutional Effects, and Institutionalism', p. 145.
22. Oran R. Young (1986), 'International regimes: toward a new theory of institutions', *World Politics*, **39** (1), 107; Donald J. Puchala and Raymond F. Hopkins (1983), 'International Regimes: Lessons From Inductive Analysis', in Krasner, *International Regimes*, pp. 61-91.
23. Young, 'International regimes', 107; and (1989), *International Cooperation: Building Regimes for Natural Resources and the Environment*, Ithaca: Cornell University Press, p. 82.
24. See Krasner, *International Regimes*, p. 18.
25. Young, *International Cooperation*, p. 82.
26. Alexander Wendt and Raymond Duvall (1989), 'Institutions and International Order', in Ernst Otto Czempiel and James N. Rosenau (eds), *Global Changes and Theoretical Challenges: Approaches to World Politics for the 1990s,* Lexington: Lexington Books, p. 60.
27. Ernst B. Haas (1983), 'Words Can Hurt You; Or, Who Said What to Whom about Regimes', in Krasner, *International Regimes*, p. 57; March and Olsen, *Rediscovering Institutions*, p. 168.
28. Alexander Wendt (1987), 'The agent-structure problem in international relations theory', *International Organization*, **41** (3), 441; Wendt (1992), 'Anarchy is what states make of it: the social construction of power politics', *International Organization*, **46** (2), 393.
29. Petter Holm, (1995), 'The dynamics of institutionalization': transformation processes in Norwegian fisheries', *Administrative Science Quarterly*, **40** (3), 416.
30. See Michael J. Shapiro, G. Matthew Bonham and Daniel Heradstveit (1988), 'A discursive practices approach to collective decision-making', *International Studies Quarterly*, **32** (4), 399.
31. Yee, 'The causal effects', 95.
32. See the ASEF website at: www.asef.org.sg
33. See Harold Sprout and Margaret Sprout (1962), *Foundations of International Politics*, New York: Van Nostrand, pp. 46-7; Philip Zelikow (1994), 'Foreign policy engineering: theory to practice and back again', *International Security*, **18** (4), 143.
34. George M. Thomas, John W. Meyer, Francisco O. Ramirez and John Boli (1987), *Institutional Structure*, Beverley Hills: Sage, p. 13.
35. Richard W. Scott and John W. Meyer (1991), 'The Organization of Societal Sectors: Propositions and Early Evidence', in Powell and DiMaggio, *The New Institutionalism*, p. 179.
36. Holm, 'The dynamics of institutionalization', 401.

37. For one of many pictorial descriptions see Serradell, 'The Asia-Europe Meeting', 187.
38. Christopher M. Dent (1999), 'The EU-Asia economic relationship: the persisting weak triadic link?' *European Foreign Affairs Review*, **4** (3), 390.
39. Gerald Segal (1997), 'Thinking strategically about ASEM: the subsidiarity question', *The Pacific Review*, **10** (1), 124-34; Camroux and Lechervy, 'Close Encounter'.
40. Simon Hix (1994), 'The study of the European Community: the challenge to comparative politics', *West European Politics*, **17** (1), 1.
41. J. Rosenau (1990), *Turbulence and World Politics*, Princeton: University Press, p. 122.
42. See Julie Gilson (1999), Japan's role in the Asia-Europe Meeting: establishing an interregional or intraregional agenda?, *Asian Survey*, **39** (5), 735-52.
43. Stuart Harris (1999), 'The Asian Regional Response to its Economic Crisis and the Global Implications', Department of International Relations Working Paper, 1999/4 (Australian National University: Department of International Relations), p. 6.
44. Alexander Wendt (1994), 'Collective identity formation and the international state', *American Political Science Review*, **88** (2), 389.
45. See Richard Higgot (1994), 'Ideas, interests and identity in the Asia Pacific, *The Pacific Review*, **7** (4), 367-80.
46. Gilson, 'Japan in ASEM'; Wendt, 'Collective identity formation', 391.

PART IV

The Politics of Economic Linkages

7. A material–discursive approach to the 'Asian Crisis': the breaking and remaking of the production and financial orders

Sum, Ngai-Ling

INTRODUCTION

The so-called 'Asia Crisis' has been constructed and explained from many viewpoints: two of the most popular are the specific defects of national 'crony capitalisms' and weaknesses in the global financial architecture (see section 2). This chapter offers a critique of these accounts and suggests an alternative, 'material–discursive' approach to the crisis that pays careful attention to its structural, strategic and discursive dimensions. This approach examines: (a) the structural background to the crisis in terms of the material interconnections between the productive and financial orders in the context of global capitalism; (b) the conjunctural factors precipitating the crisis and its implications for the current economic disorder; (c) the role of various actors in developing competing discourses to restructure the global–regional–national political economy and to remake their associated identities and interests; and (d) the subsequent interplay between these various material and discursive aspects in shaping the crisis as it has developed since 1997.

In developing the first element of this approach to the crisis, my chapter examines the development of the East Asian region since the Plaza Accord was signed in 1985. Structurally, this 'post-Plaza' period was characterized by, *inter alia*, a Japan-led *regional-national production order* financed by *export-oriented FDI* (foreign direct investment) and an American-dominated *dollar-bloc regime* linked – at least as it operated during the 1985–95 period – to a *yen-appreciating bubble*. The relations between these two orders displayed a strong and stable 'structured coherence' (see section 3.1). Despite this coherence, the productive-financial orders were structurally liable to at least three forms of crisis: overproduction–underconsumption, overborrowing, and exchange rate weaknesses (see section 3.2). This vulnerability was exacerbated by such conjunctural developments as the arrival of China as a major production site, the bursting of the 'property bubble' in Japan, and the joint US–Japan decision to depreciate the yen in 1995, for these developments disrupted the previous coherence within and between the two orders (see section 3.3). This disarticulation, in conjunction with national–local circumstances, has had differential effects on economies in the region. For example, Hong Kong and China have maintained exchange rate stability against the dollar, with the unintended development of becoming the first lines of defence of the US-dominated international currency order (see section 3.4).

Given the specificities of these orders and their differential impact in the region, the so-called 'Asian Crisis' cannot be resolved through the traditional 'rescue' programme preferred by the IMF. On the contrary, 'financial contagion' has led to a new 'domino effect' that moved from Asia to Russia and thence to Brazil. This, in turn, leads us to the third dimension of the material–discursive approach – the struggle between actors (for example, Japan, the USA, the IMF, 'Greater China') to establish new visions and identities relevant to the remaking of globalities and regionalities (section 4). The chapter concludes with some remarks on a possible research agenda on the remaking of the global–regional–national political economy (section 5).

2.   TWO POPULAR ACCOUNTS OF THE CRISIS AND THEIR CRITICISMS

The 'Asian Crisis' has been represented and explained from many viewpoints ranging from the defects of East Asian 'crony capitalism'[1] to the weaknesses of the global financial architecture and the destructive activities of hedge funds. Claims about 'crony capitalism' have been taken up by some global institutions and Western commentators to explain the crisis. For example, the World Bank narrates the causes of the crisis in terms of the 'perverse connections between lenders and borrowers',[2] inadequate bank supervision, a lack of transparency, state-directed lending, and political pressures for loans. These are held responsible for bad loans that could total as much as $660 billion. Krugman is even more explicit when he links the crisis to the 'fuzzy line ... between what was public and what was private; the minister's nephew or president's son could open a bank and raise money from the domestic populace and foreign lenders, with everyone believing that their money was safe because official connections stood behind the institutions'.[3] Together with this alleged lack of transparency and inadequacies in the regulation of financial institutions, this government-directed investment system is also accused of having produced excesses and errors. The IMF also subscribes to these views and hopes thereby to justify its bail-out package(s) for the East

Asian NICs (hereafter EANICs) even though these involve domestic austerity programmes (for example, high interest rates and restriction of domestic demand) and radical institutional change, including further liberalization of the financial sector.

A second popular account is forwarded by Jeffrey Sachs[4] and has been echoed by some East Asian national leaders/governments. Sachs explained the crisis in terms of a classic financial panic: a run on the banks and mass capital flight that was exacerbated by mismatch between Asian banks and borrowers. This was accompanied by global speculative attacks on currencies and the collapse of asset values. Sachs claims that such attacks have little to do with the underlying 'fundamentals' in these economies. Instead, he attributes the problem partly to fragile banking systems and partly to flaws in the global financial architecture. Some East Asian national leaders/governments have explicitly identified the latter flaws with the capacity of large global speculators/hedge funds to move rapidly around the world without any regulation. One notable example of such an explanation was Mahathir's speech delivered at the 30th anniversary celebration of the ASEAN in July 1997. He argued that the Malaysian crisis is an effect of global speculative trading, and, more specifically, he blamed the 'currency sabotage' conducted by George Soros. Similarly, in Hong Kong, the Financial Secretary, Donald Tsang, described the global hedge funds as 'crocodiles' and alleged that they had 'struck' Hong Kong for a second time in August 1998. Likewise, Ian Macfarlane, Governor of the Reserve Bank of Australia, described the hedge fund flows as the 'privileged children of the financial scene, being entitled to the benefits of free markets without any of the responsibility'.[5]

Both accounts of the 'Asian Crisis' are one-sided. The former focuses on some long-standing and essentially local/internal features of state–business links in specific East Asian countries. Indeed, these same features had previously been invoked (albeit with less pejorative language) to explain the success of the EANICs. In any case, these features can hardly explain the timing, degrees, volatility and diverse forms of the crisis in the region as a whole. Yet, as the crisis has unfolded, this interpretation has been strategically appropriated by the IMF to lend moral weight to its attempts to impose its well-known and long-standing structural adjustment policies on the worst-hit East Asian countries as a condition for receiving financial support. Conversely, the second account, especially in the versions promoted by local politicians, assigns too much weight to the external factors and/or global actors. Implicit in this interpretation is a global-versus-national approach that is then used to justify nationalist policy responses by East Asian states. This approach explains neither the speed nor the varying incidence and depth of the crisis. As for Sachs' argument, it highlights the healthy 'fundamentals' of the East Asian economies and relates the crisis to some behavioural and speculative features of the international financial system. He interprets the crisis as essentially a financial one and leaves both the 'real economy' and its interconnections with finance under-examined. In addition, in focusing on the national and/or the global level, both accounts miss the multiscalar complexities of the crisis.

3. TOWARDS A MATERIAL-DISCURSIVE APPROACH TO THE CRISIS

This chapter argues for an alternative, material–discursive approach to the crisis. Due to the limitation of space, it concentrates on three key aspects: a) the structural background to the crisis; b) the conjunctural factors that undermine the structural coherence[6] of the production–financial orders; and c) the struggles among global, regional and national actors to remake globalities and regionalities. We begin with the first aspect.

3.1 The Structural Background to the 'Asian Crisis': Articulation Between the Production and Financial Orders

Structurally, post-Plaza Asia has developed in the context of an increasing triadization in global capitalism.[7] Among the factors shaping this tendency in Asia we can note: (i) the increasing importance of collaboration within each part of the East Asian triad to ensure cost reduction in production, R&D, and so on, and rapid cost recovery in an era of accelerating as well as increasing competition; (ii) the information and communication technology revolution, which allows rapid transmission of production and financial information within and across triads; (iii) the impact of the 1980s neoliberal turn, which introduced financial liberalization to the region; (iv) the end of the cold war, which has increased the priority of multilateral geoeconomic concerns relative to bipolar geopolitical worries in this region; (v) the emergence of Japan as the regional hegemon and the rise of the EANICs as major players in the global economy; and (vi) the growing US–Japan trade deficits and accumulating surpluses in Japan.

These developments contributed to the emergence of complementary and stable relations between the production and financial orders in East Asia. The production order was mediated by a Japan-led regime that integrated East Asia into the wider global economy. This began in 1985, when the USA tried to reverse its trade deficits with Japan through the Plaza Agreement. This entailed a yen–dollar accord that required joint US–Japanese intervention in foreign-exchange markets to correct trade imbalances. This resulted in the yen's appreciation against the dollar. Saddled with uncompetitive export prices, the need for cost reductions and the availability of surplus capital, and fearing greater protectionism in US and European markets, Japan recognized that it needed to transfer some of its manufacturing production to other parts of Asia. Initially this occurred through industrial and trade finance. For example, Japanese FDI in 1986 was nearly double that of 1985. By 1988, the figure had doubled again; it peaked in 1989 at $67.5 billion. This process was mediated by a transregional class alliance articulated to the specificities of national–local capitals and conditions. Details of such alliances are beyond the scope of this chapter but Bernard[8] offers interesting case studies on Thailand and South Korea.

This transregional class alliance was expressed and reinforced discursively by the metaphor of a 'flying geese' region in which Japan was portrayed as the spearhead of the flock and the four EANICs were following close behind, while the six ASEAN economies were seen as the next to take off. This image of the 'flying geese', though not uncontested, aimed to reinforce a 'synergistic' division of labour. It was seen as synergistic because Japan concentrated on high-tech and R&D; South Korea and Taiwan specialized in high-valued OEM (original equipment manufacturing) related to intermediate parts; Hong Kong and Singapore developed as service centres; while Malaysia, Thailand and China focused on the production of low-value products. In this regard, the region was tightly integrated to provide semi-conductors, electronic goods, textiles and clothing, and other products mainly for the American markets. Such a synergistic intraregional relationship was also marked by competition and 'leapfrogging' behaviour. There were well-known 'leapfrogging' cases and some firms were able to compete with their Japanese counterparts (for example, Hyundai, Singapore Airlines and Hong Kong Bank). However, these examples are better treated as exceptions rather than the rule. Developing the capabilities to acquire and operate foreign technology did not necessarily lead in each country to an ability to adapt or innovate, let alone to 'leapfrog'. A study of Singapore's electronic industry showed that local firms pursued a long-term, painstaking, incremental learning path rather than leaping from one vintage of technology to the next. Their development involved a 'hard slog' rather than a 'leapfrog'.[9] In this regard, economies in the region were highly dependent on Japan. More specifically, roughly half of total trade was intraregional with a high proportion of the exports from Japan to EANICs (except South Korea) being capital goods and sophisticated parts. These capital goods were used as inputs by Japanese or Japan-related subsidiaries/subcontractors for the region's export-oriented production.

This Japan-led regional production order was complemented by the American-dominated financial order. The latter can be examined in terms of its credit and currency forms. First, regarding the credit form (concerned with the organization of credit), Japan was the major provider of industrial and trade finance. This was organized through direct lending by Japanese banks to Japanese multinationals and affiliates in the region. FDI financed a high import content of intermediate capital from Japan. Up to 1995, Japan accounted for 20 per cent of the region's FDI. Second, regarding the money–currency form (the contradictory functions as national money and international currency), all East Asian economies have their own national currencies but most of them were externally pegged to the US dollar. This confidence in the dollar created a kind of dollar-bloc regime (or pegged-rate dollar standard) which was linked to a yen-appreciating bubble. This money–currency form suited the export-oriented region in two ways. First, since most East Asian imports and exports are/were invoiced in dollars, it reduced the currency risks involved in trading with major markets in the USA or elsewhere. Second, the dollar pegs anchored domestic monetary policies. This means that the policies of Indonesia, South Korea, Malaysia, the Philippines, Thailand, Hong Kong and Singapore were loosely tied to each other. This protected each of these economies from competitive devaluations by the others and thereby stabilized their domestic price levels from the 1980s to 1996.[10]

The important question here is not so much what constituted the credit and money–currency forms, but the way in which these articulated with and complemented the post-Plaza production order. Given the 'catch-up' dynamics of the region, the EANICS were strongly oriented to investing in upgrading technologies and/or innovating for niche markets. This required high investment and, given that these economies compete/cooperate to export primarily to the US market, profits for some tended to be relatively low. The combination of export-orientation, high investment and relatively low profit meant that this production order required much external trade and finance.

In terms of external trade, a dollar-bloc regime stabilized import–export prices with little risk of competitive devaluation between 1980 and 1996. Moreover, given that this regime was also linked to the yen-appreciating bubble, export competitiveness of the EANICs, in dollar terms, was also improved relative to Japan. Under these conditions, the former not only became OEM/cheap labour sites for Japan; but export platforms could also enhance the region's external trade. As for external financing, a dollar-bloc regime under a stable yen–dollar rate encouraged foreign borrowing that involved no exchange risk. In the case of Japanese lending and FDI, the yen-appreciating bubble was also significant – especially once Japanese interest rates were lowered in 1987. The share of Japanese FDI going to emerging Asia and China rose from 12.1 per cent in 1986 to 46 per cent at the turn of the 1990s. In turn, such outflows, especially Japanese capital heading for the EANICs, stimulated EANIC investment flows to the ASEAN countries. This further deepened the regional production–financial order.

In short, the investment- and export-oriented Japan-led production order was highly dependent on external trade and financing. It was complemented by an American-dominated dollar-bloc regime that could enhance its external trade by stabilizing its import–export prices, and also providing external financing at no exchange risk. So complementary and stable were these features between 1985–95 that they produced a certain 'structured coherence' between the production and financial orders (see Table 7.1).

Table 7.1   The 'structured coherence' between the production and financial orders in the post-Plaza period, 1985–95

Post cold war/post-Plaza (Regionalization in Asia)	Later Bretton Woods (Dollar-bloc regime)
Regional–national production order	Regional–global financial order
Production form Japan	*Credit form* external finance
R&D developments	trade and industrial finance
technology exports	high import content of FDI
EANICs	*Money-currency form*
OEM	pegged-rate dollar standard
trade and financial services	stable yen-dollar rates
ASEAN/China	'yen-appreciating bubble'
labour-intensive production	
Export to ⎹_____→ USA _____⎸	Role of US dollar and FDI

Source: Author's compilation.

3.2 Crisis Tendencies of the Export-oriented Production–Financial Orders

Despite their mutual 'structured' coherence, these orders also had certain crisis tendencies in their production, credit and currency forms. These included, respectively, risks of relative overproduction–underconsumption, excess liquidity and exchange rate vulnerability. Thus, in terms of the production order, corresponding to the 'catch-up' dynamic of the region, the allocation of domestic and Japan-related credit tended to privilege investment rather than consumption. The risk here is one of overinvestment and overproduction. Rapid expansion of (potentially excess) productive capacity in the region tends to increase land and labour costs; and the resulting expansion of production can exceed market growth and thereby trigger falling prices for the resulting goods. When costs rise and prices fall, profits are squeezed. One counter-tendency to this was the shift from higher to lower cost production sites within the region, but this intensified investment demands and led to problems of excess capacity as well as profit squeeze.

This tendency for overproduction–underconsumption and profit squeeze can be aggravated by financial liberalization and the availability of easy credits at no exchange risk. The inflow of foreign investment and credit capital may exceed the absorptive capacity of economies already prone to overproduction. This (over)supply of cheap foreign credit may enter into stock market speculation, property-price inflation and even risky loans to local companies. This increases the tendency toward bad debts and even credit contraction. Speculation can make this worse by generating rapid rises in asset values (for example, shares and property). This, in turn, can induce over-production of property at mega-level prices. As speculators turn from buying to selling, the 'property bubble' bursts and banks start to call in loans and cut credit lines. This development generates non-performing loans and may even lead to potential or actual bank runs or failures.

There is no necessary link between this kind of crisis in the credit form and a currency crisis; that is, a speculative attack on a currency that forces a sharp devaluation/depreciation.[11] But this did become a problem when those Asian economies started to run balance of payments deficits and to overborrow under the dollar-bloc regime. In terms of trade balance, deficits appear when export values do not keep pace with imports to enhance industrial capacity and commercial real estates. Accumulating deficits make it hard for these economies to maintain their peg to the dollar. This pressure upon the pegged system was coupled with a declining quality of investment. Since governments in the region could no longer maintain the dollar peg and started to depreciate, the size of the foreign debt burden that local firms had to service rose in local currency terms. In other words, currency depreciation may raise the borrowing costs and can result in firms defaulting on their debt payments. These debt problems can then spread to more prudent banks and firms.

3.3 Some Conjunctural Factors Behind the Crisis: Disarticulation Within and Between the Production and Financial Orders

These crisis-tendencies were actualized by various conjunctural develop-ments. Regarding the production order, the entrance of China into global–regional production intensified the tendency towards overproduction in the EANICs. The latter's competitive edge stems from its supply of cheap skilled and unskilled labour as well as the preferential conditions it offers to foreign capital. Given the People's Republic of China's (PRC) strong competitive challenge, the EANICs were forced to respond by upgrading their technologies and/or by expanding their innovative capacities. This was associated with attempts to move higher up the value chain in established sectors (for example, clothing and electronics) and/or to move into or upgrade their position in service industries. This occurred in conjunction with the relocation of Japanese industries to the region. Together they formed part of the Japan-led production order, with each co-operating and struggling to climb the technological/innovation ladder. This 'catch-up' process and effort to upgrade/innovate, encouraged new rounds of investment in the region's economies. Between 1990 and 1995, gross domestic investment grew by 16.3 per cent per annum in Indonesia, 16 per cent in Malaysia, 15.3 per cent in Thailand, and 7.2 per cent in South Korea. By comparison, investment in the USA grew by 4.1 per cent per annum over the same period.

This 'investment rush' occurred on the basis of unrealistic projections about future global demand, and encouraged the build-up of excessive production capacities. For example, in response to a temporary shortage of 16 megabyte Dynamic Random Access Memory chips (DRAMs), Korean *chaebol* increased their investment between 1994 and 1995. However, supply shortages had disappeared by 1996, and excess capacity began to build up. The retail price of DRAMs dropped by 90 per cent in 1996. Similar excess capacity could be seen in the Thai property market, with 365 000 unoccupied apartment units in Bangkok in early 1997. In both cases, of course, overcapacity led to declining profit rates.

This 'investment rush' and falling profitability was also confirmed by a firm-based study of selected Asian economies since the late 1980s.[12] Rates of corporate investment were found to be consistently high for all economies, apart from Hong Kong (see Table 7.2). This regional 'investment rush' exposed these economies to problems of overproduction, as prices of goods fell and profitability was relatively low. The same study recorded relatively low profitability rates in Hong Kong, South Korea and Singapore as compared with Taiwan, Malaysia, Thailand and Indonesia. However, in general, all six economies, except Taiwan, were experiencing declining profits in some form (see Table 7.3).

These problems of overinvestment and overproduction were exacerbated by the limited potential to find alternative foreign markets for exports switched from the USA and/or fully to absorb any unsalable export production within the region itself. Consumption has obviously risen in the region as economic growth has continued but the weight and dynamic importance of export-oriented production makes rapid reorientation of output very difficult. The Japanese and EANIC economies have high saving ratios and the crisis may even increase the inclination to save. This is especially clear for Japan, with

Table 7.2   Capital investment in selected Asian economies (per cent, medians)

	1989	1991	1993	1995
Hong Kong	16.6	7.6	19.8	5.8
South Korea	13.8	19.6	11.2	12.4
Singapore	7.6	8.8	11.3	12.5
Taiwan	n.a.	14.3	8.4	11.2
Malaysia	7.6	9.6	13.4	14.6
Thailand	12.9	15.0	15.0	14.5
Indonesia	n.a.	12.4	8.6	13.8

Source: Adapted from Claessens et al., 1998, p. 8.

Table 7.3   Return on assets for selected Asian economies (per cent, medians, in real local currency)

	1989	1991	1993	1995
Hong Kong	5.3	4.8	3.8	3.9
South Korea	3.9	4.0	3.6	3.6
Singapore	4.5	3.9	4.6	3.9
Taiwan	n.a.	5.1	6.5	6.5
Malaysia	5.6	6.2	6.5	6.1
Thailand	11.0	11.2	9.8	7.8
Indonesia	n.a.	9.1	7.9	6.2

Source: Adapted from Claessens et al., 1998, p. 4.

its aging population and decade-long stagnation. Conversely, although the Chinese market is potentially huge, the low-wage regime in China and its low per capita income (for example, US$621 in 1998) inhibits any switch to this market of the goods produced in the region and previously exported to high-income economies.

These problems of overproduction/underconsumption were exaggerated by access to cheap credit and the bursting of the yen-appreciating bubble. In the early 1990s, cheap credit became easily available in the global–regional contexts of: (i) the liberalization of the global financial markets; (ii) the emergence of Tokyo and Hong Kong as regional financial centres; (iii) the bursting of the Japanese property/stock market bubbles and the emergence of bad debts therein; and (iv) the resultant low interest rate in Japan (reaching half a per cent). The ample supply of portfolio capital in Japan was matched by the fortuitous bursting of the yen-appreciating bubble in 1995. In that summer, the American Treasury and the Japanese Ministry of Finance agreed on a deal to help re-elect President Clinton and allow Japan to continue to export its way out of its post-bubble problems. This would be achieved by depreciating the yen against the dollar (that is, reversing the Plaza Accord), thereby increasing Japan's export competitiveness. In return, Japan would continue to supply cheap credits to the public and private sectors in America, thereby financing federal debt, domestic consumption and trade deficits.[13] The yen-appreciating bubble burst and the value of the yen fell against the dollar by about 60 per cent between April 1995 and April 1997. The speed and extent of the fall had a major impact upon FDI and portfolio capital.

A fall in the value of the yen slowed down FDI flows from Japan to the EANICs. This was matched by the outflow of Japanese portfolio capital to these economies as the falling yen created arbitrage opportunities for local and overseas banks based on low interest rates in Japan. Japanese, American and European banks began to develop new offshore practices which came to be known as the 'yen carry trade'. Godement illustrated these practices by means of the following two-part example:

> Borrowing (by banks) at 1 per cent on three-month terms while the yen stands at 100 to the US dollar, and immediately lending at 6 per cent for one year in a currency tied to the dollar, is the first part of the trick. Paying back the initial loan after the dollar has climbed to 110 yen, or even better, loaning again the money while rolling over the short-term yen, is the second part.[14]

Owing to its popularity as a credit device, most Asian economies came to depend on short-term cheap money from 'offshore' to finance long-term domestic projects. Between 1995 and 1997, Japan was the single most important source of portfolio investment and provided about 31 per cent of the total in the region. For their own political and economic reasons, some Southeast Asian governments (notably Thailand and Indonesia) started to run easy credit policies to foster growth. On balance, these portfolio credits tended to be short term and many went into property markets, speculation, infrastructural projects and corporate bonds. Thus, the Japanese property/stock market bubbles were exported to other parts of Asia. In the case of Thailand, much of the portfolio investment from Japan was poured into property speculation; by 1995, an overhang of unsold buildings led some building firms to close down. By 1996, non-performing loans in Thailand were about 9.2 per cent of its GDP. As for South Korea, a massive rise in investment increased the volume of stockpiled goods. Faced with cash-flow problems, firms obtained more short-term loans from foreign banks. By 1996, the non-performing loans in South Korea were about 6 per cent of GDP.[15]

Two incidents occurred in the end of the first quarter of 1997 that intensified the problems of overborrowing and exchange rate vulnerabilities. Japanese banks and subsidies needed to jack up their own assets towards the end of the fiscal year, and they were less willing to roll over short-term credits. This tightening of Japanese credit was coupled with a sudden rise in the yen, making short-term borrowing less attractive.[16] These created a vicious spiral of illiquidity, leading possibly to insolvency and a consequent worsening of the new asset positions of the Japanese creditors. In turn, this deterioration of financial intermediation abilities of Japanese banks exacerbated the domestic and regional credit crunches. This further prompted the increase in the amount of non-performing loans, leading some firms to sell off their products cheaply and leading international bankers and hedge fund managers to expect that the region's currencies would soon or later de-peg from the dollar and depreciate (or be allowed to float). Such depreciation would increase the size of the debt burden of local firms when measured in local currency.

Speculators first attacked the Thai bhat on 5 February 1997. To defend the currency, the Bank of Thailand raised interest rates and bought billions of bhat in the forward market. This domestic credit squeeze put more pressure on weak financial institutions and companies to close down. By mid 1997, the Bank of Thailand had used about half of its foreign reserves in defence of the bhat. On 2 July 1997, it allowed the bhat to float. Non-performing loans were estimated at 25 per cent of the total. Only two out of the 58 financial institutions that were closed have sufficient capital to reopen.[17] This triggered a financial contagion that quickly spread from Thailand to other parts of Asia between July and December 1997. It was estimated by Howell[18] that US$62.2 billion of private financial capital fled the region in 1997, and monthly data for 1998 shows that outflows have not halted.

3.4   Differential Impact of the 'Crisis' and the Case of 'Greater China'

The above conjunctural developments – the arrival of China as a competitive production site, the export of the Japanese property/stock market bubbles, the US–Japan deal to lower the value of the yen, the regional credit crunch – weakened the 'structured coherence' within and between the production and financial order. They became disarticulated when the export-oriented production order overproduced from within and failed to secure cheap and exchange-risk-free credits from without. Such disarticulation at the end of 1997 did not have the same impact on all economies in the region. Data relevant to this period reveal a differential impact of the crisis on then 'stronger' economic formations such as Singapore, Taiwan and Hong Kong, and on 'weaker' formations such as the Philippines, Malaysia, South Korea, Thailand and Indonesia (see Table 7.4). In this regard, it is perhaps more accurate to refer to Asian crises instead of the 'Asian Crisis'. Economies in the so-called 'Greater China' region,[19] especially Taiwan, seem to have escaped the worst effects of the contagion.

Table 7.4   Differential impact of the 'crisis': changes in stock prices and currency (percentage measured in USD, 1 Jan to 31 Oct 1997)

	Stocks	Currency
'Stronger' economic formations		
Singapore	–28.7	–12.3
Taiwan	6.9	–12.1
Hong Kong	–19.5	0.0
'Weaker' Economic Formations		
Philippines	–42.4	–33.4
Malaysia	–46.0	–32.8
South Korea	–28.0	–14.3
Thailand	–45.4	–58.0
Indonesia	–21.6	–53.0

Source: Adapted from *Fortune*, 24 November 1997, p. 32.

This differential impact of the crisis was largely related to the pre-existing strengths and embedded capacities of each economy. Relevant factors here include current account balances (see Table 7.5), foreign debts and reserves (see Table 7.6), degree of openness to global capital, state capacities (for example, regulatory capacities over financial institutions) and, equally important, on the balance of economic, political, and social forces with different interests. It is beyond the scope of this chapter to deal with the specificities of individual economies and their diverse strategies of restructuring. A substantial body of literature has concentrated on the cases of Indonesia, Malaysia, Thailand and South Korea, with the latter two economies showing signs of economic recovery since the end of 1998. Instead, this section seeks to examine briefly some of the 'stronger' economic formations, especially those within the 'Greater China' region.

Taiwan has escaped from the devastating impact of contagion. This is attributable to its pre-existing strengths which include: (i) a flexible small- to medium-sized manufacturing system based on cost-effectiveness; (ii) infrastructural and financial support to industries from the government and Kuomintang (KMT)-related economic forces; (iii) its position as an exporter

Table 7.5   Current account balances (as percentage of GDP)

	1995–96	1998–99ff.
'Stronger' economic formations		
Singapore	16.1	16.4
Taiwan	3.0	2.2
China	0.6	0.7
Hong Kong	1.4	1.1
'Weaker' economic formations		
Philippines	–3.7	0.3
Malaysia	–7.1	–1.4
South Korea	–3.3	7.0
Thailand	–8.0	5.6
Indonesia	–3.6	2.2

Source: Adapted from J.P. Morgan, World Financial Markets, First Quarter 1998.

Table 7.6   Asian foreign debt and reserves (US$ billion) - end 1997 estimates

	Total debt	Short-term debt	Reserves
'Stronger' economic formations			
Singapore	—	—	88
Taiwan	46	29	81
China	152	42	141
Hong Kong	—	—	75
'Weaker' economic formations			
Philippines	58	15	9
Malaysia	39	14	24
South Korea	155	60	17
Thailand	102	32	20
Indonesia	131	27	28

Source: Adapted from J.P. Morgan, World Financial Markets, First Quarter 1998.

of capital with large reserves; (iv) the associated low external debts of the government and corporations; (v) a not yet fully financially deregulated system with exchange controls on foreign investment; and (vi) an early devaluation of the New Taiwan dollar (NT$) in August 1997. Benefiting from this strong position, Taiwan is still expecting an official GDP growth rate of around five per cent. Given that private credit comprises 166 per cent of GDP and public credit takes the total to 200 per cent, it is not entirely sheltered from the contagion. The government imposed new controls on foreign exchange, cutting off speculators' access to the local dollar by restricting trade in non-delivery forward contracts. In August 1998, the government approved an NT$193.7 billion economic stimulus package covering a range of infrastructure projects.

Other 'crisis-related' symptoms began to appear in the latter part of 1998. In the corporate sector, for example, there was financial trouble at the Central Bills Finance and the Taichung Medium Business Bank, which were temporarily taken over by government-linked institutions in November 1998. Together with a series of defaults on stock payments and debts by medium-sized firms (for example, An Feng Steel, Kuoyang Construction Company), the stock index plunged by 40 per cent between its August 1997 peak and January 1999. The KMT-led government has set up a US$8 billion Stock Stabilization Fund to prop up share prices. In the case of the property sector, falling prices have also stimulated the government to introduce a $7 billion scheme to bail out the real estate market by offering low interest loans to home buyers. Given the local political context (especially with the challenge of the Democratic Progressive Party (DPP)), these KMT support packages involved a politics of redistribution when the unemployment rate also rose to three per cent in the meantime.

Up to the time of writing, China has largely escaped the worst impact of the contagion because of: (i) trade surpluses and relatively large reserves; (ii) limited financial liberalization in foreign banks – which can handle the Yuan only in Pudong and Shenzhen; (iii) a partial command economy with exchange and credit controls; (iv) a non-convertible currency that is not a good target for speculators; and (v) a domestically oriented economy with export assistance. Despite these strengths, there was frequent talk that the Chinese yuan would devalue, especially after the devaluation of the Brazilian ríal and the period when the yen was weak against the dollar. The justifications for not devaluing are: (i) the high import content of China's trade would cancel out the possible benefits on exports after devaluation; (ii) a yuan devaluation would mean greater debt-servicing and this would affect the values of H-share and Red Chip companies; (iii) devaluation would lower the inflow of foreign direct investment; (iv) it would put severe pressure on Hong Kong's currency board system; and (v) China was unwilling to devalue on the fiftieth anniversary of communist rule. Instead, the Chinese government has sought remedies by fiscal stimulus and monetary easing. For example, the Chinese government has assembled a 200 billion yuan fund aimed at financing increased public works projects. It has also raised tax rebates on exports of coal, cement, ships, textiles and steel by between 2 and 8 per cent.

Nevertheless, the economy is faced with an export slowdown from 21 per cent in 1997 to less than 1 per cent in 1998. The government has also revised expected growth rates downward from eight to seven per cent. In October 1998, the collapse of Guangdong International Trust and Investment Corporation (GITIC) exposed problems of the local trust and investment corporations (ITICs) which have total external debts of US$8.1 billion. More specifically and with reference to GITIC, its collapse has sparked off not only a foreign credit crunch; but also local–central conflict over southern 'pragmatism' and northern 'dogmatism', as well as rivalry between Guangdong and non-Guangdong cadres. In early 1999, the central government decided not to bail out GITIC and embarked on policies that seek to reform the Chinese financial system (for example, reducing the number of ITICs from 240 to 40).

In the case of Hong Kong, the dollar came under speculative pressure on several occasions in July, August and October 1997. Initially, the Hong Kong government intervened in the market by pushing up interest rates in the inter-banking sector and, later, by imposing penalty interest on borrowing of the Hong Kong dollar. Hong Kong was able to maintain the pegged system because of: (i) its high foreign reserves; (ii) its long-established prudent fiscal policy, which meant there was no external debt; (iii) its in-built mechanism for interest rate adjustment; (iv) its tight supervision of financial institutions (for example, the use of a gross simultaneous account system among these institutions); and (v) its capacities derived from acting as an industrial, financial and commercial middleman between China and the rest of the world. Despite these strengths, the pegged exchange rate is maintained under conditions of high interest rates, capital flight from the Hong Kong dollar, and reduced external demand. These pushed the local stock index and residential property prices down by over 50 per cent between October 1997 and June 1998. This asset depreciation, especially in the property sector, cut at the heart of Hong Kong's internal 'growth' dynamics as this had developed since the opening of China, for as Hong Kong firms have moved their manufacturing industries to the mainland, the service and property sectors have filled the gap created by this so-called 'hollowing-out' process. More specifically, the property sector became even more dominant. It comprised banks (in the form of credit), construction companies (in the form of property assets), the government (in the form of land and revenue), and middle classes (in the form of wealth). The bursting of the 'property bubble' has given rise to fear among this property-related bloc of further asset depreciation. In order to prevent assets from depreciating further, the government stopped land sales and refunded rates to local residents.

The Hong Kong dollar came under further attack in August 1998 when the yen depreciated against the dollar, with hedge funds selling the Hong Kong stock market short in the expectation that the index would fall as interest rates rose. Speculative attacks propelled significant amounts of capital outflow, some people believing that these attacks might also force a yuan devaluation. This time the government reacted by: (i) drawing on its reserves to buy US$15 billion worth of selected Hong Kong shares (60 per cent of these were property related – higher than the weight of this sector in the stock market); and (ii) introducing a package of technical measures to strengthen the transparency and operation of the linked exchange rate system (for example, a rediscount facility to reduce interest rate volatility). The pegged system was once again maintained but at the expense of high interest rates, weak domestic demand and rising unemployment. Hong Kong's GDP fell five per cent and the unemployment rate had reached six per cent at the beginning of 1999. However, wages and rents are still high. At the beginning of 1999, the government announced that it would resume land sales in April. This continual support of the property sector was further reinforced in the 1999 budget by two 'kisses of life' (the building of a 'cyberport'[20] and, possibly, of a Disneyland theme park), both overwhelmingly property-related projects. In much the same situation as Taiwan, the Hong Kong government's support packages for the property sector involved a politics of redistribution that has been challenged by the Democratic Party as the unemployment rate rose to 5.8 per cent in the same period.

Compared with most East Asian economies, Hong Kong and China emerged as the two non-devaluing economies. The two governments coordinated actions to maintain Hong Kong's pegged system and insulate the 'Greater China' (sub)region from currency decline. China participated by providing foreign exchange market expertise and stand-by funds to defend the Hong Kong dollar. This is because a devaluation of the Hong Kong dollar would affect the value of HKD-denominated investment and prices of Chinese H-share and Red Chip corporations. It would also increase their debt burden in the Hong Kong currency and, perhaps, lead to higher interest charges and the possibility of non-performing loans. Conversely, a yuan devaluation might not benefit China and could trigger a devaluation of the Hong Kong dollar. Through the non-devaluation of the two currencies, the Hong Kong dollar and the Chinese Yuan were seen by the USA and IMF as crucial (sub)regional nodes in maintaining the stability of the later Bretton Woods system. Despite disputes with the USA over trade and human rights issues, Beijing was being constructed as the United States's possible 'number-one ally' in the region. As for Hong Kong, its 'currency board system' pegged to the US dollar was hailed by the IMF as a possible 'cure' for monetary problems.[21] As an unintended development, the Chinese yuan and the Hong Kong dollar came to assume the role of 'first line of defence' of the American-dominated international currency order.[22]

4.   STRUGGLES BETWEEN ACTORS IN THE REMAKING OF REGIONALITIES AND GLOBALITIES

Given the specificities of the crisis and the differential impact/responses in the region, it is not surprising that actors disagreed on strategies to remake the region. This leads us to the third aspect of the material-discursive approach; that is, the role of actors in constructing competing discourses concerning possible future regionalities and globalities. Due to the vast number of actors involved, this chapter can only illustrate this approach with the cases of Japan, the USA and the IMF.

4.1   Japan's Construction of Regionality: the AMF Idea and Its Containment

Given Japan's industrial and financial involvement in the region, its firms and banks were the most exposed to economic turmoil. The Ministry of Finance of Japan was eager to bail out their overexposed banks. At the same time, the Ministry of Foreign Affairs wanted to assert a greater degree of regional leadership in the face of increasing Chinese influence. Thus, Japan was interested in constructing some kind of collective mechanisms that could lessen potential financial disturbance. In March 1997, Japan proposed such mechanisms in the first meeting of the regional bankers' group Executives' Meeting of East Asia–Pacific Central Banks (EMEAP). Two novel features in this regard were that the proposal concerned financial mechanisms to deal with the crisis and that this proposal was made in a new regional forum.

Seeking to deflect a region-centred solution to the crisis, the IMF began to construct it as a 'liquidity' problem. It also selectively appropriated the previously ignored critiques of 'crony capitalism'. This strategic appropriation put the blame on to the national and crony-ridden nature of Asian governments' business relations. It left unexamined the nature of the global–regional economic systems later organized around the later Bretton Woods regime (for example, the dollar-bloc regime) and also the fact that Japan had little control over the value of its currency. In turn, the Japanese initiative for some 'financial mechanisms' was shaped in August 1997, into a 'Thai support fund', after consultation with the IMF and domestic authorities.

Given the country-specific and ad hoc nature of this support fund, it failed to stop the 'contagion' from spreading from Thailand to Indonesia, Malaysia and the Philippines. Being the most heavily affected country in the region, Japan was eager to see a quicker, more flexible and less stringent scheme of regional 'rescue'. It thus unveiled the idea of an AMF in the IMF–World Bank annual meeting in Hong Kong in September 1997. With a possible capitalization of US$100 billion, the AMF symbolized a regional source of finance that could provide quick and flexible disbursements to alleviate regional currencies in crisis, as well as provide emergency balance of payments support to crisis-hit economies. In other words, the AMF idea constructed a new form of regionality that could bypass the cumbersome decision-making procedures of the IMF and could deepen regional cooperation under the leadership of Japan. This idea attracted considerable interest from Malaysia, Taiwan, Thailand and South Korea. China expressed some concern over the possible domination of Japan under the AMF, but was not entirely uninterested.

Unsurprisingly, the US Treasury and the IMF opposed the AMF. By constructing a new scale/arena of lending activity, the latter was seen as countering American national security/economic interests[23] and the US/IMF's hegemony. This can be understood within the context of American domestic politics. Since the White House was increasingly constrained by Congress in committing financial resources abroad, Washington was forced to use the IMF as a primary mechanism for exercising US influence on world monetary affairs.[24] Hence any challenge to the IMF would be seen as countering US interests. The creation of the AMF would also drive a wedge into a US-sponsored project dating from the early 1980s to construct an 'Asia Pacific' identity.[25] It would also marginalize the IMF's debt conditionalities and its regime of truth (see section 4.2) by creating an alternative site of action. Accordingly, US and IMF officials sought to contain the AMF idea by appropriating some of its concerns into their own agenda.

In the same Hong Kong meeting, IMF officials tackled the problem of stringent and inadequate funding of the IMF, by calling for a 45 per cent increase in members' quotas. This suggestion partly addressed the issue of inadequate funding, but it also signalled to national actors in the region that the IMF still wanted to remain sole 'international lender of last resort'. Troubled by the turmoil in the region, national actors, including Japan, reiterated the IMF's centrality in the global financial architecture. This reaffirmation could clearly be seen from the outcome of the Manila Framework Group meeting in mid-November 1997. The Framework Group endorsed 'the need and desirability of a framework for regional cooperation' but added that this 'arrangement ... would supplement IMF resources'.[26] In this regard, the Manila agreement succeeded in the following: (i) containing, at least temporarily, the regional initiative within the IMF regime; (ii) defusing the contest between the IMF and the AMF; and (iii) constructing a globality that involved global–regional cooperation and supplementation. As an indication of this cooperation, the Framework Group also welcomed the US$30 billion aid assistance from Japan.

4.2   The New 'Domino' Effect and the Renegotiation of IMF's Identities

Partly to regain the centre stage, the IMF extended its neoliberal regime, especially the 'conditionality' practices, to Thailand, South Korea and Indonesia (the so-called 'IMF 3') between August and December in 1997 (see Table 7.7). The mechanism deployed to this end was the imposition of the blanket-type contractionary economic practices associated with Structural Adjustment Programmes (for example, cutting the budget deficit by tightening of fiscal policy, restricting central bank credits to government) and an insistence on greater transparency on behalf of the banks and G7 governments.

Table 7.7   IMF's regime of truth since the 1970s

Identities	Neoliberalism (under the 'Washington Consensus')
	● Good governance
	● Accountability
	● 'International lender of last resort' with full conditionality
'Conditionality' practices	Structural Adjustment Programmes (contractionary measures)
	● Tight monetary policy
	● Tight fiscal policy
	● Higher taxes to eliminate deficits

Source: Author's compilation.

Nonetheless, the IMF's actions, backed by the US Treasury, failed to arrest the 'contagion'. Its 'domino effect' has rippled from Asia to Russia, thence to Brazil and even to the USA between July 1997 to September 1998. Thus, following the collapse of the Thai bhat and its repercussions in East Asia, a second domino fell when the rouble folded and Russia defaulted on its international debt obligations. Two further dominoes were toppled when Norway (whose currency was backed by its oil reserves) was obliged to double interest rates to protect the krone, the repercussions of which were felt elsewhere in Scandinavia; and when foreign investors began to move assets from Brazil, Venezuela and Mexico, fearing that all emerging markets were now vulnerable. Finally, in September 1998, the near collapse of the Connecticut-based Long-Term Capital Management in the USA exposed the vulnerabilities of major American and European banks and hedge funds; for example, Merrill Lynch and UBS.[27]

The IMF's failure to arrest the 'contagion' has prompted a barrage of criticisms. Even actors from the free-trade tradition began to question its regime of truth. These include prominent economists, (such as Bhagwati, Krugman, Sachs) who have deployed the pages of the *New York Times*, the *Wall Street Journal*, and the *Washington Post* to question this regime. Thus, Bhagwati argued that capital markets are inherently unstable and require controls and Krugman likewise outlined the case for exchange controls as one response to crisis.[28] Bhagwati went further by noting that free capital mobility is promoted by the 'Wall Street–Treasury Complex' which equates its interests with the 'good of the world'.[29] Sachs in turn focused more on the folly of IMF's policies during the crisis. Specifically, he criticized its austerity measures – which involved tightening money, high interest rates and tight fiscal policies under the Structural Adjustment Programmes – and argued that, in the Asian context, they transformed a liquidity crisis into a financial panic. He proposed that the IMF should revise its standard formula for economic reform, make its decision making more transparent, and become more accountable for the impact of its policies.

Such academic 'dissent' sparked off internal and external debates concerning the roles of the IMF and the World Bank. Internally, the IMF began to discuss the issue of 'capital control' and to reverse some policy targets imposed on the 'IMF 3' (for example, deficit targets for Thailand, South Korea and Indonesia were reset to 3 per cent, 4 per cent and 8.5 per cent respectively between July and September 1998). As for the World Bank, it took steps to distance itself from the IMF's structural-adjustment approach. The Bank's then chief economist, Joseph Stiglitz, was at the forefront of the IMF–World Bank split. He openly questioned the usefulness of the adjustment programmes at the WIDER Annual Lecture.[30] He argued for a 'Post-Washington Consensus' that would encompass a broader set of goals when designing adjustment policies in developing countries. He suggested that these goals should include not only increases in GDP but also sustainable, equitable and democratic development. Stiglitz's attempt to go beyond the 'Consensus' resonates with the arguments of many NGOs that have been calling for an end to the IMF adjustment programmes. The demand that the IMF and World Bank become more transparent and responsive organizations, contributing to poverty reduction, added fuel to the debate.

Partly in response to these criticisms and demands, the IMF and World Bank adopted more socially conscious discourses. Thus, at the end of 1999, the IMF renamed its 'Extended Structural Adjustment Facility' as 'Poverty Reduction and Growth Facility', and rephrased its 'conditionality' requirements in more reform-sensitive terms. Likewise, in the IMF–World Bank Meeting in September 1999, the World Bank highlighted 'poverty reduction' as a 'main objective' and suggested that 'debt forgiveness' should be delivered 'with participation of civil society' and 'social safety nets'.[31]

Apart from these internal renegotiations of IMF–World Bank identities, many proposals have been made concerning the future of these two institutions. They include reports and rebuttals from the G24, the US Congressional Panel of the International Financial Institutions Advisory Commission (the Meltzer Commission), the Clinton Administration (for example, the US Treasury), and Washington-based thinktanks (for example, the Institute of International Economics). A detailed discussion of these reports and their implications for globality is beyond the scope of this chapter. However, close attention needs to be paid to how the IMF–World Bank identities are being renegotiated and re-embedded within an unequal power structure and to how these global players are seeking to legitimize a regime of economic truth that still remains grounded in orderly (as opposed to disorderly) 'liberalization, good governance, and accountability'.

4.3 Reinventing Regionalities: From the AMF to the 'New Miyazawa Initiative' and Beyond

Concurrent with the remaking of the IMF/World Bank's regime(s) of truth, the AMF idea was reinvented by Japan in October 1998 at a meeting of Asian Finance Ministers. Tactically, Japan sought to disentangle this initiative from the original AMF and the latter's struggle with the IMF. It thus adopted the following strategies: (i) to give the idea new names – the 'New Initiative to Overcome the Asian Currency Crisis'/'Resource Mobilization Plan for Asia' (more popularly known as the two stages of the 'New Miyazawa Initiative') (see Table 7.8); (ii) to redefine it as a new aid package (and not a currency stabilization scheme) that would be part of a multilateral G7-sponsored US$90 billion 'contingency' facility with an Asian focus; and (iii) to route the 'New Initiative' through the G7. The USA benefited from this, insofar as the 'New Miyazawa Initiative' enabled it to exert quasi scrutiny over Japan's regional initiative under the IMF–World Bank regime. At the same time, the initiative enabled Japan to install a regionally focused initiative with the support of the USA and related international agencies such as the IMF and Asian Development Bank.

For Japan, the regional space created by the 'New Miyazawa Initiative' was appropriated by the Ministry of Foreign Affairs and Ministry of Finance in the following ways: (i) as new resources to carry out financial diplomacy in the region; (ii) as an opportunity to bail out crisis-hit Japanese firms; and (iii) as a chance to provide loans in yen, as part of an effort to 'internationalize the yen'.

We look briefly at each in turn. First, the initiative armed the Ministry of Foreign Affairs with extra resources to carry out its financial diplomacy. Just before the APEC summit in Kuala Lumpur in November 1998, pressures were building up over the possible US–Japan trade deficit of US$300 billion in the

Table 7.8 Two stages of the 'New Miyazawa Initiative' 1998–99

Stage I: Total financial support amounted to US$30 billion	Stage II: Resource mobilization plan for Asia of up to US$17 billion

Medium- to long-term financial support: US$15 billion
(i) to provide funds for policy measures
    • supporting corporate debt restructuring
    • strengthening the social safety net
    • stimulating the economy
    • addressing the credit crunch
(ii) to provide direct official financial assistance
    • extending loans from Export–Import Bank
    • acquiring bonds issued by Asian countries
    • extending ODA yen loans
(iii) to support Asian countries in raising funds from international financial markets
    • using the guarantee functions of Export–Import Bank
    • providing export insurance
    • providing interest subsidies
(iv) to co-finance with the World Bank and the Asian Development Bank
(v) to provide technical assistance on debt restructuring
 	
Short-term financial support: US$15 billion
(i) to facilitate trade finance
(ii) to take the form of swap arrangements
	Assistance measures to mobilize private-sector capital
	(i) to assist fundraising in international financial and capital markets by Asian countries
	(ii) to assist investment in Asian private-sector enterprises via equity funds
	
	Construction of a stable financial system resistant to currency crisis
	(i) to upgrade and foster Asian bond markets
	(ii) to provide assistance for a stable financial system

Source: Adapted from Ministry of Finance of Japan, 3 October 1998 and 15 May 1999.

following year. Being a trade-oriented forum, the APEC summit was one of the arenas in which the USA pushed to open markets in the region, especially that of Japan. More specifically, this meeting saw a move to open up US$1.5 trillion in international trade in nine key sectors (the so-called Early Voluntary Sectoral Liberalization Plan). Some of these sectors (for example, fishery and forestry products) were precisely those that Japan is eager to protect. Given their divergence and Japan's strong resistance, US officials jacked up the aid discourse on 'Japan not doing enough to help Asia', thereby constructing Japan as the 'villain'. At the same time, China was hailed as 'hero' and 'number-one ally' because it helped to maintain the stability of the dollar-bloc regime by not devaluing its currency (see section 3.4).[32] Partly in response to the American challenge that 'Japan is not doing enough for Asia' and partly to rally support to delay APEC's trade liberalization plan, the Ministry of Foreign Affairs deployed the aid-related 'New Miyazawa Initiative' to gain support from Thailand, Indonesia, Malaysia, Taiwan and China. The Kuala Lumpur Summit thus ended with: (i) trade ministers voting to refer Early Voluntary Sector Liberalization to the World Trade Organization; (ii) finance ministers calling for new measures (such as supervision of banking systems and securities markets) to be discussed in the G22; and (iii) President Clinton and Prime Minister Obuchi launching a US$10 billion 'Asian Growth and Recovery Initiative' to aid bank restructuring and trade finance in the region.

Second, adopting the discourse of 'Japanese and Asian economies recovering together', the initiative disbursed the first stage of loans to Thailand (US$1.85 billion), Malaysia (US$1.5 billion), and the Philippines (US$1.4 billion) through a new global–regional network comprising the Asian Development Bank, the World Bank and the Japan Bank for International Cooperation (created by merging the Export–Import Bank of Japan (JEXIM) and Japan's Overseas Economic Cooperation Fund (OECF)). This network provided Japanese tied loans to crisis-hit countries. The nature of the tie can be seen in the fund's guidelines which 'prescribe that qualified proponents for identified projects be wholly-owned Japanese companies. Or if a tie-up with a counterpart exists, such as US companies, more than 50 per cent of the total man-months devoted for a specific project should be undertaken by the Japanese counterpart. This departs from the traditional approach of simply tying loans to either Japanese companies, or companies belonging to any of the DAC-member countries'.[33] In this regard, the tied nature of the initiative may have the effect of enabling the Ministry of Finance to use public funds to bail out Japanese crisis-hit private corporations.[34]

Third, Tokyo also viewed the 'New Miyazawa Inititiatve' and its second stage as an opportunity to provide loans in yen as part of an effort to internationalize its currency. In December 1998, the Ministry of Finance announced the launching of an Asian yen-bond market based on auctioning of Financing Bills and exempting Treasury Bills and Financing Bills from a witholding tax. The launching of the Asian yen-bond market was reinforced in the second stage of the 'New Miyawaza Initiative' in May 1999. The latter involved an injection of two trillion yen in credit guarantees for borrowing/ acquiring bonds by private-sector capital in Asia. These measures would enable Japan to: (i) facilitate the internationalization of the yen; (ii) counteract Asia's excessive dependence on the US dollar; and (iii) actualize Miyazawa's idea, borrowed from France, of a tripolar currency system based on the dollar, euro and yen. This plan to 'internationalize the yen' seemed to gain some initial support from the ASEAN countries. However, up to the time of writing, limited interest has been shown from within the region because of: (i) the already very high levels of public debts issued by Asian governments; (ii) the uncertain benefits of a possible yen-based currency system where America (and not Japan) is still the major export market for most countries in the region; (iii) the well-established frameworks in Asia assuming the use of the US dollar (not the yen) in international trade; (iv) the continuing problem of memories from the Japanese military occupation; and (v) the implied requirement that Asian countries reorient their geopolitical allegiances to Japan.

As the second stage of the 'New Miyazawa Initiative' emphasized the building of a regional capital market and general apprehension about Japan's growing hegemonic influence in the region, regional–national actors are also seeking to rebuild regionality in other directions. Seeing that the IMF was not effective in dispensing loans/maintaining monetary stability during the crisis, finance ministers in the region are looking for new ways of building a regional currency cooperation that would be acceptable both to Japan and China. The ASEAN, especially the ASEAN Plus Three (the ten members of the Association of Southeast Asian nations plus Japan, China and the Republic of South Korea) offers a new scale of activity to escape this impasse. Using the 33rd ADB annual meeting in Chiang Mai in May 2000, the finance ministers of ASEAN Plus Three agreed on a bilateral currency pact. The latter came to be known as the 'Chiang Mai Initiative' and is intended to establish a web of bilateral currency pacts that supplement the IMF and to engage in the swapping and repurchasing of central bank reserves between member countries in times of crisis. This initiative, together with ideas such as the AMF and a proposed free-trade zone between Japan and the Republic of Korea, are agenda topics in various bilateral and regional/international forums. They are powerful symbols in developing future regional discursive networks and policy practices that may contribute to the building of new regional institution(s).

5.   CONCLUDING REMARKS: A POSSIBLE RESEARCH AGENDA

The above discussion suggests that discursive and material struggles are emerging over the new 'global–regional–national financial architectures', as the established global and (emerging) regional hegemons (that is, the USA and Japan) engage in conflict/cooperation with other actors. Among other things, these involve struggles to establish and codify the nature and purposes of new globalities and regionalities (for example, 'New Bretton Woods', 'Post-Washington Consensus', AMF, 'New Miyazawa Initiative', 'ASEAN Plus Three) and their associated identities and practices. These competing discourses/practices can be constructed and appropriated by different global–regional–national networks of actors for their own purposes. At the time of writing, the USA, Japan and, to some extent, China and Malaysia are building their respective discursive networks. These tendencies towards conflict/cooperation and their respective discursive codifications and otherizations of what constitute the 'future' are crucial to any remaking of globalities and regionalities (Sum, 2000).

Given that some Asian countries are caught in a vicious circle of overproduction, falling profit, overborrowing, exchange rate vulnerability, bursting of property-/stock- market/currency bubbles, tight credits and unemployment; escaping from these chains is often the target of national leaders searching for 'quick fix' and also scholars seeking to reassert their preferred models of analysis (for example, a 'developmental state' that can impose capital controls and/or neo-Keynesian measures). This paper argues that, since the crisis involves a structural disarticulation between regional-national production and global–regional financial orders, it is not susceptible to speedy resolution and/or uniscalar solution. Thus my own brief intervention in terms of a material–discursive approach is not only concerned with crisis analyses (for example, symptoms and causes) but also the ongoing restructuring processes. On the latter, this chapter highlights the processes that are involved in the remaking of global–regional–national political economy and its complexities. Such complexities could be translated into a possible research agenda in three interrelated ways: discourses, scales and materiality.

On the first, section 4 demonstrated the importance of discourses in mediating changes. Much more work needs to be done on networks of actors involved in constructing and appropriating new globalities and regionalities. On this issue, there are emerging discursive networks centred upon the USA and Japan generating fresh meanings of what constitute the new global–regional–national political economy (for example, the 'New Financial Architectures', 'Post-Washington Consensus', the 'New Miyazawa Initiative', the 'internationalization of the yen', and the 'Chiang Mai Initiative'). They are jostling to generate diverse objects of globalities and regionalities in and through the (re)construction and (re)combination of symbols, codes and practices. This creates a strategic field in which alternatives are constructed and alliances can be built to shape and be shaped by structural constraints that are related to the post-Plaza, the later Bretton Woods, and the 'Washington Consensus' regimes.

On the second point, this chapter also reveals the importance of scale in the restructuring process. Section 4 shows that this process is marked by newly emerging scales of action (for example, G20, ASEAN Plus Three, the 'New Miyazawa Initiative', a free-trade zone between Japan and the Republic of Korea) that are beyond national- and global-level concerns. Such emerging scales raise two issues. On the theoretical level, they question traditional arguments such as the 'development state' thesis. The latter attempts to explain economic success in terms of qualities of nation-states. In this regard, it is less equipped to explain crisis/failure and restructuring that involve new scales of actions. Rather than chanting the chorus to 'the model is dead, long live the model', it is an appropriate time to rethink such approaches and possibly combine them with other approaches to transcend internal/external and national/global distinctions. On the policy level, the coexistence of old and new scales of actions (for example, IMF and 'New Miyazawa Initiative'/ AMF; G7, G20 and G22, APEC and ASEAN Plus Three, IMF practices and national capital controls, and so on) may pose problems of interscalar articulation and issues of the 'fit' across them. Resort to national 'quick fixes' may miss important issues regarding new scales and their articulation with the national. To help take these changes into account, this chapter calls for a shift from a binary way of thinking (for example, national and/or global, internal and/or external) to a more multiscalar level of analysis both theoretically and in terms of policy consideration.

Finally, section 3 demonstrates the (dis)articulation between the production and financial orders of the post-Plaza regime. The breakdown of such complex structures raises questions beyond those of financial 'quick fix' and social afterthought (such as microeconomic reforms or building social safety nets). Here one should rethink the materiality of global–regional–national political economy by moving from a financial 'quick fix' to a finance/industry/trade 'fit'. This latter may be related to the following questions: (i) what are the relations between industrial, financial and commercial circuits and their new linkages? (ii) what are their scales of activities and how are they being deepened? (iii) what are the social implications of such deepening? (iv) what structural constraints and conjunctural opportunities are involved in remaking the above (for example, power of global/regional hegemon?) (v) what is being selected under the changing power relationship between old and new institutions (for example, the IMF, the World Bank, G7, G20, the ABD, the

ASEAN Plus Three)? (vi) what are the emerging identities and regimes of truth associated with these institutions ('orderly liberalism', 'Post-Washington Consensus', national protectionism)? and (vii) what power relations are involved in the latter?

NOTES

1. Krugman, P. (1998), 'Asia: What Went Wrong', *Fortune*, 2 March, World Bank 1997.
2. World Bank (1977), 'Are Financial Sector Weakness Undermining the 'East Asian Miracles?', *News Release* No. 98/1417/EASIA, << http://www.worldbank.org >>
3. Krugman, ibid. p.19.
4. Sachs, J. (1997), 'Personal View: Jeff Sachs', *Financial Times*, 30 July.
5. Yam, J. (1999), 'Causes of and Solutions to Recent Financial Turmoil in the Asian Region', Speech delivered at a symposium in Commemoration of 50 Years of Central Banking in the Philippines, organized by the Bangko Sentral ng Philippines, Manila, 5 January 1999, p. 3, << http://www.bis.org/review/r99108c.pdf>> accessed on 8 March 2001.
6. Harvey, D. (1982), *Limits of Capital*, Oxford: Blackwell.
7. Ohmae, K. (1990), *Borderless World*, New York: Harper Perennial.
8. Bernard, M. (1999), 'East Asia's Tumbling Dominoes: Financial Crises and the Myth of the Regional Model', in C. Leys et al., *Global Capitalism vs Democracy, Socialist Register 1999*, pp. 190–8.
9. Sum, N-L. (1996), 'The NICs and Competing Strategies of East Asian Regionalism,' in A. Gamble and A. Payne (eds), *Regionalism and the World Order*, London: Macmillan, pp. 228–30.
10. McKinnon, R.I. (1999), 'Exchange Rate Co-ordination for Surmounting the East Asian Currency Crises', *Journal of International Development*, **11** (1), pp. 97-9.
11. Liew, L.H. (1998), 'A Political–Economy Analysis of the Asian Financial Crisis', *Journal of the Asia Pacific Economy*, **3** (3), 313.
12. Claessens, S., S. Djankov and L. Lang (1998), 'East Asian Corporates: Growth, Financing and Risks over the Last Decade', World Bank Discussion Paper, 27 October.
13. Johnson, C. (1998), 'Economic Crisis in East Asia: the Clash of Capitalisms', *Cambridge Journal of Economics*, **22**, 658.
14. Godement, F. (1999), *The Downsizing of Asia*, London: Routledge, p. 44.
15. Sparks, C. (1998), 'The Eye of the Storm', *International Socialism*, **78**, 25–7; Liew (1998), op. cit. p. 306.
16. Godement (1999), op. cit. p. 45.
17. Sparks (1998), op. cit. pp. 25–8.
18. Howell, M. (1998), 'Asia's "Victorian" Financial Crisis', <<http://www.ids.ac.uk>>, accessed 23 February 2001.
19. 'Greater China' is interpreted here to include Taiwan, (southern) China, and Hong Kong.
20. In the 1999 Budget Speech, the Financial Secretary of Hong Kong proposed to develop a $13 billion 'Cyberport' that would provide the essential infrastructure to develop Hong Kong into an e-commerce hub of the region. It is expected to provide 12,000 jobs upon completion in 2007.
21. Enoch, C. and A.-M. Gulde (1999), 'Are Currency Boards a Cure for All Monetary Problems?', *Finance and Development*, December, p. 40.
22. In this regard, the Hong Kong dollar and Chinese yuan can be compared with the pound sterling as a first line of defence for the US dollar from the 1950s to 1970s.
23. LaFalce, J. (1998), 'The Role of the US and the IMF in the Asian Financial Crisis', Address given before the Institute of International Economics, Willard Hotel, Washington, 27 January.
24. Altbach, E. (1997), 'The Asian Monetary Fund Proposal: A Case Study of Japanese Regional Leadership', *Japan Economic Institute Report*, **47A**, p. 9.

25. Sum, N-L. (2000), 'Three "Kinds of New Orientalism": The Construction of Trans-Border Identity of the Asia-Pacific', in C. Hay and D. Marsh, *Demystifying Globalization*, London: Macmillan.
26. Manila Framework Group (1997), 'A New Framework for Enhanced Asian Regional Cooperation to Promote Financial Stability', Meeting of Asian Finance and Central Bank Deputies Agreed Summary of Discussion, Manila, Philippines, 18-19 November, <<http//www.dfa-deplu.go.id/archives>>, accessed on 5 March 2001.
27. Graham, G. (1998), 'Stark Staring Bankers', *Financial Times*, 5 October.
28. Krugman, P. (1999), 'Depression Economics Returns', in *Foreign Affairs* ,**78**, 1.
29. Bhagwati, J. (1998), 'The Capital Myth: the Difference Between Trade in Widgets and Dollars', *Foreign Affairs*, **77** (7), p. 12.
30. Stiglitz, J. (1998), 'More Instruments and Broader Goals: Moving Toward the Post Washington Consensus', WIDER Annual Lectures, No. 2, Helsinki, 7 January.
31. Wolfenson, J. (1999), 'Coalitions for Change', Address to the Board of Governors of the World Bank, Washington DC, 28 September, <<http://www.worldbank.org>>, accessed on 5 March 2001.
32. The talk of a 'strategic partnership' between the USA and China was disturbed by the 'mistaken' bombing of the Chinese embassy in Belgrade and USA–Japanese proposals for a Theatre Missile Defence System, with implications for China's eventual reunification with Taiwan.
33. Palma, A. (1999), 'Miyazawa Fund: A New Japanese Tied Fund Approach', International Market Insights, December, <<http://www.ita.gov/td/untiedaid/phil-miyazawa699.htm>>. Accessed on 14 February 1999.
34. Greenfield, G. (1999), 'The World Bank's Bigger Brother?', *Alarm Update*, **37**, October–December, <<http://is7.pacific.net.hk/amrc/alarm/AU37/993701.htm>>.

8. China: the politics of 'rational authoritarianism'

Zhao, Chenggen and Sean McGough

INTRODUCTION

This chapter tracks political and economic reforms within China, in order to cast light upon a key national actor in the future development of Asia–Europe relations. It demonstrates how Western models of democracy and governance may be ill suited to conditions within Asia, and that, therefore, a novel form of accommodation needs to be sought in order to place Europe–Asia linkages on a more equal footing. In defining their future relations, the need to find compromises between these different systems will be crucial, even in an era of globalization. An analysis of China's domestic changes, and the difficulties inherent in its attempted transitions, should serve as a lesson for future interaction between European and Asian counterparts.

Political and economic reforms were a widespread feature of the 1980s, both for liberal democratic countries and Communist countries. The reforms were put in place in a response to political and economic crises in these countries. In the late 1970s, all the main countries in the world faced a deep crisis. Western liberal democratic models based on the Keynesianism of the 1930s, and emphasizing state intervention in the economy and social welfare, were challenged by the decline of economic growth, governmental overload and ungovernability. The legitimacy of democratic governments and even the capitalist system itself was being challenged by its apparent failure to meet the demands of the contemporary world.

At the same time, like capitalism, communism was also undergoing a period of radical change. In its response to the crisis of highly centralized, socialist (political and economic) systems and the decline of economic growth, China began its economic reform in the late 1970s under the aegis of the authoritarian statesman, Deng Xiaoping. To satisfy the demand for democratization and political liberalization, China reformed its economic systems and administrative systems, thereby providing powerful leadership and stable political circumstances for the necessary economic reform and development. From a long-term perspective, such a reform strategy had serious shortcomings.

THE DUALIZATION OF A STRONG STATE AND FREE ECONOMY

In 1949, Mao, through the Communist Party, established socialist political and economic systems where the state controlled all the political, economic and social powers. The communist state controlled all enterprises and managed them with a highly centralized planning mechanism. The state also controlled all important resources, such as housing, healthcare and education, and distributed them solely in the name of the state. In such a political and economical system, the state was indistinguishable from the economy and society. From the outset, such a highly centralized economic and political system served to impede productivity and depressed the people's political liberty, eventually requiring fundamental reform. As time passed, the defects inherent in the totalitarian socialist system grew more evident. First, the state adopted too tight a control over enterprises, and the definition of administrative and management powers was rather vague, thus making the enterprises mere adjuncts of governmental agencies, with no autonomy. Second, China rejected the functions of commodity production, the laws of value and the market. Third, egalitarianism existed in distribution, with everybody 'eating from the same big pot'. Fourth, China's unique system of ownership and economic structure seriously undermined productivity and severely dampened the creativity, initiative and enthusiasm of regions, enterprises and their workers. Fifth, government of the country, by relying on the ideas of political 'movement' and 'class struggle', was a recipe for political disorder, and created the right conditions for a series of political calamities, especially during the Cultural Revolution. Finally, an outcome of the highly centralized systems was that everything was controlled and distributed by the state, the people themselves having no political and economic freedom, and social choice subordinated to the interests of the state. Such a society was a lifeless one and everybody had to have a dual personality. The people's outward compliance covered an inward rebellion against the regime's economic and political shortcomings. By 1976, the Chinese national economy was on the verge of collapse. Dissatisfaction with the radical-leftist line reached a critical level. The highly centralized system fell into deep political and economic crises.

Mao's death in 1976 provided an opportunity for a reform of the totalitarian state, and this came about with the return to power of Deng Xiaoping. Deng, who had been dismissed by Mao from the power centre during the Cultural Revolution, was rehabilitated to the leadership position. Deng then grasped the highest power of the party with the support of the old generals who were his comrades during the revolutionary war. Under his powerful leadership, China began twenty years of reforms.

The main tasks of the economic reform in the late 1970s were to reform the centralized socialist economic and political systems. There was to be a separation of the economy and society from the totalitarian state and thus an establishment of a state-free economy and an economic-free state. The Chinese economic reform was a process of marketization, but it did not lead to radical privatization of state-owned enterprises as happened in the Soviet Union and Eastern Europe in the late 1980s. Such a radical reform of the public sector in these places led to a redistribution of all interests, giving rise to social and political conflicts. Such radical reform is thus accompanied by high risks. Instead, Chinese reforms walked along an incremental road, choosing the easiest place as a starting point for reform. Instead of the privatization of state-owned enterprises, the first step of Chinese economic reform was to permit the establishment of small personal enterprises, village and town enterprises, and foreign capital-owned projects through the introduction of foreign capital.

Most of the marketization policies with which Deng is associated were not planned in detail in advance but were improvised according to the particular circumstances and opportunities encountered by the reformers. The great attractiveness of the benefits of such an opportunity soon caused increasing movement of capital and human resources to the private sector. As advantages of economic marketization and liberalization became clearer, more sectors, regions and enterprises were involved in the process, and increasing numbers of people supported it. The resistance of the radical-left to this process was easily defeated. As the results of free and fair competition between non-state-owned enterprises and state-owned ones became clearer, the heavy defects of state-owned enterprises in ownership and management led to an increasing number of state-owned enterprises falling into decline or deficit. From 1984, China began the marketization reform of its state-owned enterprises. After Deng Xiaoping's speech during his visit to southern China in the spring of 1992, the Communist Party finally decided to establish a socialist market economy. Thus, through incremental stages, institutional change occurred, a socialist market economic system was gradually established and the communist state abandoned direct control of production and trade. The changes this involved are identified and explored further in the following subsections.

The Strengthening of the Market Mechanism

During the twenty years of reform and opening up in China, the gradual weakening of the traditional planned allocation and the strengthening of the market mechanism have caused profound and revolutionary changes to the means of resource allocation. According to the calculation of two Chinese scholars, Lou Zhongyuan and Hu Angang, the index of marketization rose from 24.91 per cent in 1979 to 63.23 per cent in 1992 (and to 77.32 per cent in 1997), indicating that the market economy has begun to take a dominant position in economic life since the early 1990s (see Table 8.1).

Table 8.1   Marketization indices in China (%)

Year	Indices of marketization	Indices of investment marketization	Indices of price marketization	Indices of production marketization	Indices of trade marketization
1979	24.91	23.10	11.60	21.53	46.01
1980	32.13	38.90	17.70	24.03	48.57
1981	33.66	39.60	20.90	25.24	50.15
1982	35.77	45.00	21.70	25.56	51.30
1983	42.57	64.00	23.90	26.64	53.01
1984	45.56	63.00	32.90	30.91	54.45
1985	54.23	63.90	63.00	35.14	59.58
1986	55.67	64.30	64.70	37.73	60.59
1987	57.61	64.00	70.60	43.20	60.90
1988	61.33	70.20	76.00	43.20	60.54
1989	62.62	64.40	64.70	43.94	60.90
1990	62.17	71.70	74.80	45.40	60.41
1991	62.55	69.70	77.80	47.06	59.81
1992	63.23	71.70	81.80	45.39	58.71

Note: Indices of investment marketization refer to the proportion of foreign investment, fundraising and the other investment to total investment. Indices of price marketization refer to the proportion of the quantity of agricultural products whose prices are set by non-state sectors to that of agricultural products. Indices of production marketization refer to the proportion of non-state-ownership economy to gross industrial output value. Indices of trade marketization refer to the proportion of non-state-ownership economy to total retail sales of consumer goods. Indices of marketization refer to the weighted means of the above four indices.

Source: Hu Angang (1995), *The Next Step of China*, Sichuan People's Publishing Press, pp. 3-5.

The reform in the price management system is obvious. For example, in the total volume of purchase of the farm products and sideline products, those prices set by the state have fallen from 94.4 per cent in 1978 to less than 15 per cent in 1997. Except for cotton and corn, the prices of other farm products are all regulated by the market mechanism. Among the total volume of retail sale, those goods with state-set prices also fell from 97 per cent in 1978 to less than five per cent now. Concerning the ex-factory prices of the industrial products, the means of production sold with the market prices has accounted for 96 per cent of the total volume. In addition, the varieties of goods distributed by the state through mandatory instructions have been reduced from 791 in the early stage of reform to only five now, which are kept for military demand. Other materials have all been brought into the circulation of the market mechanism.[1] Obviously, the pattern of allocating resources by the market mechanism has now been formed.

The Growth of Non-state-owned Enterprises

Various non-state-owned enterprises have developed very quickly since 1978. The former pattern of unitary and rigid public ownership in China has been greatly altered and a new pattern, focusing on public ownership but allowing the mutual development of various other economic factors, has been formulated. Tables 8.2 and 8.3 show, from the perspective of ownership structure of China's GDP, that the output value of state-owned enterprises (SOEs) has decreased from 56 per cent in 1978 to 40.8 per cent in 1996, and that of non-SOEs has increased sharply from 44 per cent in 1978 to 59.2 per

Table 8.2   The ownership structure of China's GDP (%)

Year	State-owned economies	Collective units	Non-public-owned units
1978	56.0	43.0	1.0
1993	42.9	44.8	12.3
1996	40.8	35.2	24.0

Source: For the figures in 1978 and 1993, see Chen Yuansheng (1997), the Tendency of Change and the Key Reform in China's Ownership System, *The Theory Frontier*, Vol. 24. For the figure in 1996, see *The People's Daily*, 14 September 1997.

Table 8.3   The development of private economies from 1993 to 1996

Year	Households (1000)	People (1000)	Turnover (million yuan)
1993	17 669.9	29 393.0	330 920
1994	21 866.0	37 759.0	421 140
1995	25 285.0	46 139.0	897 250
1996	27 037.0	50 171.0	1 155 420

Source: Zhang Zhuoyuan (ed.) (1988), *The Retrospect and Prospect of the Twenty Years of Economic Reform in China*, Planning Publishing Press of China, p. 37.

cent in 1996. It is estimated that the share of the SOEs' output value in China's GDP will shrink further to 37.2 per cent by 2000 and to 34.7 per cent by 2010. Corresponding to this, China's employment structure in those economic units with different ownership also changed profoundly. Table 8.4 shows that 112.44 million workers were employed by SOEs in 1996, while those working for various non-SOEs also reached 63.06 million and the latter was growing far more quickly than the former. The non-state-owned economy has exceeded the state-owned sectors, becoming the mainstream of the national economy in modern China. So China is no longer a socialist country according to the traditional definition of socialism. In the amendment of the Chinese Constitution in 1997, the legal position of the private sector in the national economy was written into the constitution.

Table 8.4   Employment in the cities in 1996

Total	SOEs	Collective units	Joint- ventures	Stock company	Foreign company	Hong Kong, Taiwan and Macao invested	Private- run units	Household economy	Others
198 150	112 440	30 160	490	3630	2750	2650	6200	17 090	90

Source: Same as Table 8.3.

The Reform of State-owned Enterprises

The SOEs were subordinate organizations of the state and were put under the direct control of government under the planned economic system. The reform of SOEs has always been one of the most important parts of Chinese economic reform. Today, SOEs have achieved almost all their power through their autonomous business operations, becoming relatively independent economic organizations as a result of economic reform. The state does not control SOEs directly, except through the appointment of the main leaders of SOEs and the supervision of SOEs' owners. A modern corporation system is being established in Chinese SOEs, especially in large and medium-sized SOEs. The separation of state and state-owned enterprises has made great progress since 1984.

The Wider Implications

China's market-oriented reform and its successful transformation from a highly centralized planned economy to a market economy has been a crucial influence upon both China and the world. It has vastly altered the lives of the Chinese people and changed its economic and social structures. Free marketization provided a channel for latent capacity to be fully utilized, much of this having been stifled in the planning mechanism since 1949, and it has thus facilitated high economic growth over the past twenty years. Once again the free market mechanism created an economic 'miracle' in an eastern country. Economic privatization and marketization also led to an improvement in political results, and thus changed the relations between state, economy and society.

Marketization made a breach in the totalitarian communist system and provided chances (*chulu*) for social vigour and capacity. Along with the development of the market sector in the Chinese national economy, an increasing number of technical and managerial elites left the lifeless state-owned enterprises and communist bureaucratic offices and participated in the free market economy. Marketization thus provided chances for everyone to enjoy the rights of free choice from a free economy in a politically dictated communist state. The people voted with their feet in their economic activities, although they were denied the right to vote with their hands in political affairs. They had the right to decide for themselves on the enterprises they owned and managed, although they were still denied the right of democratic representation.

Many scholars advocate democracy as the precondition of liberty. Yet, for the theorists of the New Right, marketization and economic liberalization are the most important factors for liberty. According to Freidrich A. von Hayek (in Gamble, 1979), a democratic state may protect liberty if it is properly organized, but it is not the only kind of state that can do so. Liberty is defined as the condition in which there is the least possible coercion of the individual. Coercion by individuals can be greatly reduced if one social agency/structure, the state, is able to punish individuals who infringe laws governing individual exchange. A problem then arises as to how to reduce coercion by the state itself. The answer is in the state's ability to construct a private sphere free from state interference. Such a private sphere can only come into existence if there are certain protected activities and rights that cannot be infringed by the government.[2] The case of Chinese marketization and economic liberalization shows that the private sphere created by the existence of non-state enterprises provided a space for social choice. Such a free-market mechanism provided a place for people to escape from state coercion and thus led to the decline of the dictatorship of the state.

The destruction of political liberty is always regretful. Yet, clearly it is not to be compared to the far more serious loss of economic freedom for capital and labour. Economic liberalization and liberty is very important, and its role in national development and social outcomes is quite different from that of political liberty. Economic liberty leads to good accumulation of resources and capital, and will promote economic growth. It can also limit political dictatorship by limiting the scope of the dictating state and influencing the operation of the state. When we further examine the political influences of economic liberalization, we find that people's free social choice in economic activities is one important part of political liberty. If you have a right to choose and change your employer, or to decide to invest your capital in different economic areas, it means you have a greater chance of shaping your future. You are then an autonomous person.

FROM TOTALITARIAN STATE TO THE NEW AUTHORITARIAN STATE

China's market-oriented economic reform was led by the communist state. The transformation of the totalitarian state itself was the precondition of the transformation from a highly centralized planned economy to a market economy.

The death of Mao in 1976 provided an opportunity for Deng Xiaoping and his old revolutionary colleagues to gain control of the highest levels of political power and transform a Chinese totalitarian state that, at the time, was experiencing deep political and economic crisis. Generally speaking, the response to such a crisis in a totalitarian state is democratization and political liberalization. The first important reform, when Deng was rehabilitated, was to transform the totalitarian state and its radical-leftist policies. However, what he undertook was not democratization and political liberalization in the Western sense, but a gradual replacement of the totalitarian state with an authoritarian state.

As the result of the coup that cracked down on 'the gang of four'– headed by Mao's wife, Jiang Qing – and the political struggle with Mao's successor, Hua Guofeng, Deng was 'rehabilitated' and eventually became the highest political leader of the communist state. Under his aegis, the ruling Communist Party successfully transformed its political programmes from the radical class struggle to one in which the work of the party was centred on economic reconstruction, especially in the years from 1978 to 1982. The party re-established the institutions of state and party destroyed by Mao during the Cultural Revolution, and created a 'democratic' system in the party, establishing a collectivist leadership and rehabilitating many of the old cadres. Deng and his supporters replaced the radical-left, creating a consolidated and powerful policy-making centre composed of reformers. This was the political power centre that led China during its ensuing twenty years of reforms.

Deng's political reform in the late 1970s and early 1980s began the rationalization of the Communist Party. It led to the end of the totalitarian state, providing a stable political order and an efficient and strong core executive that launched and managed the whole process of economic reforms, administering various sets of reform policies in different fields. The transformation from a totalitarian to an authoritarian state was one of the essential preconditions for successful Chinese economic reform. Without such a transformation we cannot imagine what would have happened in the past twenty years. This does not mean that Deng was a 'messiah' of change and reform, for a more complex interaction between structures and agencies was involved in the reform process. Economic and political reform had become essential if crisis was to be avoided, and Deng chose the best course for an authoritarian state to succeed in the midst of the collapse of the totalitarian state. His transformatory strategies indicated an optimal use of resources and conditions in that particular temporal and spatial setting.

The economic reform initiated and led by the state also led to the reform of the state itself. If Deng's efforts to reform the radical-left totalitarian state after his rehabilitation was the beginning of the end of that totalitarian state, it was twenty years of economic reform that finished the process of its transformation from totalitarian socialist state to the new authoritarian socialist state. Such a new authoritarian state was quite different from both the traditional totalitarian state and a liberal democratic state. It is to the main characteristics of such a state that we now turn.

The Leadership of the Communist Party

The Chinese Communist Party is the only ruling party in the state, although there are many other parties that can participate in the governance of the state. The party has an organization system corresponding to different levels of government, and has representatives in every ministry of the State Council. The party enjoys leadership of the legislature, executive and judiciary, and is the highest state-ruling organization. It also controls the state's military forces, and makes all important public-policy decisions, commanding the process of legalization and its implementation by the government. The existence of this highly disciplined Communist Party, together with its highly centralized leadership and control of state agencies and activities, is one of the most important characteristics of the Chinese authoritarian state.

In the years of reform, the party transformed from a revolutionary class-struggle party to a rational ruling party, displaying a readiness to respond to the demands of various interest groups and the outside world. Although the name of the party is still the Communist Party, it is not the traditional revolutionary Communist Party but a pragmatic ruling party, unfettered by the radical-left communist ideology and dealing with the concrete concerns of the contemporary world. It is a ruling party that is flexible and open to the changing world. This is the core of the new Chinese authoritarian state.

An Authoritarian Statesman

One authoritarian statesman became very important in the new regime, especially in the early years of political struggles when intense debate broke out among the party leaders. Deng Xiaoping personified the process of change, establishing and strengthening his personal authority over the party, government and military forces, despite not having any formal position in the party or government during most of the time of his rule. His role was taken over by Jiang Zeming after Deng's death in 1997. Deng's sovereign power was very important for China's market-oriented reforms. According to classical communist ideology, market economy means vicious capitalism. Anyone who wants to connect the market with the communist economic system is the enemy of the whole party. China's market-oriented reform aroused great resistance from the radical-left faction in the Communist Party. The reform also aroused major debate on the reform strategy among reformers. It was Deng's sovereign power that balanced and supervised the struggles in the party and state, and that provided a stable and efficient power centre to promote the whole process of economic reform. Deng's sovereign power was also used to reverse the fundamental policy line. When economic reform stagnated after 1989, it was he who revived it and who led the way to the great transformation of policy in 1992 with his speech during a visit to southern China that spring. He was a powerful man who had the ability to bring about radical change, and he was able to deter anyone who dared challenge his autarchic position in both state and party.

State, Party and Society

The authoritarian state established institutional relations between the Communist Party and the state, and between the state and society. During the Cultural Revolution, almost all state institutions were destroyed and the party directly controlled the People's Congress and judiciary system, society left with no institutional channels to participate in China's governance. In the twenty years since Deng's rehabilitation, the party and its government have taken a series of measures to promote the establishment of institutional relations between party and state, and between state and society.

The separation of state from party ensured that the various state organs performed their important functions to maximum effect as part of China's governance reform. Before 1982, there was no distinction of functions and institutions between the party and government, the party taking the place of government in the making and implementing of public policies, and in the administration of daily affairs. Since 1982, the separation of party from the authoritarian state, both in functions and institutions, created the opportunity for the Chinese government and other institutions to administer the affairs of the country more or less independently. Professional bureaucrats, instead of party cadres, became the main actors in Chinese governance. The level of administrative efficiency was thus greatly improved.

The Free Economy and the New Rational Authoritarian State

The free economy limits the size and scope of the state as shown by the 1982, 1988, 1992 and 1997 public administrative reforms. One aim of such an economy is to establish an administrative system appropriate to the market economy. Another is to establish small government in a big society, to use the market mechanism to manage that state, and to try to strengthen state capacity and competence in good governance. A small government, and a strong and relatively independent society, have been established in China in preparation for the new century.

The Chinese government has maintained its policy of modernization through recent years. The state modernizes itself while simultaneously modernizing the economy and society. Today's Chinese state could be defined as a new rational authoritarian state. It is not only different from the Western democratic state but also different from the authoritarian states existing in many developing countries. In some senses, it is different from any other kind of state. It is the direct result of a particular process of Chinese economic and political reform. These reforms are a product of a relationship between the longevity of Chinese civilization and of Western influence upon it since 1840. The authoritarian state that has managed Chinese economic reform since 1980 will continue to be an active factor in Chinese development in the new century.

REFORM WITHOUT DEMOCRATIZATION AND POLITICAL LIBERALIZATION

Deng's reform of China's highly centralized totalitarian socialist state did not mean political liberalization and democratization. His critique of Mao's radical-left mistakes during the Cultural Revolution was moderate. He did not want to change Communist Party leadership of the state. His intention was to make the party more pragmatic and more appropriate to the needs of new governance. He corrected all the mistakes of the Cultural Revolution, and knew that the most important thing was economic reconstruction and the improvement of people's living standards. Thus, economic reconstruction and reform were policy priorities.

From the beginning of Deng's rehabilitation and reforms, there existed a strong demand for political liberalization and democratization. When many dissidents expressed their wish for democratic rights, both on the Xidan democratic wall in Beijing in 1978 and in the demonstration for democratic elections in Beijing in 1980, Deng cracked down on them. In 1979, Deng put forward 'four basic principles' of which the most important was the insistence that the Communist Party continue to lead the state, and demolish the Xidan wall. The purpose of Deng's 'principles' was to provide stable political circumstances and the powerful leadership necessary for economic reform, following the death of Mao.

Along with economic reform in the 1980s, the pressures of democratization and political liberalization became stronger, both in the party and society. Many people hoped that democratization would encourage opposition to the political corruption that increasingly dogged the progress of economic reform. When economic reform foundered in 1986, the demand for democratization ran high and some party leaders hoped democratization would end the passive state of economic reform. Yet, when democratic demonstrations were staged in 1986 and 1989, Deng did not want to compromise with the dissidents and dealt with them with an iron hand.

The aim of democratization is to destroy the old authoritarian state and to build a new democratic state. So the process of democratization is full of sharp political struggles between different interest groups and the authoritarian state. Democratization often stimulates different kinds of conflicts, such as religious, regional, class and racial conflicts. It also undermines the government's authority and legitimacy and can then lead to political disorder. So democratization has an important influence on economic development.

If a new democratic order begins to operate, it also needs a long period for the pluralist political forces unleashed to learn how to work together peacefully in the new institutions. In such a transitional period, governmental authority and competence will be heavily affected and will have an important impact upon economic growth. Even if China had begun its democratization and tried to establish a liberal democratic system in the late 1970s, we cannot be sure that the economic and political reform that followed would have been successful.

Since the beginning of the twentieth century, China has long been ravaged by war, political disorder and famine, sometimes caused by foreign aggression and sometimes by social movements that the political system could not contain. For many, the protection of a stable strong state able to preserve human lives and protect property ownership rights is more important than their political rights and freedom.

Further, when we look at what happened in many developing countries after their democratization, we find that new democratic regimes often fail to deliver efficient government free from political corruption and enjoying high levels of economic growth. Democracy is not always a panacea for all ills. The modern political regime is a complex system that is composed of many different kinds of sectors of influence and power. In our judgement, the key ingredients of good government are as follows: the legitimacy of the government and its policies; a visionary leadership with strong power and authority; an efficient bureaucracy and institutions open to public criticism. As we said above, the new authoritarian state in China is a rational state, working hard and efficiently in the interests of the Chinese people, making and implementing many rational policies. The Chinese government is supported by most Chinese people today.

THE CRISIS OF THE NEW AUTHORITARIAN STATE

The success of Chinese economic reforms, the collapse of the Soviet Union after the relative failure of its political reforms, and the subsequent decline of Russia has encouraged increasing numbers of Chinese scholars and statesmen to believe in the new conservatism, supporting a traditional and incremental process of change. Today, many famous political dissidents have become believers in the new conservatism. Nevertheless, many scholars are concerned about how long the new authoritarian state can coexist with the liberalized economy. At present, the Chinese authoritarian state is governing China quite well. However, the government's negative response to democratic demands and pleas for economic and administrative reform could now have a detrimental impact upon Chinese economic development, going against rational decision making. The authoritarian state will have to endure many potential crises, and the lack of democratization can only hinder the sustainable development of the Chinese economy from a long-term perspective.

New pluralist forces will not tolerate being denied access to the political process, because removal from political power means removal from many economic interests. Such forces, therefore, will challenge the Communist Party's rule and try to replace it with a competitive regime that will create equilibrium among pluralist interests. Along with this will go increasing demands for the trappings of political liberty, including free speech and free press.

The rationalization of the Communist Party since 1979 was, in some senses, the byproduct of the political and economic disorder following communist rule since 1949, especially during the period of the Cultural Revolution. In many ways, the transformation of China over recent years is a revival of Chinese civilization following political disorder and war stretching back over the past one hundred years. As a statesman who was attuned to the complexities of Chinese history, Mao commented on China's sequential dichotomy of disorder and order in Chinese dynasties as being one in which, 'great calamity is accompanied by great development' (*da luan da dao da zhi*). Mao is right. Chinese economic development since 1979 is, in many ways, the byproduct of long periods of disorder. Nevertheless, without sustainable political stability and good governance, the present economic achievements may be destroyed. With this in mind, one has to balance democratization against the possible costs to the Chinese economy and society as a whole.

An authoritarian state without free democratic elections and a competitive political party system is a polity without balance. In a liberal democratic state, a correct response to new social and economic problems, and a respect for public opinion during governance, is the lifeblood of the system. The demands that drive the political system become the interests of the ruling party (parties), and its government is interrelated with the interests and demands of the people. By contrast, in an authoritarian state, the response to the people's demands is decided by the logic of the political system, one in which there is a constant quest for political and sovereign power. Very little can constrain that thirst for power and it is, inherently, an extremely dangerous political system. Many special interests, especially the bureaucrats' interests, greatly influence the state's policy making. Political corruption is, consequently, a structural problem in the Chinese authoritarian state's governance.

MARGARET THATCHER; THE STRONG STATE AND THE FREE ECONOMY

There are crucial distinctions between the strong state and the free economy often associated with Margaret Thatcher and her Conservative governments of the 1980s, and that envisaged and sought after by Deng Xiaoping. Whilst Margaret Thatcher's strong state appeared to depend on a democratic and populist perception of the state, Deng's free economy rested upon the foundations of a strong state born from authoritarian rule. Nonetheless, an analogy between the two can be drawn, for in this case it was the degree of perception that was important. Margaret Thatcher personified the image of strong 'authoritarian' leadership and dramatic economic change. The degree of accuracy regarding authoritarianism was secondary to the belief that she represented the legitimate use of force for economic ends. For example, the dispute with the miners in the 1980s embodied the assumption that state force could legitimately be used to accomplish economic ends. For many of China's elite, the period of Thatcher's rule was one that China could learn much from, not least in the dichotomy of strong rule and economic freedom. The important aspect here is not the accuracy of the comprehension of the Thatcher 'model', but the received image in China of Thatcherism as a balance between force and freedom. The outcome was that China applied its own unique version of a free economy and a strong state, yet the influence of Western 'models' was always evident in the construction and management of this Chinese hybrid.

The strong state and the free economy are recognized as coterminous with democracy, yet democracy is not essential in the early development of this duality. In contrast, it may even be impossible, illogical or unhelpful to insist on a simultaneous marketization and democratization. This is not to say that democratization is discarded or that it is of less importance than economic change. In contrast, it is seen as a vital and unavoidable step in development. Nevertheless, the right environment is needed to ensure successful democratic reform. In China, the 'right' environment is a balanced and expanding economic structure that can accommodate and serve political transition. Successful economic reform can dictate the pace of democratic change, and care is needed to prevent economic failure feeding the demands for immediate, radical political changes. The safest form of democratization is developed within a stable, free economy. Margaret Thatcher was aware of the delicate balance between democratization and achievement of the right economic conditions necessary for political change to take place. This was clearly shown in her memoirs, where she observed that:

> At some point the increasing momentum of economic change in China itself will lead to political change. Keeping open the channels of trade and communication, while firmly pressing for human rights in China to be upheld, are the best means of ensuring that this great military power, on the verge of becoming a great economic power, becomes also a reliable and predictable member of the international community.'[3]

Yet it must also be understood that a populist force against democratization remains possible in an authoritarian China enjoying increasingly higher advances in standards of living. Many people will become afraid of or just resistant to changing a system that is providing material benefits, even if this is at the cost of enjoying full democratic liberties. At present, as Thatcher noted, 'Chinese socialism is whatever the Chinese Government does; and what it has been doing amounts to a thorough-going embrace of capitalism.'[4] The continued material success of economic liberalization without democratization could engender a problematic scenario; one in which the problem would not then just be one of convincing the political elites of the necessity for change, but instead one requiring the conversion of large sections of the population.

CONCLUSION

We are sure that China will become a democratic state in the future. In the meantime, we should understand that the new authoritarian state is still very positive in Chinese economic reform and development. China's democratization will take a long time before it finally succeeds. The best path for it to take is probably that of a gradual evolution, similar to China's experiences of economic reform.

NOTES

1. See *The Economic Daily*, 26 September and 1 October, 1998.
2. A. Gamble (1979), 'The Free Economy and the Strong State: the Rise of the Social Market Economy', *The Socialist Register*, London: Merlin Press, p. 7. See also A. Gamble (1994), *The Free Economy and the Strong State*, Macmillan: London.
3. Margaret Thatcher (1993), *The Downing Street Years*, London: HarperCollins, p. 495.
4. Ibid; p. 494.

REFERENCES

Birch, A.H. (1984), 'Overload, ungovernability and delegitimation: the theories and the British case', *British Journal of Political Science*, **14**, 135–60.

Cristi, Renato (1998), *Carl Schmitt and Authoritarian Liberalism*, University of Wales Press.

Crozier, Michel J., Samuel P. Huntington and Joji Watanuki (1975), *The Crisis of Democracy*, New York University Press.

Diamond, Larry and Marc F. Plattner (1996), *The Global Resurgence of Democracy*, Baltimore: Johns Hopkins University Press.

Gamble, Andrew (1979), 'The Free Economy and the Strong State: The Rise of the Social Market Economy', in R. Miliband and J. Saville (eds), *Socialist Register 1979*, London: Merlin, pp. 1–25.

Gamble, Andrew (1994), *The Free Economy and the Strong State* (2nd edition), Basingstoke: Macmillan.

Gao, Shangquan (1996), *China's Economic Reform*, Basingstoke: Macmillan.

Habermas, J. (1975), *Legitimacy Crisis*, Boston: Beacon Press.

Held, David (1993), *Prospects for Democracy*, Cambridge: Polity Press.

Hirst, P. (1990), *Representative Democracy and Its Limits*, Cambridge: Polity Press.

Lieberthal, Kenneth (1995), *Governing China*, London: W.W. Norton & Co.

Rose, Richard (1984), *Understanding Big Government*, London: Sage.

Shirk, Susan L. (1993), *The Political Logic of Economic Reform in China*, University of California Press.

Thatcher, Margaret (1993), *The Downing Street Years*, London: HarperCollins.

White, Gordon (1991), *The Chinese State in the Era of Economic Reform*, Basingstoke: Macmillan.

Wu, Jinglian (1998), *On Competitive Market System*, Guangdong Economic Press.

9. The European Union's commercial policymaking towards China[1]

Tseng, Su-Ling

INTRODUCTION

How to describe the development of European Union (EU)[2] commercial policymaking in respect of China? How best to analyse this policy process? What are the characteristics of this policymaking? Who are the players in this decision-making process? Which players are influential? How to assess the competence of players in this policy process? What affects and shapes the policy outcomes? These questions deserve answers.

In the case of China, the major driving force of policymaking has kept on changing: from the EU's internal dynamism in the early days to the complicated entanglement of internal and external dynamism in recent years.[3] Given its technical and symbolic nature in the early days, EU commercial policymaking in respect of China was, to a great extent, a reflection of EU structure, particularly the EU institutional settings relevant to the making of EU external policy. Along with the increasing engagement of China in the world economic system, the gradual strengthening of EU–China economic relations and the growing politicization of policymaking in relation to China,[4] implications of developments (considerably) outside the EU have become more important. Nevertheless, this does *not* mean that the impacts of external developments are, and will be, more important than those of EU internal dynamism. The impacts of EU internal dynamism upon policy outcomes are as important as they were two decades ago, while the impacts of external dynamism have gradually increased since the last decade. In recent years, this policy process has become even more complicated, since the internal and external dynamism have been increasingly entangled. Given that China is expected to enter into the WTO in the near future, such complicated entanglement is likely to be the future trend. Obviously, the questions which deserve answers are no longer whether the impacts of EU internal dynamism are more important than those of external developments, or the other way around. The questions needing to be answered are how internal and external dynamism are entangled and how this entanglement affects the competence of players, and subsequently, policy outcomes.

Moreover, the implications of EU-China commercial agreements also deserve examination. These agreements, together with the EU legal framework that guides over all EU external commercial policy, provide the guidelines for EU commercial policy towards China. Before the conclusion of the EU-China trade agreement in 1978, EU internal and external dynamism affected the outcomes of EU negotiating positions and subsequently shaped agreement outcomes. After the conclusion of the 1978 agreement, it, in turn, affected, to a greater or lesser degree, the future negotiating positions of the EU and future EU commercial policymaking towards China. It is in this sense that EU-China commercial agreements are considered as factors affecting the outcomes of EU commercial policy in respect of China.

In brief, the development of EU commercial policymaking in respect of China since 1975 is best analysed from four aspects: EU internal dynamism, external developments, the entanglement of internal and external dynamism, and EU-China commercial agreements. However, this paper does not aspire to examine every development in relation to China since 1975 but rather to single out key factors and to analyse the implications of these in relation to China.[5] The examination of implications is twofold: how a factor affects the scope of EU commercial policy in respect of China, and, how it affects the competence of players in the decision-making process and the contribution of players to policy outcomes.

EU INTERNAL DYNAMISM

Internal dynamism is discussed from three perspectives: the EU legal framework relevant to the case of China, institutional practices shaped by organizational structure, and the implicit norms and routines long established in EU decision-making.

The Legal Framework

The legal framework determines the formal powers of players and provides the guidelines for EU external commercial policymaking. The framework which is relevant to the case of China is enshrined in Articles 131-4, 300 and 301, Treaty of Amsterdam.[6] It is worth noting that, although this chapter focuses only on the articles which are relevant to the case of China, the examination of these articles can ultimately be applied to not only the case of China but also to other trading partners of the EU. This is so because those articles are designed to guide the EU's commercial policymaking towards *all* of its trading partners rather than only China.

Articles 131–4 are the so-called Common Commercial Policy (CCP). Article 131 sets out that member states, acting in common interest, aim at progressive abolition of restrictions on international trade and reduction of customs barriers. Article 132 provides the principles of CCP during the transitional period and the procedures to move from the transitional period to the completion of CCP. Article 133 is the basis of negotiations on EU trade agreements with third countries or international organizations. The proposals are initiated by the Commission, negotiated by the Commission based on Council mandates upon a qualified majority vote (QMV), and concluded by Council QMV. Article 134 specifies the circumstances and procedures in and through which one or more member states may adopt protective measures in the case of economic difficulties.

Among these articles, Article 133 is the most contentious and frequently used. Article 133 does not provide a clear definition of CCP, but only lists some examples: changes in tariff rates, the conclusion of tariff and trade agreements, measures of liberalization, export policy and protective measures such as those to be taken in the event of dumping or subsidies. This has aroused many disagreements between the Commission and the Council on the scope of CCP. The Commission takes the view that measures and issues related to commercial activities, be they listed in the CCP or not, are subject to Union competence. The Commission asserts that the scope of CCP should be consistent with that of EU internal commercial policy, in which the Commission enjoys great competence. The Council argues that only those that are listed in Article 133 are subject to EU competence and the rest remain subject to national competence. The Commission has often referred arguments to the European Court of Justice (ECJ), and the Court has ruled that aid for exports to third countries, export credits and generalized tariff preferences are Union competence.[7] The most controversial issue recently was aroused by the GATT Uruguay Round on the General Agreement on Trade in Services (GATS) and intellectual property rights (IPR). The ECJ ruled that the GATS and IPR are 'mixed competence' to be shared by the Union and the member states.[8] Thereafter, an amendment to Article 113 (Treaty of Rome) was made: '[t]he Council, acting unanimously on a proposal from the Commission and after consulting the European Parliament, may extend the application of paragraphs 1 to 4 to international negotiations and agreements on services and intellectual property insofar ...'.[9] Since the definition, and scope, of CCP remain unclear, more disputes between the Commission and the Council are likely to be raised in the future.

Clearly, the CCP is not a sufficient legal base and thus the Union has to rely increasingly on its other powers.[10] One of the powers is the Union's secondary legislation, such as Council Regulations and Commission Regulations.[11] Since the implications of Council Regulations are among the most significant ones and the procedures to make Council Regulations are the most complicated procedures of all, we focus here on Council Regulations. These need to be adopted by the Council, unanimously or with QMV depending on the issues (Articles 250 and 251 Treaty of Amsterdam[12]). In practice, the Council often adopts Commission proposals without much disagreement, since the Council Regulations are subject to relevant EU treaties and agreements and are normally administrative and technical. In this sense, the Commission gains de facto competence in EU secondary legislation, but this does not imply that the Council simply 'rubber-stamps' Commission proposals. For example, EU anti-dumping policy is primarily governed by Council Regulations, and definite dumping duties need to be approved by the Council based on Commission proposals. The Council does not often reject the Commission's proposals to impose definite dumping duties,[13] but a controversial case on the imports of cotton from certain countries, including China (as one of the major targets), demonstrated that the member states, through the Council, would reject a Commission proposal if their perceived national interest is at stake.[14]

Article 300 provides the procedures of negotiations on agreements between the EU and third countries or international organizations. Where it is applicable, the procedures are identical to that of the CCP: proposals initiated by the Commission, negotiated by the Commission based on Council mandates upon a QMV and concluded by Council QMV. This Article is the EU's legal base for the EEC–China trade and economic cooperation agreement concluded in 1985. Since Article 300 does not provide for the scope of agreements, the players involved in the conclusion of a particular agreement enjoy relatively greater freedom to define the scope.

Article 301 provides that, for consistency with the Common Foreign and Security Policy (CFSP), the economic relations with one or more third countries can be interrupted or reduced. Where this article is applied, the Council's competence in the external commercial policymaking can be greater than the Commission's, since the CFSP remains national competence and the Commission can only be informed by the Council. Although such kinds of economic interruption are based on Commission proposals (Article 301, Treaty of Amsterdam), the Commission can hardly resist the political pressure from the Council (if the member states reach consensus at the Council). Clearly, there is an entanglement of CCP and CFSP. The Council's influence in external commercial policymaking can be enhanced as a result of its dominance in the CFSP. In the case of China, such economic interruption has happened once. Following the Council's 'Declaration on China'[15], official EU–China relations were interrupted for almost two years because of the Tiananmen Square event in 1989. Nevertheless, strong political intervention as such is rare, as this has serious economic implications. Since 1975, when the EU and China established formal diplomatic relations, such economic interruption has been the only occasion.

The Union's legal framework provides some, but not comprehensive, insights into its commercial policymaking in respect of China. Firstly, our understanding of the scope of EU external commercial policy is patchy, because the existing legal framework does not provide a clear definition but piecemeal illustrations. The commercial issues that are not listed in the CCP and that have not been clarified by the ECJ often become the battlefield where the Commission and member states contend for power. Secondly, the legal framework determines the formal powers of players and the procedures of policy process, but these formal powers are not necessarily comparable to the competence and contribution of players in practice. Neither are those who are given formal powers necessarily the only players in the policymaking process. The contribution of the European Parliament (EP), the European Court of Justice (ECJ) and interest groups also deserves attention, although they are not given formal policymaking powers. Thirdly, the whole process of policymaking is often more complicated than can be enshrined in formal procedures. All these phenomena can be observed in the case of China. In addition, an examination of the legal framework does not tell us whether there are peculiarities of policymaking in the case of China. If 'yes', what are they? If 'no', why? However, the usefulness of the legal framework should not be ignored, even if it does not provide a sufficient explanation of the policy process. The legal framework provides the general idea and guidelines behind decision making and, under this framework, further details can be supplemented by looking at the institutional practices which are shaped by the institutional and organizational structure, and by implicit norms and routines long established in EU decision making.

Institutional Practices

A feature in the case of China is that the scope of EU policy in practice often goes beyond the illustrations given in the EU legal framework and the interpretation added by the ECJ. For instance, before the ECJ's ruling on the General Agreement on Trade in Services (GATS) and on Intellectual Property Rights (IPR) in 1994, these two issues have been conducted at EU rather than the national level in relation to negotiations on China's entry into the WTO. Trade promotion aimed at enhancing the competitiveness of EU industry in the Chinese market remains an issue of national competence but the Commission's involvement in this issue has been gradually increasing since the early 1980s. However, the Union's legal foundations do not tell us explicitly how this 'go-beyond' happens. A starting point is to explore how and why the players are able to extend their influence, since the legal framework which is loosely set up leaves relatively more room than before for the players to exert their influence on the final decisions.

The legal framework confers the formal powers of EU external commercial policymaking onto the Commission and the Council, while also requiring close cooperation between them. Does this framework depict daily practice in relation to China? Partially, but not entirely.

Firstly, the influence of the EP and ECJ has been very limited, because they do not have formal power in the decision-making process. The ECJ's competence does not lie in decision-making but in jurisprudential interpretation. For example, the ECJ's interpretation of CCP scope clarifies what should or should not be conducted at EU level. Subsequently, the ECJ's interpretation shapes policy outcomes. However, the ECJ's role is essentially passive because it cannot offer any interpretation without a request first being made by, for example, the Commission. The EP's limited influence in the case of China is also attributable to its lack of formal powers. Although there are informal and personal networks within the EP, the Commission and the Council, this has not helped to strengthen the EP's influence. The EP's opinions have been ignored by the Commission and Council. This, in turn, discourages MEPs from giving opinions concerning EU commercial policy towards China. In the last ten years or so, the EP's concern about China has shifted considerably from commercial to political issues, particularly the human rights issue. Such development has generated a vicious circle that has gradually weakened the EP's influence in commercial issues related to China. Many MEPs believe that the only way to reverse this vicious circle is to give the EP formal powers in the Union's external commercial policymaking (which can obviously be applied to all the EU trading partners, including China).[16]

Secondly, the influence of interest groups has been minor in commercial issues related to China, not because of their lack of formal access to the decision-making process or of contacts with the Commission and the Council but due to the insufficiency of organized lobbying. The Commission and national governments have always paid more attention to interest groups' opinions and demands than to the EP's, because of the need occasionally for information from interest groups in order to shape the policy agenda. In general, interest groups are able to exert greater influence than the EP in the decision-making process. However, their influence should not be exaggerated for at least two reasons. First of all, it is unavoidable that various interests are sometimes in contradiction (for instance, producers' interests against consumers' interests and/or importers' interests against exporters' interests). To a certain extent, it is up to the Commission and national governments to decide what positions they take. In this sense, what an interest group wants is not necessarily reflected in policy outcomes. Moreover, no (non-governmental/independent) interest groups from either the EU or China have represented the commercial interests specifically of China.[17] In the EU, there are many 'issue-oriented' rather than 'country-oriented' interest groups. These interest groups are concerned with particular issues, such as anti-dumping, consumer welfare, imports, exports or trade in general. China is one among many countries, but not the only country, of concern to interest groups. The fact that no interest group has represented China's commercial interests from the Chinese side is, to a large extent, attributable to China's political system, which has discouraged the formation of 'public gathering' and hence non-governmental/independent lobbying groups. The insufficiency of organized lobbying has limited the influence of interest groups on policy outcomes.

Thirdly, the contribution of the Commission and Council to policy outcomes is affected in practice not only by their formal powers but also by many other factors, such as institutional cohesion, expertise and the ability to grasp opportunities to exert influence. It is to these that, briefly, we now turn.

Internal cohesion
The higher the degree of internal cohesion an institution can reach, the more likely this institution is as a whole effectively to utilise available instruments and to exert its influence in the decision-making process. Potentially, the Commission can reach a relatively higher degree of cohesion than the Council, for the following reasons: (i) it is not supposed to be politically or nationally partisan; (ii) the Commissioners serve full time on the Commission and thus tend to attach themselves to the success of the Commission, whereas their counterparts in the Council are primarily concerned with affairs in their home countries; and (iii) the Commissioners' term of office is longer than their counterparts in the Council, in which national representatives may change frequently following changes of government in their home countries. However, the coherence of the Commission should not be overestimated. Inside the Commission, there are various preferences, policy styles and working cultures. Inter- sectoral/departmental competition and hierarchical conflicts cannot be avoided, particularly in areas where policy responsibilities overlap and different sections develop different views on certain issues.[18] For example, the dispute between Directorate General (DG) I (External Economic Relations) and DG VI (Agriculture) on which DG should lead the negotiations on agriculture issues in the GATT Uruguay Round weakened the Commission's role as the EU's negotiator.[19] In the case of China, such tensions and negative effects have not been seen, because most issues related to China, including the sensitive textile trade, are managed by DG I. On the other hand, the fragmentation of the Council should not be exaggerated. Hayes-Renshaw and Wallace argue that, in the Council, there is shared culture which is

embedded in formal and informal contacts and reinforced by forms of socialization, in spite of the publicized tensions amongst the member states.[20] In the case of China, the perception of Council cohesion has been reinforced, particularly because member states realise that 'China was very good in dividing us' by offering better conditions to some member states than others, thus rendering member states too divided to make decisions. Being aware of the game of 'divide and rule', the member states have tried, and been able, to reach consensus in issues related to China in recent years.[21] Overall, the internal cohesion of the Commission in the case of China has been relatively more consistent than that of the Council over the past two decades.

Expertise
Expertise often implies persuasive power. The EU's institutional design depicts the Commission as the major source of technical expertise and information about the content and impact of most EU policies. In order to initiate policies, the Commission needs to have expertise and knowledge in most EU policy areas and to be able to evaluate what policies are workable and the extent to which policies can be accepted by member states. With its expertise, the Commission is in a better position to persuade member states to accept Commission proposals. Of course, the extent of Commission expertise varies from one policy area to another. In policy areas where EU competence is long established, such as external trade, the Commission is more likely to develop better knowledge.[22] Textile policy, for example, involves mathematical calculations, technical terms and professional knowledge (such as the chemicals and natural materials used to made cloth). In order to deal with such matters, a textile section has been set up in DG I of the Commission. Within this section, there is a subsection specializing in EU–China textile trade. Most of the Commission's proposals concerning this EU–China textile trade are drafted according to this subsection, whereas there is no counterpart to this sub-section, or even the textile section, in the Council. The EU-China textile trade is normally dealt with by the Asia group of the Council, which is concerned not only with China but also with many other Asian countries, and not only the textile trade but also political issues. In this case, the Commission has better expertise than the Council does. Although member states can collect information from industries, national representatives sometimes find it difficult to deal with technical terms and mathematical figures. With regard to the EU–China textile trade, Commission proposals are normally approved by the Council without much change. Nevertheless, this does not imply that the Council simply 'rubber-stamps' Commission proposals. The Commission has to provide evidence and explanations to convince the Council, and the Council has to trust the Commission. In addition, the Commission also relies on advisory committees, in which the Commission and the Council have

representatives respectively, to ensure that its proposals will be accepted by the Council. Through those committees, the Council is frequently informed about what is going on. Although the Commission, with its expertise, enjoys an advantageous position in policy initiatives and developments, there is no guarantee that the Commission will always get what it wants. For example, EU anti-dumping policy also involves expertise and technical calculation, but the increasingly politicization of this policy led to the Council rejecting a Commission proposal imposing definitive duties on imports of cotton from certain countries, including China (as one of the major targets).

Windows of opportunity

The better an institution can grasp opportunities to exercise its powers, the more likely it will be to influence policy outcomes. Cram argues that 'the Commission's ability to influence any policy sector is its ability to respond rapidly to any "windows of opportunity" ripe for EU intervention, or indeed to facilitate the appearance of these windows'.[23] Her study on EU IT policy demonstrates how the Commission can facilitate and encourage the emergence of EU interest, and obtain support from industries, thus enhancing its competence in this policy area. Her study on EU social policy demonstrates how the Commission can make use of non-binding legislation and small-scale direct expenditure programmes in order to create precedent and establish Union competence in this policy area. She gives examples: 'in areas in which it proves impossible to get a *policy* accepted, the Commission may propose a *programme*; [o]r where the use of a directive or regulation would prove unacceptable to the member states, DG V might propose a recommendation or an opinion.[24] She argues that 'these soft policy options are an important means of preparing the ground for future regulatory action'.[25] Similar strategies are used by DG I in the case of China, although the long-term implications remain to be seen. Trade promotion has long been regarded as an issue of national competence but, since the 1980s, the Commission has been coordinating EEC–China Business Week, organizing seminars on doing business in China for EU bankers, traders and officials of the member states, making financial contributions to those who promote EU exports to China, and organizing a specialized trade fair. The Commission's experience in organizing trade promotion activities has laid the ground for future regulatory action.

In addition, it is worth assessing the implications of the Commission's organizational structure that gives the Commissioner in charge a greater say in his/her responsibility. Firstly, the proposals drafted by the sections or subsections of the Commission need to be accepted by the Commissioners in charge. The positions of Commissioners can, to a certain extent, affect the selection of draft proposals (although the Commissioners should be as impartial and neutral as possible). Thereafter, the Commissioners in charge are in a position to ensure the adoption of proposals at the College level. Finally, the Commissioners in charge are at the forefront of efforts to convince member states to approve the proposals. For example, Sir Leon Brittan, the External Economic Relations Commissioner of the Delors III Commission and the Santer Commission, paid great attention to the Union's relations with China. He contributed greatly to many Commission initiatives on policies related to China, most importantly the Commission Communication on long-term policy for EU–China relations. This Communication was soon adopted by the Council. It has become the basis for the EU's long-term China policy (COM(95) 279). Brittan was also active in setting up the EU–China Summit.[26] The aim here is not to examine Brittan's record in promoting EU–China relations, but to demonstrate the potential influence of the External Economic Relations Commissioner's position in relation to China.

Implicit Norms and Routines

A good example of implicit norms and routines is the preference of member states to achieve 'consensus' rather than call for (formal) voting at the Council. Since the Luxembourg Comprise in 1966, 'consensus achieving' has been regarded as a better way than voting, particularly where QMV or simple majority is required. Although there are legal bases for QMV and simple majority, both ways might force one or more countries in the minority group to accept a decision which it can hardly fulfil in practice. In order to avoid such difficulty, 'consensus achieving' has become a norm in Council decision making and voting is considered a last choice, used to push for a decision in the case of deadlock. It should be noted that such 'consensus' does not imply unanimity. The achievement of consensus often involves persuasion and compensation payments. Such is the case for commercial issues, which can mostly be decided by QMV. It often becomes very difficult for a minority of countries to block a policy proposal if a simple majority of member states take the same line as the Commission. Since a minority of countries often oppose a proposal on different grounds, it is relatively difficult for them to be 'united'. Once the Commission and majority group reach a compromise with one or two countries of the minority group, these countries shift their positions and join the majority group. Such shifts of position often turn a simple majority into a qualified majority. QMV can then be reached if a vote is called for. This leaves the 'genuine' minority group in the position of having to accept compensation, which often involves trading off one issue with another, or getting nothing (as the majority group can push through the agenda by voting). Thus, 'consensus' can be reached within the Council without the need for a vote. In this sense, voting should be seen as the last tool used to reach collective decisions, especially difficult ones, in the Council. It is hard to avoid confrontation among member states on sensitive issues, but in most cases member states are able to reach collective decisions in the Council. In the case of China, most collective decisions are made, and consensus reached, at the level of working groups.

EU EXTERNAL DYNAMISM

This section focuses on the implications of international context and GATT/WTO regulations.

The International Context

In the first decade of EU–China trade, the bilateral trade relationship was largely symbolic, since the trade volume was not significant.[27] In addition, although China opened its market to the outside world in the late 1970s, China's economic weight remained light compared to many other countries. Therefore, EU commercial policy in respect of China was not considered important. Since the mid-1980s, EU–China economic relations have been gradually strengthened in two ways: deepening and widening. Relations have been deepened as bilateral trade and economic cooperation programmes have gradually increased. They have widened since commercial activities have extended from textile trade to service trade.[28] Moreover, China has become the EU's fourth largest trading partner in recent years and the EU trade deficit against China has increased every year since 1988. An implication of the growing EU–China economic interdependence, and China's growing economic weight is that the importance and sensitivity of EU commercial policy in respect of China has increased. In the past decade, it has become more difficult to reach agreement on EU commercial policy towards China. A well-known example is the argument over inclusion of a 'human rights clause' into EU–China commercial agreements. For several years in the early 1990s, member states were divided between the hard-liners, who believed that the inclusion of such a clause would force China to take human rights more seriously, and the soft-liners, who doubted the effectiveness of such a clause. China, of course, has resisted the inclusion of a human rights clause, arguing that political matters should be separated from economic issues. In recent years, the hard-liners have realized that China will not concede on the human rights issue. Although they remain critical of China's human-rights record, they are unable to push for the inclusion of a human rights clause in EU–China commercial agreements, which requires China's concession in the end.[29] In addition, to insist on the human rights issue only hinders the Council's cohesion and the whole decision-making process (in the case of China). As a result the hard-liners have finally softened their positions.

Impacts of GATT/WTO Regulations

During the period between 1978 and March 1987, neither the EU nor China was a GATT contracting party, and thus neither was bound by GATT regulations. However, the EU's commercial policy towards China was consistent with GATT regulations, since EU member states are GATT contracting parties. Where should member states stand if EU legislation contradicted GATT regulation? Clearly, the EU and its member states would avoid such a contradiction. This implies that the EU did not necessarily have to take into account all GATT regulations but only needed to avoid a contradiction with these. In addition, China's reluctance to comply with GATT rules left the Commission and the Council room to exercise their powers in the formulation of EU commercial policy towards China. Consequently, the impact of GATT regulations was minimal during this period. This is evident from the fact that the most-favoured-nation (MFN) clause in EU–China trade and economic agreements is more restrictive than the MFN clause in the GATT.[30]

China's application to the GATT in March 1987 showed its willingness to comply with GATT regulations. At this stage, the EU and China were still not bound by GATT regulations but, with the vision of China becoming a GATT contracting party, both sides took GATT regulations more seriously than before. The impact of GATT regulations became substantial. For example, the EU had always been protective of its textile trade, especially with China (as a major textile producer). Although the Multi-Fibre Arrangement (MFA) has been gradually relaxed and the EU has slowly liberalized its textile market since the mid-1980s,[31] the Commission and certain countries (the hard-liners) remained protective in EU–China textile trade. In negotiating the EU–China textile agreement in 1988, the hard-liners and the Commission attempted to decrease, or at least not to increase, the import quotas of Chinese textile products.[32] This attempt was in contradiction to the MFA. Partially because of China's application to the GATT, the hard-liners softened their position and quotas on certain products were increased in accordance with the MFA.

With the EU as a WTO founding member, and with China's application to the WTO, the impact of WTO rules is even greater. Now, the EU is bound by WTO rules. Since China has been urging to expedite its WTO application, there is no reason why the Chinese should not take full account of WTO rules in managing their economic relations with the EU. The impacts of WTO rules have already been seen in the case of GATS and IPR negotiations in the Uruguay Round. In the EU, GATS and IPR had always been issues of national competence. However, the Commission argued that it cannot represent the EU at WTO negotiations if these remain issues of national competence. Therefore, the Amsterdam Treaty provides that, subject to Council unanimity, the scope of CCP can be extended to services and IPR (Article 133). Although this does not guarantee the Commission's competence in GATS and IPR, in practice the Commission, on behalf of EU member states, has been negotiating both issues with its Chinese counterparts.

With the conclusion of China–USA and EU–China WTO negotiations in November 1999 and May 2000 respectively, China is expected to become a WTO member in the near future. Once China becomes a WTO member, both the EU and China will be bound by WTO rulings should trade disputes between the EU and China arise.

EU-CHINA COMMERCIAL AGREEMENTS

Any agreement between the EU and China has to be concluded by both parties, and is then binding on each of them. During the course of decision making leading to the conclusion of the first EU–China trade agreement in 1978, many factors had to be taken into account. This agreement, in turn, became a factor influencing the conclusions of subsequent EU–China agreements; and those agreements, in their turn, will influence future decisions. It is in this context that EU–China commercial agreements must be considered.

EU-China Trade and Economic Agreements

In general, there are two types of EU–China commercial agreements: trade and economic cooperation agreements that lay down the foundations of EU–China commercial activities, excluding textile trade; and textile agreements which provide the basis of textile trade. On the EU side, the trade provisions of EU–China trade and economic cooperation agreements[33] are mostly covered by the examples listed in the CCP, and thus are clearly subject to EU competence. The economic cooperation provisions are not exhaustive, but list some examples: industry and mining; agriculture, including agro-industry; science and technology; energy; transport and communications; environmental protection; and cooperation in third countries. Strictly speaking, EU competence can be limited to the listed fields, and thus the Commission plays no role in unlisted fields, which may be considered to be of national competence. When the 1985 agreement was concluded, member states were reluctant to completely renounce their powers in concluding economic cooperation agreements with China. Article 14 states that, without prejudice to EU treaties and EU–China agreements, the member states retain the power to conclude bilateral economic cooperation agreements with China. In practice, the Commission has been the engine in developing various forms of economic cooperation with China, largely in the fields listed above. In terms of the areas which are not listed, a growing amount of Commission proposals has been adopted by the Council without much controversy. This coincides with the trend that the number of bilateral agreements between member states and China has gradually declined since 1985, although member states are not prohibited from concluding certain kinds of economic agreements with China.[34] This development implies an increased willingness on the part of member states to conduct economic cooperation with China at the EU level. As a result, the Commission's competence has been de facto enhanced.

EU-China Textile Agreements

EU Textile agreements[35] give detailed definitions of products, list products which are subject or not subject to quantitative restrictions (QRs), lay down safeguard measures, and specify which imported products are subject to regional limits and national quotas in the EU. One feature of these agreements is that the regulations are very strict and thus, once the agreements are concluded, their implementation is rarely distorted.[36] Therefore, the competence of the Commission and the Council on EU textile trade policy towards China is best examined from assessing how competent they are in concluding textile agreements with China.

CONCLUSION

In 1978, when the first EU–China trade agreement was concluded, China had just started its 'open market' policy and EU–China trade relations remained to be developed. The first trade agreement did not reveal more than a willingness on both sides to establish formal trade relations. More substance for conducting trade relations was not provided in this agreement. Of course, it was not difficult to reach consensus within the Commission and the Council respectively, or between the Commission and the Council. In 1985, when the EU–China trade and economic cooperation agreement was concluded, the intentions of both sides were similar to what they had been in 1978: to show a willingness to extend formal trade relations into economic relations. This is part of the reason why economic cooperation provisions do not provide clear definitions but instead list some examples.

   EU–China economic relations have dramatically intensified since the late 1980s,[37] and thus commercial problems and disputes have substantially increased. Owing to China's application to the GATT/WTO, the EU and China shifted their negotiating forum to GATT/WTO in turn. From March 1987 onwards, China's application was discussed in *every* EU–China meeting. Neither the EU nor China intend to negotiate another bilateral trade and economic agreement until China enters the GATT/WTO. Both sides have been discussing bilateral economic relations and trade problems under the GATT/WTO framework. Since the EU is a WTO founding member and China is expected to join the WTO, the impact of WTO rules will become very important.

With China's growing economic weight and intensified EU–China economic relations, China's response to the EU becomes ever more crucial. The dispute on inclusion of a 'human rights clause' into EU–China commercial agreements is a good example. Even if the EU reaches an internal consensus (especially a common line between the hard- and soft-liners) to take a hard line on this issue, China may still resist. EU hard-liners softened their position recently, because of their perception that China's economic weight has considerably increased in recent years. The EU is no longer in an absolutely advantageous economic position *vis-à-vis* China. In addition, the Chinese market remains attractive to European business and industries, despite the Tiananmen Square event. Only if there is another case with equivalent political implications will the EU be able to push for the inclusion of a 'human rights clause'.[38]

Within the EU, textile-trade policymaking is highly technical and requires expertise. Therefore, the Commission has a more advantageous position than the Council in this policy sector. In the early days of EU–China textile trade, the Commission had a relatively free hand in concluding textile agreements with China, since the impact of the MFA was minimal and China's bargaining power was not strong. Since China has been a major textile supplier wanting to enter the GATT/WTO, the room left for the Commission to move has been substantially reduced.

EU anti-dumping measures are also highly regulatory and technical, but they are not insulated from political influence. Definite duties need to be concluded by the Council. Holmes and Kempton argue that the Council remains 'unwilling or unable for the foreseeable future to devise a purely legalistic and depoliticized set of rules which would be necessary for application of the anti-dumping regime to be solely delegated to the Commission'.[39] In terms of Commission versus Council influence in this area, the Commission does not have the advantageous position it has in EU trade policymaking. Although EU anti-dumping regulations were in line with GATT anti-dumping guidelines, the EU was not bound by GATT regulations, nor was China a GATT contracting party. These two factors gave the EU excuses to impose anti-dumping duties against Chinese products in order to protect the EU internal market,[40] and the EU has been accused of being one of the most frequent users of anti-dumping measures. With the vision of China being a WTO member, the EU has to be more careful in using anti-dumping measures in the future.

As we have demonstrated, EU policymaking in respect of China is complicated and intricate. The major factors affecting policy outcomes often change across different sectors and in accordance with different stages of development of EU–China economic relations. Therefore, it is difficult to identify the major driving force of EU commercial policymaking overall towards China. This chapter sets out EU internal dynamism, external dynamism and EU–China commercial agreements as the three major factors which should be considered in any examination of EU commercial policymaking in respect of China. It suggests that before these major factors can be properly analysed, particular sectors and stages of development need to be specified. It would be arbitrary to draw the conclusion that one factor is more important than the others without such specification.

NOTES

1. I am grateful to Beate Kohler-Koch and Peter W. Preston for the comments on the earlier version of this chapter and to many members of the European Parliament (MEPs), governmental representatives at the Council and Commission *fonctionnaires* who shared their time with me, while the responsibility for the content rests with the author.

2. Strictly speaking, it should be the 'European Community's' commercial policy, since the relevant treaty articles retain the name 'European Community' (EC) rather than 'European Union' (EU). This question caused by the Treaty on European Union (TEU) has not been answered by the Amsterdam Treaty. Further confusion arises in the cases of EU–China trade and economic agreements, since agreements were signed in the name of the 'European Economic Community' (EEC). Another question to clarify relates to the fact that the commercial policy towards China discussed in this chapter covers the period dating back to the late 1970s when commercial relations formally started but the 'EU' did not even exist! Nevertheless, since the EU is 'founded on the European Communities' (Article A , TEU), it is acceptable to use 'EU' to encompass 'EC' and 'EEC'. For the sake of simplicity, 'EU' is used throughout this chapter.

3. The terms 'internal' and 'external' are best understood in a *relative*, rather than absolute, manner. Since the EU is not a closed system, the evolution of EU 'internal' structure (that is the EU's institutional settings) are often entangled with the development of the 'external' environment. Likewise, the 'internal' dynamism and the 'external' dynamism are often interwoven in the case of China. In practice, it is difficult to trace what is sheer internal and what is sheer external. However, a caveat needs to be introduced for the purpose of analysis. In this chapter, internal dynamism relates to the EU legal framework, the institutional practices shaped by organizational structure, and the implicit norms and routines long established in EU decision making. External dynamism focuses on the international political and economic environment, and the regulations of the General Agreement on Tariffs and Trade (GATT)/World Trade Organization (WTO).

4. In fact, there is politicization of overall EU commercial policymaking, the case of China being only one among many EU commercial policies towards third countries or international organizations. John Peterson and Elizabeth Bomberg (1999) (*Decision-making in the*

European Union, London: Macmillan, pp. 90–119) and Stephen Woodcock and Michael Hodges (1996) ('EU Policy in the Uruguy Round', in Helen Wallace and William Wallace (eds), *Policy-making in the European Union,* 3rd edn, Oxford: Oxford University Press) observe that although EU commercial policymaking remains essentially technocratic, it has been gradually politicized.

5. As mentioned above, the entanglement of internal and external dynamism has become a very important factor in the case of China in recent years. The best example to demonstrate this argument is the triangular relationships among the EU, China and the USA on the negotiations of China's WTO membership. What happens in the EU–China negotiations affects China–USA negotiations, and vice versa. However, examination of this factor is not included in this chapter because of the insufficiency of information at the time this chapter was published. For years, both China–USA and EU–China negotiations have been conducted under great secrecy. Even the negotiation outcomes have not been published fully, in spite of the conclusion of USA–China negotiations in November 1999 and EU–China negotiations in May 2000.

6. The Amsterdam Treaty renumbers most EU Treaty articles. With some amendments, Article 113 (Treaty of Rome) becomes Article 133 (Treaty of Amsterdam) and Article 228 (Treaty of Rome) becomes Article 300 (Treaty of Amsterdam). Without change of content, Article 228a (Treaty of Rome) becomes Article 301 (Treaty of Amsterdam). However, the familiar label, 'Article 113 Committee', which is set up according to Article 113 (Treaty of Rome), was not clarified. It is widely accepted that this committee receives its new label, 'Article 133 Committee'. For simplicity, I use the new numbering of treaty articles and 'Article 133 Committee' throughout this chapter.

7. For more examples and details of the arguments between the Council and the Commission on the definition of CCP, see Nicholas Emiliou (1996), 'The Allocation of Competence Between the EC and Its Member States in the Sphere of External Relations', in Nicholas Emiliou and David O'Keeffe (eds), *The European Union and World Trade Law: After the GATT Uruguay Round,* Chichester: John Wiley & Sons, pp. 31–45; Richard Lauwaars (1988), 'Scope and Exclusiveness of the Common Commercial Policy – Limits of the Powers of the Member States', in Jürgen Schwarze (ed.), *Discretionary Powers of the Member States in the Field of Economic Policies and Their Limits under the EEC Treaty,* Baden-Baden: Nomos Verlagsgesellschaft, pp. 73–90.

8. The GATS envisages four modes of trade in services. The Court rules that one of the modes is covered by the CCP, but not the other three modes. Likewise, one type of IPR is covered by the CCP, but not the rest. For details, see Chalmers, Damian (1996), 'Legal Base and the External Relations of the European Community', in Nicholas Emiliou and David O'Keeffe (eds), *The European Union and World Trade Law: After the GATT Uruguay Round,* Chichester: John Wiley & Sons, pp. 59–61; Baroness Elles (1996), 'The Role of EU Institutions in External Trade Policy', in Nicholas Emiliou and David O'Keeffe (eds), *The European Union and World Trade Law: After the GATT Uruguay Round,* Chichester: John Wiley & Sons, pp. 28–30; and Emiliou (1996), pp. 34–5.

9. See the four paragraphs of Article 113, Treaty of Rome and the amendment (paragraph 5) form Article 133, Treaty of Amsterdam. For development of this case after the Court ruling in 1994 and before the amendment added to the Treaty of Amsterdam, see Peterson and Bomberg (1999), pp. 100–101.

10. Chalmers (1996), p. 61.

11. For the secondary legislation, see Article 249, Treaty of Amsterdam and Neil Nugent (1994), *The Government and Politics of the European Union,* 3rd edn, London: Macmillan, pp. 210–15. For the same reason given in note 4, this article was previously Article 189, Treaty of Rome.

12. For the same reason given in note 4, these articles were previously Articles 189a and 189b, Treaty of Rome, respectively.

13. Peter Holmes and Jeremy Kempton (1996), 'EU anti-dumping policy: a regulatory perspective', *Journal of European Public Policy,* 3 (4), 653.

14. For the 'cotton row', see Peterson and Bomberg (1999), pp. 112–15.

15. This Declaration was made at the Madrid European Council meeting (point 1.1.24., *Bulletin*

of the European Community **6**, 1989, p. 17; points 828 and 924, 23rd *General Report of the European Community*, 1989, pp. 347 and 393.

16. Interview with the MEPs, May 1999.
17. According to many Commission *fonctionnaires*, MEPs and governmental representatives at the Council, they have never been lobbied by Chinese interest groups. The officials from China's Mission to the EU also recognize the absence of non-governmental/independent lobbying groups from China. In the case that lobbying is considered as efficient, the Chinese officials even have to rely on the interest groups from the EU. For example, in the case of anti-dumping against Chinese products, the Chinese government often counts on the free trade associations in the EU.
18. Laura Cram (1994), 'The European Commission as a multi-organization: social policy and IT policy in the EU', *Journal of European Public Policy* **1** (2), 195–217; Nugent (1995), pp. 611–12.
19. Thomas Christiansen (1997), 'Tensions of European governance: politicized bureaucracy and multiple accountability in the European Commission', *Journal of European Public Policy* **4** (1), 78–81; Jens L. Mortensen (1998), 'The Institutional Challenges and Paradoxes of EU Governance in External Trade: Coping with the Post-hegemonic Trading System and the Global Economy', in Alan Cafruny and Patrick Peters (eds), *The Union and the World: The Political Economy of a Common European Foreign Policy*, The Hague: Kluwer Law International, pp. 218–19; Nugent (1995), p. 612; Woodcock and Hodges (1996).
20. Fiona Hayes-Renshaw and Helen Wallace (1995), 'Executive power in the European Union: the functions and limits of the Council of Ministers', *Journal of European Public Policy*, **2** (4), 564–6; see also Fiona Hayes-Renshaw and Helen Wallace (1997), *The Council of Ministers*, London: Macmillan.
21. Interviews with national representatives to the EU, May 1999.
22. Nugent (1995), p. 608.
23. Cram (1994), p. 193.
24. Ibid p. 210.
25. Ibid.
26. Interviews with Commission *fonctionnaire*, May 1999.
27. Bilateral trade was always less than 5 billion ECU in terms of both imports from China and exports to China every year from 1975 to 1984. For figures, see Eurostat.
28. See Christopher M. Dent (1999), *The European Union and East Asia: An Economic Relationship*, London: Routledge, p. 133 for the diagram in which the emergence of new sectors in EU–China trade can be observed; and Dent (1999), p. 134 for the growth of EU–China trade.
29. For an examination of the human rights clause in EU commercial agreements and a comparison between the case of China and other EU trading partners, see Marise Cremona (1996), 'Human Rights and Democracy Clauses in the EC's Trade Agreements', in Nicholas Emiliou and David O'Keeffe (eds), *The European Union and World Trade Law: After the GATT Uruguay Round*, Chichester: John Wiley & Sons, pp. 62–77.
30. China was persuaded to accept the more restrictive MFN clause. China's bargaining power was limited at that time, since its economic weight was less significant. See Yuanxiang Hu (1991), *Legal and Policy Issues of the Trade and Economic Relations between China and the EEC: A Comparative Study*, Deventer: Kluwer Law and Taxation Publishers, pp. 19–24; Francis Snyder (1996), 'Legal Aspects of Trade between the European Union and China: Preliminary Reflections', in Nicholas Emiliou and David O'Keeffe (eds), *The European Union and World Trade Law: After the GATT Uruguay Round*, Chichester: John Wiley & Sons, pp. 365–6; Zhi Yue Xiao (1993), *Current EC Legal Developments: The EC and China*, London: Butterworth, pp. 22–7.
31. Mehmet, Ugur (1998), 'Explaining protectionism and liberalization in European Union trade policy: the case of textiles and clothing', *Journal of European Public Policy*, **5** (4), 652–70.
32. Xiao (1993), pp. 82–3.
33. There are two agreements of this type: the EEC–China Trade Agreement (1978) and the EEC–China Trade and Economic Cooperation Agreement (1985). The former was incorporated, without change of wording but with a renumbering of the articles, into the

latter. In implementing the agreements, numerous Council Regulations (1766/82; 3420/83; 3421/83) were adopted. For competence of the Commission and the Council on the adoption of Council Regulation, see pp. 3–4. For detailed examination of the agreements and Council Regulations, see Hu (1991) and Xiao (1993).

34. For bilateral agreements between China and EU member states, see Wolfgang Bartke (1992), *The Agreements of the People's Republic of China With Foreign Countries 1949– 1990*, 2nd edn, Munich: Saur.

35. The first textile agreement was concluded in 1979, and was then incorporated into the Supplementary Protocol in 1984. In 1988, the EU and China concluded a new textile agreement in order to renew and replace the 1979 agreement. The 1988 agreement has been amended frequently.

36. Hu (1991); Xiao (1993).

37. Although official relations were interrupted after the Tiananmen event, private business and trade continued. In fact, the EU trade deficit towards China continued to grow from 1990 to 1992.

38. Interviews with Commission *fonctionnaires*, MEPs and governmental representatives at the Council, May 1999.

39. P. Holmes and J. Kempton (1997), *EU Anti-Dumping Policy Towards China*, London: The Royal Institute of International Affairs, p. 647.

40. Many studies suggest that in a period of high unemployment, EU politicians are under pressure to demand anti-dumping action against Chinese products simply to deny the competitiveness of Chinese products. See Piet Eeckhout (1997), 'European Anti- dumping law and China', *European Integration Online Papers (EIoP)*, **1** (7), <<http://eiop.or.at/eiop/texte/1997-007a.html>>; Holmes and Kempton (1997); and Edwin A. Vermulst and Folkert Graafsma, (1992), 'A decade of European Community anti- dumping law and practice applicable to imports from China', *Journal of World Trade*, **26** (3), 5–60.

10. The European Union and China: the benefits of openness in international economic integration

Tong, Jia-Dong

INTRODUCTION

There are two kinds of model in international economic integration. One is the institutional model, the so-called policy-oriented model, and the other is the non-institutional model, the market-oriented integration model. These two models show one shared characteristic when we consider the interdependence of nations. That is, that any kind of economic integration must have some attraction to the participating states.

The European Union is a typical example of the institutional model of integration. In the past, it was a rather closed system, and it was difficult for third countries to enter it in order to trade. It can be argued that the EU should now become more open to trade in order to boost its rate of economic growth. In this context, we can note the importance of expanding trade with China. I would argue that the EU should open its trade more widely and strengthen its economic contacts with countries outside the EU. In theoretical terms, the EU should adjust the balance of its economic system and move away somewhat from the present rather closed system towards a stance which is more open to the world.

MODELS OF ECONOMIC INTEGRATION

There are two kinds of international economic integration in the world. One is institutional integration, the other is non-institutional integration oriented to the mechanism of the marketplace. The two strategies have distinctive benefits and disbenefits.[1]

The model of instutional integration means that member states should transfer some legislative regulative power from the national level to the supranational level. In return, the member states receive trade facilities or other benefits from the organization. The benefits derived by members will flow not merely from trade linkages and basic economic integration but also from other fields of integration; for example, technical cooperation. This improved economic environment is the main attraction to members if they are willing to hand over elements of their national state power to the supranational body.

Generally speaking, the deeper international economic integration among the members becomes, the more scope there will be for the organization to open its doors to the wider world. It is clear that non-members will, in general, face discrimination, and if regional economic integration among the members is deep then the discrimination faced by non-members could be serious.

One way in which successful institutional integration can generate additional economic energy, and thus growth, is to open its system to non-members from the outside world. The key factor here, for the members, is the extent of the additional benefits to be derived from any new arrangement in contrast to the old system.

The other model of international economic integration is non-institutional integration, also called market-oriented integration. This kind of model means that the member states do not need to transfer any legislative regulatory power from the national level to the supranational body. The process of trade liberalization generates the desired additional economic benefits for participants. The participants can also take the position that any trade facility or trade liberalization measure, once agreed by the participating members, can be shared with non-members. One problem generated here is that of the 'free rider'. It might be asked, if this is the case why do the member economies still want to join the organization? The answer is very simple. There are some other, further benefits which the members can secure by virtue of their cooperation. If there were not, then all the countries would be free riders.

In my view, market-oriented economic integration stems from particular opportunities or benefits that attract the member states. If an organization fostering market-oriented integration can maintain this characteristic, no matter what the individual particular opportunities and benefits might be, then it can be kept stable and successful.

Generally speaking, this kind of attraction can change from low class to a higher one. There are two particular kinds of relationship between the lower and the higher. The first form is supplement. This means that higher-class attraction is based on the lower one. For example, a single currency is based on monetary policy harmonization, otherwise the single currency cannot be accepted by member states. The other form is replacement. For example, trade barriers can be replaced by a further equivalent facility among the member states, and then the new facility will form a new discrimination against third countries. Any strategy of international economic integration must have some schedule of particular discriminations against non-member states, no matter what kind of integration is pursued, whether an open market-oriented non-institutional strategy or an institutional strategy.

THE EUROPEAN UNION MODEL VERSUS THE APEC MODEL

The organization named Asia Pacific Economic Cooperation (APEC) is focused upon market-oriented economic integration. In particular, it has affirmed the notion of open regionalism. It has announced that any agreements on trade between its members will be extended to non-members; that is, there is no exclusion of non-member economies. However, whilst this applies to trade relations, it does not extend to other forms of cooperation between the members. Otherwise, there would be no particular reason to join the organization. In fact, APEC economic and technical cooperation amongst member economies is an exclusive field. So the organization is not afraid of free riders in trade or trade liberalization.

The European Union is a typical instance of institutional integration. The aim of the organization is to foster economic and political union. The EU realized a small part of the overall objective first, in the form of a customs union. At that time and stage, the European Community (EC), as it then was, was focusing on the establishment of its internal market, so its strategy of exclusion of other non-members was very successful. The EC encouraged the development of internal trade. Even though it had some external trade with non-member countries, it mainly concerned itself with the internal market.[2] These matters are illustrated in Table 10.1.

Table 10.1   The EC/EU's dependent rate to trade by region

Year	East Asia	North America	EC/EU	Others
1975	3.0	8.7	51.2	36.3
1980	4.5	8.5	52.4	34.6
1985	5.5	10.5	53.5	30.7
1990	7.3	8.4	59.2	25.1
1992	8.0	8.0	59.8	24.2

Source: Derived from Masami Yoshida, Masayaki Nohara and Kimitoshi Sato (1994), *Regional Economic Integration in East Asia*, Royal Institute of International Affairs.

If we consider this table we find the following points of note. The European Union's internal trade increased gradually. This change was the result of trade diversion from other countries to member states. Trade with North America decreased by 0.7 per cent from 1975 to 1992, and by 2.5 per cent from 1985 to 1992 respectively. In this data we can see the effects of trade diversion. In the meantime, trade with East Asia increased by 5 per cent from 1975 to 1992. Trade increases with East Asia mainly came from the transfer from other partners to East Asia. The increases in internal trade most likely came from the transfer from North America to the member states. In the light of these data, it seems to me that the EU could become the 'European fortress' often posited. In this condition, the EU would be so closed that no other country able to compete with its member states could enter easily.

The situation of a relatively closed European Union economic system would cause two results of particular note. First it would create a relatively stable internal market for all its members, especially for those members who would be disadvantaged by competition from non-members. The second, negative, effect would be that competition with non-members would be discouraged. If we believe that competition is an engine for economic advance and growth, then the EU might lose an impulse to innovate in production. It can be argued that this is one reason why the EU lagged behind Japan and the USA in the 1980s and early 1990s.

In recent years, almost all economies have become more and more internationalized. It is widely granted amongst analysts and policymakers that economic and trade liberalization is one of the more important factors which can stimulate economic growth and development in national economies. It might be noted that the WTO plays an important role in encouraging its members, and even non-members, to reduce their trade barriers. It seems to me that, in this matter, the EU should follow the trend. It is necessary, therefore, for the European Union to adjust its model. Five points can be made in this regard.

Some Recommendations for European Union Policy Change

First of all, the European Union's integration has been steadily upgraded over the last fifteen years, from a customs union to a single market, and from a single market to an economic union, including a monetary union. This kind of systematic upgrading allows the EU to generate a lot of opportunities and benefits for its member states. In this situation it is clear that the opportunities for free trade within the member countries, and excluding third countries, are significant, but the benefits of monetary union and policy harmonization are playing a more and more important role in securing the adherence of the member countries.

Second, the enlargement of the European Union and the long process of integration reveals that the EU can tolerate different levels of integration amongst the member countries. If this is a report on how the EU has operated internally over the years, then it is clear that the EU could offer concessions to other countries which presently cannot adopt similar policies.

Third, even though the European Union is committed to the principle of internal free trade, the organization has gone beyond this goal. The single currency, the free movement of capital and labour, as well as policy harmonization have created new opportunities and benefits for member countries and, at the same time, new discriminations against non-members. Internal competition has become stronger and the economy as a whole has benefited.

Fourth, the European Union needs a new engine of growth from the rest of the world. In the last twenty years the trans-Pacific area has developed very fast, both in economic levels and trade. According to data from APEC, its member countries make up 45 per cent of total world trade. Even the recent financial crisis of 1997–98 has not significantly damaged the region as a whole. APEC is still committed to trade liberalization. As APEC is committed to open regionalism, continuing trade liberalization will benefit members and non-members. It might be noted that some experts have argued that open-region trade liberalization is better than free trade within the region. Others say that the 21st century should belong to the Pacific area. At the present time it is not clear how these arguments will be resolved. However, in my view, the EU should open its market to the rest of the world and, in return, EU members' access to other markets would be assisted.

Fifth, the European Union should pay a more important economic role after the end of the cold war. This means that the EU should accept imports from the rest of the world, not just from less-developed countries but also from the developing and developed countries. It can be argued that the EU has already adjusted its policy to the new situation, and has good results from this kind of policy change. These points are illustrated in Table 10.2.

The table shows that European Union trade in both imports and exports has had a lower growth rate than the world average over the period 1990 to 1997. The situation changed in 1998. At this time the EU enjoyed a positive growth rate whilst the world average rate was negative. One of the reasons for this was that the EU was not influenced by the East Asian financial crisis. A further reason is that the EU exports little raw material or fuel. In addition the policy that the EU adopted played a very important role. As is shown in Table 10.3, in 1998 EU imports from the rest of the world were larger than its exports for the first time.

The table shows that the European Union has increased its imports from the rest of the world, mainly from the four countries named in the table. It also

Table 10.2 *World and EU trade*

	Export value in FOB and growth rate					Import value in CIF and growth rate				
	1998	1990–95	1996	1997	1998	1998	1990–95	1996	1997	1998
World Total	5225	7.5	4.5	3.5	−2.0	5410	7.5	5.0	3.0	−1.0
EU15	2171	6.5	3.5	−0.5	3.0	2163	5.5	3.0	−2.0	5.5

Source: Derived from WTO trade reports, 1999.

Table 10.3   EU trade with main partners (in billions of euro)

EU15 Exports		Growth rate, %	Partners	EU15 Imports		Growth rate, %
1998	1997			1998	1997	
159.6	141.3	13	USA	150.7	137.8	9.36
57.0	53.0	7	Switzerland	492.0	45.1	9.58
31.4	36.1	−13	Japan	65.5	59.8	9.53
17.3	16.5	5	China	41.8	37.5	11.5

Source: EU <<http://europa.int/en/comm/eurostat>>

seems clear that it is good for the EU to stimulate competition in its internal market. The conclusion to be drawn is that the EU should adjust the model which informs its trade and economic policies, changing from the closed model to one which is a little more open to the rest of the world. An implication of this kind of change would be that the EU would have more levels of activity. These are: (i) the core level, namely the 11 Euro-zone members; (ii) the second level, the EU15, where the rest of the members participate; (iii) the third level, the candidates for entry to the EU; and (iv) the rest of the world. It can be argued that the EU should adjust its present policy so as to adopt a policy of freeing trade with the rest of the world, for example by attending to the issue of non-tariff barriers. In terms of the fourth level of activity, with the rest of the world, the EU should be prepared to establish a preferential trade area with APEC, or with the Asian members of the ASEM.

THE EUROPEAN UNION AND CHINA

The European Economic Community (EEC) established normal relations with China in 1975. Since then two-way trade has increased very rapidly. In 1980 the total value of trade was 2.425 billion ECUs. The cumulative growth was 437.1 per cent from 1980 to 1990. The trade value reached 40.3 billion ECUs in 1995, 39.8 billion ECUs in 1996, 44.4 billion ECUs in 1997 and 48.9 billion ECUs in 1998. In 1999, it was even better, the total value of two-way trade 59.1 billion euro. So trade between the European Union and China has been developing very fast, with China's economic growth continuing and the economic recovery in the EU also advancing. This kind of two-way trade benefits both partners. But it is not enough, since the value of the trade is still very small, as compared, for example, with Japan. As is well known, Japan is the first trade partner with China. The EU is the third, following Hong Kong.

However, there are fifteen countries in the EU and most of them play very important roles in world trade. In this context, the present levels of trade with China do not look high. There are a number of reasons for this situation. First, the EU pays too much attention to its internal trade and to some associated members' trade. Second, there are some trade barriers, especially non-tariff barriers (there were a series of anti-dumping cases which Chinese companies have had to deal with in the last five years). Third, there has been some political disturbance in the relationship. In short, it would seem that the EU has not realized how important the East Asian market is, especially the Chinese market (it might be noted that in 1996 the EU had just formulated a new strategy on trade with Asia and China). However, the Asia–Europe Meeting (ASEM) was set up in 1996. It is a good mechanism for the EU if it wants to compete in the East Asian market, which is a new potential market. If the East Asian area moves towards a policy of open regionalism it will still need to trade with the EU. So this kind of trade liberalization is very important for the EU if it wants to enter the East Asian market. It might be argued that, as one pillar of the post-cold war world, the EU should play a much greater role in the world economy, and not restrict its attention or activities to Europe.[3]

CONCLUSION

The two models of economic integration noted at the outset, the institutional oriented and the market oriented, must offer those who participate a schedule of benefits and opportunities. The two models offer different schedules of benefits and opportunities. However, they are similar in one crucial respect, that they both offer benefits and opportunities to members and, by implication, deny these to non-members. In general, the greater the degree of economic integration the greater the difference between the situations of members and non-members. At this point, the member countries will be in a position to offer access to non-members.

The European Union is a typical example of institutional integration. This is the objective of economic and monetary union. The EU is in a position to adopt a relatively open policy towards non-members. The policy is not only necessary for the levels of domestic economic activity within the EU but also preferable to a closed strategy if the EU wants to play an important role within the world economy. In this context, we can note that China is a key trade partner with the EU. However, even though two-way trade has developed very quickly, it should be larger, given that the EU is an economic organization that embraces fifteen nations. The EU, then, needs to move from a relatively closed to a relatively open model.

In the future, it can be argued, the EU should pay attention to two broad spheres of economic and political activity: the domestic and the international. On the one side is the internal market and the project of its deepening and enlargement. On the other side, the EU should establish more stable relations with countries outside of Europe. It is possible for the EU to establish normal international economic relations or some kind of open integration organization. The role of ASEM is relevant here. The EU should go further, namely pursue a kind of open integration. Both the EU and APEC could take trade liberalization to each other, or the EU could offer some Asian countries preferential treatment in trade in order to establish stable relations with Asian countries. China is one of these target countries, since it has a very large potential market.

NOTES

1. On this, see Jeffrey A. Frankel (1998), *The Regional Integration of the World Economy*, University of Chicago Press; R. Lawrence (1996), *Regionalism, Multilateralism and Deeper*, Washington, Brookings; OECD (1995), *Regional Integration and the Multilateral Trading System: Synergy and Divergence*, Paris, OECD; David Henderson (ed.) (1994), *The Trade Blocks? The Future of Regional Integration*, The Royal Institute of International Affairs.
2. On this, see Frank McDonald and Stephen Dearden (1992), *European Economic Integration*, London: Longman; Franz Somers (1998), *European Union Economics: A Comparative Study*, London: Longman; Willem Molle (1991), *The Economics of European Integration: Theory, Practice and Policy*, Aldershot, Dartmouth.
3. Jiadong, Tong (2000), 'The upgrading of the European economic integration', in *Nankai Journal*, 2.

11. East Asia: emergent regional dynamics

Peter W. Preston

INTRODUCTION

At the turn of the new millennium the East Asian region is subject to close attention from political agents, policy analysts and scholars. It is clear that the region is undergoing widespread economic and social change. This chapter will present a broad survey of the salient economic and political changes presently underway in the region. It will seek to complement the detailed work presented in earlier chapters with a synoptic overview of emergent regional dynamics. The discussion will be ordered around the notion of complex change. We might speculate that it seems likely that the future of the region over the next few years will be shaped by the intermingled logics of the continuing shift to the modern world, the drive towards regionalism and finally the continuing effects of the recent financial crisis.[1]

READING CHANGE IN THE GLOBAL SYSTEM

The end of the cold war has had a series of remarkable consequences for European observers. As the obfuscations of the period fell away, leaving politicians, policy analysts and scholars free to contemplate the world directly it became apparent that the global system had taken a distinctly tri-polar form. It was clear that the USA constituted one key power within the global system, indeed this was a familiar matter, however what was new was the relatively abrupt realization that the European Union also constituted a distinctive sphere, and that, moreover, East Asia, hitherto regarded as one of the arenas of cold war competition[2] had been undergoing a somewhat similar long drawn out process of macro-regional integration.[3]

A series of reactions to the newly recognized situation were offered, including, to pick a spread of the more obvious, the following quartet: (i) 'retrospective denial'; the attempt to co-opt the novel situation to familiar hegemonic aspirations (thus Huntington's arguments that the West should rally to the leadership of the USA in a world made up of competing civilizations); 'prospective denial', where the attempted co-option is more subtle and superficially inclusive (thus the proponents of globalization, who have enthusiastically recycled the old fifties ideas of the inevitable convergence of presently disparate economic and political systems upon the model of the West or the USA); (iii) 'politically active affirmation', which directly celebrated the new circumstances, thus the enthusiasts for the federal political–cultural project of the European Union who saw the EU as the only game in town in Europe, or again, the enthusiasts for East Asian regionalism; for example, Dr Mahathir's proposal for an East Asian Economic Caucus or, again, Ishihara insisting that Japan can say no to the USA[4]; and (iv) 'pragmatic affirmation', that is, the recognition that something certainly was going on, which might have things to be said for it, but whose status was unclear (that is, just what was going on and where it was leading to were unclear).

The last noted reaction could be unpacked a little further, in particular. It could be argued that, whatever the substantive concerns addressed or indeed the methods used to further enquiry, all these debates have a common concern in the analysis of change; the attempt, made by politicians, policy analysts and scholars to grasp the logic of unfolding events. It might also be argued that the variously pursued concerns for change share a formal/substantive or constitutive premise, namely that the rough outline of the future is clear; that is, an industrial–capitalist system of global reach[5]. It is this package of concerns which lies at the heart of the classical European tradition of social theorizing. It is this tradition which can be turned to the analysis of complex change as it presents itself within the current global system.

CHANGE IN EAST ASIA

The classical European tradition of social theorizing affirms a particular conception of theorizing (interpretive/critical) and a spread of core substantive concerns in the analysis of complex change in the ongoing shift to the modern world. The approach has roots which lie in the very earliest periods of the shift to the modern world in Europe. An extensive repertoire of concepts has been developed.[6] There are a series of key debates, and in this context two are of particular interest: first, the nature of the global system as a whole and the related issue of regions; and second, the business of temporality, or how change runs over time.

The notion of a 'region' is not straightforward. It is not a simple matter of geography; rather, the notion of a region must be taken to be an elaborate social construction.[7] In terms of the classical European tradition, a region is constituted in the historically unfolding interplay of political–economic, social–institutional and cultural structures, and the ways in which these are read by key agent groups. In terms of the familiar idea of the dynamic of structures and agents, the development of a region will require both structural change, the development of practical linkages (economic, social and cultural) and agent response. The element of agent response is crucial. The idea of a region has to figure as an element in the political-cultural projects of key agent groups; it has to be an element of their expectations and plans for their future. This means that regional projects are contingent upon the political commitment of participating agent groups. The boundaries of a region can alter as commitment is made or withheld. The boundaries of a region can alter over time as these complex processes unfold. One might speak of configurations, the pattern of regions that exists at any one historical time. One might speak of phases, the historical and discontinuous sequence of configurations whereby a particular region has been lodged within the changing wider system. One might also note that these regional projects have had their own discursive schemas, their own ways of understanding their worlds. One might also note that any political, policy or scholarly interest in regions is similarly contingent and, at the present time, such interests flow from the practical and cognitive upheavals associated with the end of the cold war.[8]

It is clear that the boundaries of the regions with which we concern ourselves today have been quite different in the past. In the case of Europe it is possible to point to a whole series of different versions of Europe – the Greco-Roman world, the Holy Roman Empire, medieval Europe, the Europe of nation-states, and cold war Europe. The current preoccupation is the European Union. The sequence has been noted by Delanty, who considers the way in which contemporary Europe, the Europe centred on the project of the European Union, is being invented in a subtle interchange of economic, social and cultural structures and elite political commitment.[9] In the case of Asia, a similar story can be told. In the years prior to the arrival of the Europeans, the East Asian region had an economic, social and cultural core in China. As Frank[10] has recently argued, the Sinocentric system was a prosperous civilization and it was not until the rulers of the late Ming Dynasty turned inwards in the mid-fourteenth century that the European powers had the opportunity to gain a real foothold in the area. The expansion of European capitalism – initially mercantile and later industrial – extensively remade the forms of life of the region and it was in the context of the ongoing exchanges with European colonizers that the various territories of East Asia began their shift to the modern world. The USA became a part of the process in the late nineteenth century.[11] The Pacific War destroyed the European, American and Japanese empires in East Asia, and the states of the region were able to pursue the objectives of growth and development under the guidance of indigenous elites. It was these national projects which were eventually to generate regional linkages and, in time, the idea of an East Asian region.

In East Asia, over the long years following the end of the Pacific War, it is possible to identify a series of key episodes which have, in broad terms, facilitated the establishment of a measure of regional integration: first, the decision of the Chinese leadership, under Deng Xiaoping, to initiate economic reforms and engage with the wider regional/global economy; second, the deepening Japanese economic involvement within the region following the Plaza Accord which agreed the revaluation of the yen; and third, the political–cultural and security implications of the dissolution of the USSR, which further reduced the salience of the divisive cold war apparatus within East Asia and simultaneously encouraged various actors in North America and the European Union to look at East Asia as a region.

Overall, in East Asia, at the present time, the keys to economic integration can be found in the twin circuits of Japanese capital, on the one hand, and Chinese capital (Greater China and the Overseas Chinese), on the other. These flows of capital have generated a regional pattern of economic linkages. These patterns of economic activity are paralleled by the development of social networks. There are extensive contacts between regional political leaders, policy analysts and business personnel. There are also informal contacts between people found in leisure and tourism. Thereafter, in a multiplicity of formal regional meetings, East Asian elites meet to discuss common concerns. It is these patterns of structural change which provide the basis, or occasion, for the construction of a region. The extent of regional integration can be disputed. It is possible to make arguments which suggest that the diversity of the region is too great to allow much by way of integration, or, in a related fashion, to suggest that the countries of the region have better developed contacts with the global system than they do with each other. It is clear that it would be wrong to overstate the extent of macro-regional integration in East Asia. However, the arguments for regional interlinkages and elite acknowledgement and action are plausible.

The current situation in East Asia can be analysed in terms of three broad timescales[12], where each embraces a distinctive logic of change: modernity, regionalism and crisis. The first, modernity, points to the historically drawn-out process of institutionalizing the priority of sceptical reason, fostering the development of industrial capitalism and building nation-states. The shift to the modern world in East Asia was accomplished in the process of the irruption of European capitalism throughout the area and the establishment of formal colonial empires. The process involved the radical reconstruction of indigenous patterns of life in line with the demands of metropolitan capital. The colonial territories were subject to a process of reconstruction and peripheralization, as the colonial systems revolved around the series of metropolitan cores, with capital cities in Europe, America and later Japan. It was a quite particular route to a quite particular modernity. The end of the Pacific War saw the systems of colonial holdings collapse. The postcolonial period has seen a shift to the modern world in East Asia consolidated under the direction of Asian elites in the form of prosperous new nation-states. Thereafter, the second logic, regionalism, points to the more recent emergence of a regional dimension to economic, social, cultural and political advance. In respect of the shorter-run process of regionalization, the post-cold war phase has seen the slow, partial and incomplete dismantling of the East Asian system of blocks (where relevant dates would be 1978, 1985 and 1989/91), such that East Asia has experienced some interregional integration and intraregional identification (in other words, the emergence of something that looks like an East Asian region). Finally, the third term, crisis, points to the recent abrupt upheavals in long-established dynamics occasioned by problems within the global financial system. In respect of the recent episode of the Asian financial crisis, the implications for the region, the global system and European tradition social theorizing are still emerging.

In this section we will consider the current situation of East Asia in terms of the logics of change running in four areas: Japan, China, the NICs and the countries of ASEAN. A final area of concern relates to the changing global system and its interactions with East Asia.

Japan's Developing Regional Role

The three timescales noted above, modernity, regionalism and crisis, have found recent acknowledgement in renewed debates about the fundamental nature of the Japanese political–economic, social–institutional and cultural structures, and the country's position within wider regional and global systems. The debate can be schematically unpacked in terms of the divergent views of neoliberals and those working with reference to the classical European tradition, with its stress on historical and structural analysis, in respect of the nature of modernity in Japan, the country's role in the region and the implications of the financial crisis.

Thus the neoliberal view, to summarize, could assemble the trio of elements in various ways, but the core position would probably suggest that, in the case of Japan, the shift to the modern world was incomplete, the role in the region inappropriately developed, and the means by which this could be remedied being financial-crisis-occasioned structural reforms; that is, liberalization and deregulation. The neoliberal view argues that as the logic of economic activity is universal then the sooner the Japanese economy is reordered the better for both Japanese consumers and the country's trading partners. Thereafter, the proponents of change identify two great episodes of reform within Japan, the

Meiji Restoration and the SCAP (Supreme Commander for the Allied Powers) reforms, and they go on to suggest that a third major reform is in prospect; that is, the reforms required by the recession of the 1990s coupled to the shock of the 1997 Asian financial crisis.[13] In this way, so the argument runs, the project of modernity in Japan could take a necessary and long overdue step forwards.

In contrast, the historical/structural view, to summarize, would offer a core position which stressed the historical particularity of the Japanese transition to the modern world, their role as core economy of the nascent region and the likelihood that the country's experience of the financial crisis (where post-bubble concerns weighed more heavily than regional issues) would reinforce rather than weaken an already evident disposition to advance nationally within the context of an East Asian region. The historical/structural view argues that as the economic, social and cultural logics running within a country are products of long-term historical trajectories then it is appropriate to note that the economy, society and culture of Japan has been developed over the modern period within the context of an elite political–cultural project oriented to national growth and security. The roots of Japanese modernity are traced back to the commercialization of Edo-period Japan which, thereafter, modulated into the emphatic concern for growth and security that marked the Meiji Restoration. So far as these theorists are concerned, the political-economic, social–institutional and cultural structures of contemporary Japan were given their characteristic form in this early modern period. The proponents of this view speak of a deep-seated continuity within the Japanese system.[14] The subsequent history is one of great success. Sheridan argues that there is no particular reason for the Japanese to abandon styles of working which have served them well.[15]

The balance of debate favours the latter group. One might, therefore, follow those who argue, in respect of the business of organizing economic recovery, that the Japanese bureaucrats will continue to 'muddle through'.[16] More broadly, one would expect Japanese policymakers to continue to advance their concern for growth and security, and in this case we might look to four particular issues: first, their economic role within East Asia (where they are the regional core economy in terms of gross output, trade, aid, foreign direct investment and technological sophistication); second, their cultural role within East Asia, where the influence of Japanese popular culture in consumption is growing[17]; third, their political/diplomatic role within the region (where the legacy of the Pacific War has displaced their diplomatic activities, which now find indirect expression within the structures of the UN[18] and some regional bodies[19]); and fourth, their economic, security and political relationship with the USA (which is both important, awkward and increasingly likely to change, and where any changes could have important regional implications[20]).

China and the Regional/Global System

The logics of change marked in terms of the three timescales noted above – modernity, regionalism and crisis – find different expression in the case of China. It is in the intersection of the two timescales of modernity and regionalism that we can consider the present situation of China. What is quite clear is that the Asian financial crisis, the third timescale, did not impact significantly upon China.

The modern world impressed itself upon China in the nineteenth century as the European (and later American and Japanese) powers ruthlessly pursued their commercial interests.[21] The Quing Dynasty was unable to comprehend the nature of the demands of the foreign trading nations and underwent a long drawn-out process of collapse. Over this period, from the Opium Wars to the revolution of 1911, China became a quasi-colony of the imperialist powers. The removal of the dynasty led to further confusion as conflict developed between nationalists, communists and the increasingly prominent imperial Japanese army. It was not until the communist victory in 1949 that political stability was regained. The overall political stability inaugurated in 1949 has been sustained. The economic and political stance of the Chinese government in the period of Mao's rule was inward-looking, a mixture of economic autarchy, socialist nation-building and cold-war-occasioned tensions. The change of leadership from Mao to Deng Xiaoping coincided with changes in the West and marked a significant turn in policy, as a series of market reforms were inaugurated, and an opening to the region and, thence, to the global system, was made. The market-oriented reforms established in 1978 by Deng continue to move forwards, despite significant problems (rural–urban migration, corruption, state-owned enterprise reform, and the problems of legitimacy presently experienced by the state/party). The reform programme has been hugely successful and has seen dramatic economic advance and social change throughout China.[22]

The Chinese economy is now one of the largest national economies. A familiar spread of issues surrounding rapid economic growth might be noted, in particular: first, the policies necessary to ensure sustained growth within the country (planning, finance, infrastructure and personnel); second, the requirement to attend to the negative consequences of growth (migration, inequality and corruption); third, the development of trade linkages within the sphere of Greater China (thus, it should be noted that there are burgeoning and powerful economies in Hong Kong, Taiwan and amongst the Overseas Chinese); and fourth, the relationship between Chinese and Japanese capital within the region (where Japanese capital centres on manufacturing whereas Chinese capital has centred on service sectors). Thereafter, in the social sphere, the employment and welfare consequences of economic growth in

China present acute challenges to the present leadership, as reforms to the state sector, that is, marketization, continue.[23] And in the political sphere there are a complex mixture of issues to consider, as contemporary national problems (the power of regions and the demands of minorities), the legacies of the cold war (the issue of Taiwan and a divided Korea) and the novel demands of regionalization and globalization all bear down upon political actors whose overriding concern is with stability.

Clearly, the dynamics of change within China have implications not only for the Chinese people but also for regional and global-system dynamics.[24] The development of relations within the region; that is, among the Asian Tigers, Japan and China; is of great interest. In Hong Kong, Taiwan, South Korea and Singapore (and the overseas diaspora) many people are rich and enjoy high levels of consumption. The Asian Tigers have made significant investments in China. The development of Sino–Japanese relations is crucial to the development of the region.[25] In a similar way the development of Sino–US relations is critical to the issue of peace and stability in East Asia.

The Situation of the NICs

The earliest experience of the four Asian Tigers, the region's NICs (South Korea, Taiwan, Hong Kong and Singapore), with the modernist project was as willing/unwilling trading partners of the Europeans and then, rather quickly, as colonized territories. The subsequent historical development experience of these countries has been shaped by the long colonial period (with the territories lodged within, respectively, the Japanese and British empires). The shift to the modern world was consolidated in the process of decolonization and nation-building. In the postcolonial and cold war period they were favourably treated by the USA in the context of its anxiety to contain communism. The project of regionalism is newer and is an historical experience less tainted by the demands of outsiders.

The South Korean and Taiwanese economies benefited directly from US involvement in the provision of aid, reform packages and access to its consumer markets.[26] The economies of Hong Kong and Singapore grew within the context of the postwar economic 'long boom', the latter as an independent nation-state and the former with a distinctly anachronistic colonial status. However, all these countries have found themselves in potentially novel contexts in the wake of the end of the cold war. The US policy of containment contributed to dividing the East Asian region into two groupings of states: the socialist, centred on China, and the nominally free market, centred on the USA. The US strategic interest in the region found expression not merely in political and diplomatic activity but also in economic and development policy where, to put the matter most simply, the USA gave its allies open access to its domestic market in return for political/strategic support. It is clear that whilst this represented no particular problem for the USA in the 1940s, 1950s and 1960s, there were signs of economic difficulties in the 1970s. The subsequent decade of the 1980s saw the issue of trade relations or, more particularly, trade imbalances, assume a central importance, with the USA unable to deal with its trade deficit with East Asia and increasingly dependent upon capital from the region. The unhappy debates between the USA and its East Asian allies continued through the 1980s and it is difficult to imagine that they will cease in the post-cold war environment.

It might be argued that these matters have been made more problematical by the uneven impacts of the Asian financial crisis, where there is evidence that, the more East Asian elites were disposed to give credence to US-sponsored arguments in favour of deregulation and liberalization, the greater was the impact of the crisis.[27] Singapore and Taiwan, both strong states, maintained close control of their economies and both weathered the financial storm relatively well. Hong Kong was fortunate to receive the support of Beijing in its struggles with financial speculators. However, in South Korea the financial crisis had a devastating impact upon an economy which had undertaken a measure of deregulation and liberalization, and one result, which might well prove awkward in the future, has been a contested increase in the influence of US-dominated international financial institutions, the IMF and the World Bank.[28]

A series of general points can be made: first, commentators have spoken of a shift in US policy orientations from geostrategy to geoeconomics, in which case the extent to which the USA is prepared to tolerate asymmetries in trade relations is now in question; second, the recent Asian financial crisis has clearly been used by Washington as a pretext to force 'market opening' on the East Asian economies; and third, more generally, the differential impact of the crisis in the region can be related to the robustness of their state machines, with the region's developmental states generally performing well as they adjusted to the demands placed upon them by the unfolding crisis.[29] In this context, if we reject, as seems sensible, the claims of neoliberal convergence theorists, the interesting questions in respect of the NICs will revolve around their perception of the importance of regional economic networks, the flows of Chinese and Japanese capital, and the extent to which any new political–cultural expectations find expression within regional organizations.

The Countries of ASEAN

In terms of the trio of timescales that frame this review (modernity, regionalism and crisis) we can note, first, that the shift to the modern world within the subregion was accomplished via the experience of colonial rule.

The experience of colonialism was diverse. The experience of decolonization was similarly diverse, as are that period's contemporary legacies. The postcolonial period saw the achievement of an uneven success. At the present time we can note two interrelated sets of concerns: first, the post-cold war concern amongst the countries of the subregion with the development of the wider East Asian region (the nature of the economic role of Japan, the advance of China, the wider-related issue of security (and the position of the USA), the important reforms to the 'ASEAN way', and more broadly the role of APEC, the WTO and the demands of globalization). Secondly, we must note the recent dramatic impact of the Asian financial crisis.

The shift to the modern world in Southeast Asia centres upon a common experience in colonial rule. Indonesia, Malaysia, Singapore, the Philippines, Cambodia and Laos are direct legatees of the colonial era in the sense that they were constituted as nation-state projects in the process of colonization and decolonization (the efforts of colonial rulers and the nationalists they generated). The other countries of the region were similarly shaped by the experience of colonial rule but are able (arguably) to reach back to political patterns antedating the colonial era (thus the kingdoms of Thailand, Burma, Brunei and Vietnam). The removal of foreign empires saw domestic elites securing control and pursuing growth and welfare goals (in diverse ways and with differing results). Yet there have been contradictory processes at work in Southeast Asia. The subregion saw conflict and confusion in respect of the future amongst the newly constituted nation-states. In this regard, ASEAN has provided both subregional security and an institutional mechanism which has served to affirm the identities of these new nations. The subregion also saw a long drawn-out war in Indo-China as the USA endeavoured to secure its objective of containing the threat of communism by military means. However, the long years of prosperity within the US-oriented sphere eventually saw all the countries of ASEAN bound into the East Asian region (in particular, via links with Japan[30]) and the wider global system (in particular, via the USA).

The post-cold war period has seen extant debates within the ASEAN countries reordered. In brief, we can point to a greater concern for the nature of the East Asian region and the implications of regional dynamics for the countries of Southeast Asia, which together unpack as a series of issues: the nature of the economic role of Japan; the nature of the growing role of China; the issue of security (and the related issue of the role of the USA); and the wider issue of the implications of the development of APEC, the WTO and the drive for globalization (issues made more urgent by the crisis).

In the 1980s there has been significant Japanese investment in Thailand, Malaysia, Singapore and Indonesia. There has also been inward investment from the Northeast Asian NICs, Taiwan and South Korea. The links between the countries of ASEAN and Greater China are both historically well established, growing and economically significant. It is clear that there are now extensive economic linkages binding the countries of ASEAN into the developing East Asian region. In the discussions surrounding these developments, the possible leadership role of Japan is familiar, and familiarly problematical.[31]

Yet, at the present time, in the context of Southeast Asian politics the emergence of China is the more awkward issue. The four modernizations inaugurated by Deng in 1978 have seen the Chinese economy expand rapidly. China has a growing role within the East Asian region. However, there are problems in the relationship of China with the countries of ASEAN; symptomatically, the disinclination of China to deal with the ASEAN countries on a multilateral basis in respect of the putative oil reserves in the area of the South China Sea, implausibly claimed by China and bordered directly by Vietnam, the Philippines and Malaysia. The issue of the relationship of the countries of ASEAN with China is made more awkward by the security concerns of the ASEAN countries in the context of American post-cold war thinking. China continues to upgrade its armed forces (one of Deng's four modernizations) and the countries of ASEAN are also investing in advanced weapon systems.

In recent years a key challenge has been made by the proponents of globalization. The routine demands of the USA have found a particular institutional vehicle in APEC. The role of APEC has been problematical for the ASEAN countries as the political elites of the region have felt obliged to run with the American agenda whilst simultaneously nursing anxieties about the apparently negative implications for ASEAN. A common formal affirmation seems to have been made to the goal of 'open regionalism'. However, the APEC project may turn out to be a victim of the recent setbacks to the neoliberal project of global deregulation, liberalization and free trade, namely the Asian financial crisis and the WTO debacle in Seattle in November 1999.

It is clear that the Asian financial crisis has had a dramatic impact upon the countries of ASEAN. There has been economic damage throughout the region. In Thailand, there has been economic retrenchment and social distress. In Malaysia, an independent-minded prime minister has rejected the orthodox Washington Consensus model and secured a measure of economic success. In Indonesia, economic crisis has run over into social and political crisis. The ASEAN countries were not able to respond collectively to the demands of the financial crisis. However, the organization has held together and there are signs that it might be changing. The accession of Burma occasioned a rethink about the 'ASEAN way' principle of non-interference. The principle has been called into question further by the participation of regional forces in the UN peacekeeping mission to East Timor. Overall, ASEAN now embraces all the countries of Southeast Asia and there are, perhaps, signs that the organization is reordering its concerns to meet novel challenges.[32] Again, one might anticipate the countries of ASEAN paying rather more attention to the situation of the East Asian region in the future.

EAST ASIA: THE INTERMESHING OF GLOBAL, REGIONAL AND LOCAL

The changes within East Asia considered above have been discussed in terms of a trio of intermeshing historical logics (the long drive for modernity, a developing concern for regionalism and the recent abrupt eruption of systemic crisis). The interplay of these historical logics has shaped domestic national patterns of change and regional changes. It is also clear that there is a wider aspect to these logics, one that embraces the broader dynamic of the global system. The relationship of the East Asian region to the wider global system has been the subject of much recent discussion. At first these debates were somewhat abstract (talk about globalization) but, more recently, they have become intensely practical (as the shock of the Asian financial crisis unfolded). In broad terms the recent patterns of change in the global system have opened up a series of interrelated issues: first, the nature of globalization; second, the aetiology of the Asian financial crisis; and, third, the character, role and desired reform of key international financial institutions.

The Debate about Globalization

The fashionable 1990s' idea of globalization purports to capture the essential character of the contemporary global system, namely that the reach of the liberal-market system is now worldwide and that an integrated global system is in process of construction. The advocates of globalization base the core of their efforts within the intellectual territory of orthodox market-liberal economic theory and thus represent their work as positive social science. The literature on globalization is vast. However, two points can be made: first, the core of the arguments advanced relate to claimed changes in patterns of economic life (here, as Hirst and Thompson[33] make clear, the empirical plausibility of the claims is low, indeed it is better to speak of a relatively restricted set of internationalized economic activities); and, second, the broad globalization package of ideas recalls the earlier 1950s' 'logic of industrialization' material, and it is better (if social scientific knowledge is our concern) to view the core assertions of globalization theory as the political rhetoric of the servants of the US-centred liberal-market system.[34] The talk is, therefore, prescriptive rather than descriptive. All of which has been rehearsed in the context of discussions about the nature of the development experience of East Asia.[35] It is a debate which has been revisited in recent years in the wake of the episode of the financial crisis in East Asia.

The Debate about the Asian Financial Crisis

The debate about the Asian financial crisis can be grasped in terms of two broad lines of reflection; the first speaks of crony capitalism, and the second looks to the problems of inappropriate liberalization. The first line of argument, deeply informed by the nostrums of the Washington Consensus, has suggested that the rapid economic growth of recent years fostered a peculiarly ill-disciplined version of capitalism, so called 'crony capitalism'. In this perspective the root cause of the financial crisis was to be found in those fundamentally corrupt Asian business and political practices which militated against the efficient functioning of the market. The crisis was therefore seen as a necessary corrective, an occasion for the establishment of more market-liberal informed institutional structures and policy stances.

The second line of argument, informed by the resources of historical/structural analysis, looks to the intermeshing of the different economic logics of the competitive liberal-market capitalism of the USA and the developmental capitalism of East Asia in the particular context of financial market liberalization (urged upon East Asian governments by the proponents/institutions of the Washington Consensus). In this perspective, the root cause of the crisis was an inappropriate financial liberalization which exposed otherwise successful economies to the vagaries of the international speculative financial market.

The arguments of the proponents of the Washington Consensus are of limited interest (notwithstanding genuine domestic problems in some East Asian countries) as they are cast in terms of a putatively universal market-liberal model which is not intellectually credible. The Asian financial crisis is not leading (and will not lead) the countries of East Asia to converge upon the American model; rather elites will read, react and adjust as new domestic agendas are established. However, one new area of reflection, as elites read and react, is the nature of the fundamental architecture of the global trading and financial system.

The Debate about Global Trading and Financial Architecture

In the years following the end of the Bretton Woods system, the project of the New Right, advocated in a number of countries and international financial institutions in the 1980s, pressed for deregulation of the sphere of economic life in the expectation that the vigour of marketplace activity would benefit the broader populations of countries (improving material levels of living, social organization and political life). The global financial system has seen extensive deregulation and liberalization in the 1980s and 1990s. The Washington Consensus has encouraged this process. The results have been mixed and serious problems have emerged.

It is possible to identify deep-seated problems and more acute crises. A series of examples of deep-seated problems could be noted: first, in the UK, Keynesian theorists have pointed out that the deregulated 1980s and 1990s have seen more financial instability, higher unemployment and lower long-term growth rates than the earlier 1950s and 1960s, when the model of the state-regulated mixed economy informed policymaking; second, in the less-developed countries of sub-Saharan Africa there has been a regression in levels of living; and third, at a macro-level there have been widespread environmental problems (the consequences of underregulated economic activity). It is also clear that the era has seen a series of more acute crises; there have been serious problems in the European Union (the exchange rate mechanism crisis of 1992), in Mexico (the currency crisis of 1995), in East Asia (the financial crisis of 1997) and in the USA (the collapse and government-led rescue of the Long Term Capital Management hedge fund, in 1998). The future of the global financial architecture is now in question, as the recently unquestioned dominance of the free market position is challenged.

The debates about the deep-seated problems are important (and often rather familiar; for example, issues of development and environment). The debates about the recent series of crises are less routinized (even if the debates of today repeat those of earlier years). In particular, the financial crises of recent years have occasioned debate about revisiting the residual machineries of the old Bretton Woods system in order to fashion a set of institutions which could govern the contemporary global economic system. In this context, the claims of the market-liberals to the inevitability of deregulation, liberalization and ever-freer trade (the Washington Consensus position) have been challenged by those who would claim that the global system is both malintegrated and made up of a diversity of forms of life with differing economic logics, patterns of social organization and cultural expectations, and who therefore suggest that necessary revision to the residual machineries of the Bretton Woods system might best be secured through dialogue amongst all the interested parties.

In respect of East Asia, this opens up a wide agenda and two general points can be made; first, the East Asian region is powerful, and second, the issue of regional interlinkages is complex. On the first point, Zysman[36] argues that each macro-region has a powerful economy, a secure social structure and a strong science base, and can generate autonomous growth. The regions are different and internally diverse, especially East Asia. Therefore, on the second, Zysman captures the difficulties of the issues surrounding trade liberalization by suggesting that 'in the years to come, the politics of trade, defined broadly, will be about reconciling differently structured political economies that express different values'.[37]

In general, if we want to speculate about the future of East Asia, then, analytically, it seems that we need to grasp the logics of historical change running through the region, and, thereafter, substantively, we must elucidate the detail of what seems to be a slow movement towards a regionalized future.

CONCLUSION: EAST ASIAN LOGICS OF CHANGE

In the wake of the collapse of the political–cultural project of state socialism in the former USSR, the related ending of the cold war in Europe, and its further reduction in salience within East Asia, commentators working within or with reference to the classical European tradition of social theorizing have been faced with the unexpected task of coming to terms with a global system that presents a number of competing analytical challenges. Thus, it is clear that the global system is home to a great diversity of forms of life, where particular patterns of economic life are embedded within distinctive social institutional structures and reflexively grasped in terms of the resources of specific cultural and political traditions. It is also clear that the global system can be described in terms of the existence of three macro-regions; that is, East Asia, North America and the European Union. At the same time, in opposition to this, the proponents of globalization routinely affirm the convergence of the diversity of available forms of life upon the single model of liberal industrial capitalism found in North America.

The classical European tradition of social theorizing is concerned with the critical elucidation of the dynamics of complex change in the ongoing shift to the modern world. The central preoccupation of the tradition is with grasping the structural logics of change that order the lives of distinct communities, states and regions. In this perspective the enthusiastic proponents of globalization look foolish at best or, more critically, merely narrowly partisan.

The logics of change which have shaped patterns of development in East Asia over the long years following the Pacific War can be summarily grasped in terms of three timescales: first, the business of the ongoing shift to the modern world; second, the post-cold war reordering of blocs in favour of a regionalized system; and third, the abrupt confusions of the financial crisis. The political elites of the states within the region must endeavour (as they always have) to read and react to changing structural circumstances. The pursuit of national political–cultural projects rooted in the domestic aspirations to modernity conceived by elites in the exchange of indigenous cultural resources with the demands of the irruption of industrial capitalism (almost invariably variations on the themes of economic growth and social welfare), have found expression in recent years in deepening economic, social and cultural linkages within the region. An element of elite selfconsciousness is evident in the proliferating round of meetings devoted to the business of East Asia and the region's relationships with North America and the European Union. The confusions of the episode of financial crisis are likely to reinforce both a sense of solidarity within the region, and an appreciation of the continuing vigour of the North American-sponsored drive towards globalization.

The contemporary situation in East Asia can be characterized in terms of the logics of change underpinning patterns of life within particular countries and their complex regional intermeshing. The economic core of the regions is, at the present time, Japan, and while the political elite has received a wealth of advice (from the USA, in particular) urging the necessity of radical liberal-market-oriented reforms, there is little reason to suppose that there will be any significant change. The logic of the modern Japanese system was put in place during the Meiji Restoration. It has been a success. Indeed, the most recent expression of this success, the planned export-oriented drive for national reconstruction following the Pacific War, which has given us the notion of the 'developmental state', has been exported around the East Asian region. In China, which has borrowed the strategy of export-oriented development and moulded it to its own historically specific circumstances, we might expect the slow process of economic reform and opening to the wider system to continue. This is also true of the NICs, where we might anticipate modest domestic reform in the wake of the financial crisis and greater interest in the region. Finally, in the ASEAN countries, which were the most badly hit by the recent crisis, we can expect a renewed affirmation of the goals of growth and development, along with a greater concern for the context of the region. Overall, it seems that the nascent region of East Asia will continue to crystallize, following its own logics and assuming its own patterns.

NOTES

1. A longer differently focused version of this argument appeared in *Contemporary Southeast Asia* (2000), **22** (2).
2. For an overview see M. Yahuda (1996), *The International Politics of the Asia-Pacific*, London: Routledge.
3. See P. W. Preston (1998), *Pacific Asia in the Global System*, Oxford: Blackwell.
4. S. Ishihara (1991), *The Japan that Can Say No*, London: Simon and Shuster. See also Mahathir Mohamad and S. Ishihara (1995), *The Voice of Asia*, Tokyo: Kodansha.
5. These matters are illuminatingly discussed by Ernest Gellner (1964), *Thought and Change*, London: Weidenfeld.
6. I have pursued these matters at length elsewhere. For a short discussion see P. W. Preston (1996), *Development Theory*, Oxford: Blackwell; in particular, parts one and two.

7. See M. Bernard (1996), 'Regions in the global political economy: beyond the local–global divide in the formation of the East Asian region', *New Political Economy*, **1** (3).
8. See P. Karhonen (1997), 'Monopolizing Asia: The politics of a metaphor', *The Pacific Review*, **10** (3). See also R. Higgot and R. Stubbs (1995), 'Competing conceptions of economic regionalism: APEC versus EAEC in the Asia Pacific', *Review of International Political Economy*, **2** (3).
9. G. Delanty (1995), *Inventing Europe: Idea, Identity and Reality*, London: Macmillan.
10. A. G. Frank (1998), *Re-Orient: Global Economy in the Asian Age*, University of California Press.
11. An interesting review of US involvement is offered by Bruce Cummings (1999), *Parallax Visions: Making Sense of American–East Asian Relations at the End of the Century*, Duke University Press.
12. An idea I derive freely from the work of Ferdnand Braudel.
13. See, for example, F. Gibney (1998), *Unlocking the Bureaucrats Kingdom*, Washington, Brookings.
14. See, for example, the work of Chalmers Johnson, Ron Dore or Robert Wade. Kyoko Sheridan argues directly that the Japanese should seek local solutions to their problems rather than aping outsiders with their calls for market solutions. See K. Sheridan (1998), 'Japan's Economic System', in K. Sheridan (ed.) (1998), *Emerging Economic Systems in Asia*, St Leonards: Allen & Unwin.
15. Ibid.
16. R. Taggart-Murphy (2000), 'Japan's economic crisis', *New Left Review*.
17. J. Clammer (1997), *Contemporary Urban Japan: A Sociology of Consumption*, Oxford: Blackwell.
18. Ron Dore (1997), *Japan, Internationalism and the UN*, London, Routledge.
19. Julie Gilson (1999), 'Japan's Role in the Asia Europe Meeting', *Asian Survey,* **39** (5), pp. 735–52.
20. Cummings (1999).
21. See Barrington Moore Jnr (1966), *The Social Origins of Dictatorship and Democracy*, Boston: Beacon.
22. F. Christiansen and S. Rai (1996), *Chinese Politics and Society*, London: Prentice Hall; K. Lieberthal (1995), *Governing China: From Revolution Through Reform*, New York, Norton.
23. E. J. Perry and M. Selden (eds) (2000), *Chinese Society: Change, Conflict and Resistance*, London: Routledge.
24. H. W. Maull (1997), 'Reconciling China with International Order', *The Pacific Review*, **10** (4).
25. R. Taylor (1996), *Greater China and Japan: Prospects for an Economic Parnership in East Asia*, London: Routledge.
26. It might also be noted that this US involvement had its price: (i) in Korea in the form of an unnecessary catastrophic war (see Bruce Cummings (1997), *Korea's Place in the Sun*, New York: Norton); and (ii) in Taiwan in the form of the unlooked for arrival of the remnants of the Kuomindang.
27. M. Rhodes and R. Higgot (2000), 'Introduction: Asian crises and the myth of capitalist convergence', *The Pacific Review*, **13** (1).
28. Ibid. See also R. Higgot (1998), 'The Asian economic crisis: a study in the politics of resentment', *New Political Economy*, **3** (3).
29. L. Weiss (2000), 'Developmental states in transition: adapting, dismantling, innovating, not "normalizing"', *The Pacific Review*, **13** (1).
30. On this see, for example, Denis Yasutomo (1986), *The Manner of Giving: Strategic Aid and Japanese Foreign Policy*, Lexington: Heath; Alan Rix (1993), *Japan's Foreign Aid*, London: Routledge; Peter Katzenstein and T. Shirashi (eds) (1997), *Network Power: Japan and Asia*, Cornell University Press.
31. P. W. Preston (1995), 'Domestic inhibitions to a leadership role for Japan in Pacific Asia', *Contemporary Southeast Asia*, **16** (4).
32. H. Mutalib (1997), 'At thirty ASEAN looks to challenges in the new millennium', *Contemporary Southeast Asia*, **19** (1).

33. P. Hirst and G. Thompson (1996), *Globalization in Question*, Cambridge: Polity.

34. The 1950s saw a period of enthusiams for the model of the USA (within the USA, certainly) which found expression in an interrelated set of social scientific theories. The key was the notion of the logic of industrialism which, it was claimed, best grasped the core of the modern system (rather than talking about capitalism or socialism). The logic was universal and all variant economic systems could be expected to converge. The system, it was claimed, would also be successful and high levels of consumption would lead to an end of ideology. The poor countries of the Third World would also be subject to this universal logic and they would experience modernization. The approach had little intellectual merit and it was fatally undermined by the confusions of the 1960s and 1970s.

35. See World Bank (1993), *The East Asian Miracle*, Oxford University Press; Robert Wade (1996), 'Japan, the World Bank and the art of paradigm maintenance', *New Left Review*, **217**.

36. J. Zysman (1996), 'The myth of a global economy', *New Political Economy*, **1** (2).

37. Ibid., p. 180.

PART V

Conclusion

12. Europe–Asia linkages: notes towards an historical/structural research agenda

Peter W. Preston

INTRODUCTION

The chapters in this volume presented above have made it clear that there is much to debate in the matter of Europe–Asia linkages, for not only do the two regions have a wealth of substantive connections but the very conceptual language which can be used to grasp these matters is in question. The precise characterization of Europe, Asia and their interconnections is not a simple matter; rather it is clear that there are radically different strategies available. Indeed, this point might be made more generally. Thus it can be asserted that social theorists have no direct access to 'reality' and that the world we inhabit is given to us in terms of the conceptual machineries which run through the cultures we inhabit; in brief, theorizing the social world is deeply interpretive. In this concluding chapter I will return to the issue of theorizing regions and their interlinkages, and sketch the outlines of an historical/structural agenda for scholarly enquiry. Such an agenda will represent a particular interpretation of the still-unfolding exchange of commentary and events. It will reflect the subtle interchange between the onward rush of events and the ways in which we grasp and order these patterns of activity.

We might begin by noting that, at the present time, a series of recent and ongoing changes within the global system have been identified: (i) the very sharp reforms in the hitherto socialist states of Central and Eastern Europe (1989/91); (ii) the sequence of broadly integrative changes in East Asia (1979/1985/1991); (iii) the accelerating integration of the European Union (1985/1991/1999); and (iv) the slow relative decline of the USA. The sequence of changes have seen the intermingling of the very dramatic (as with the opening of the Berlin Wall, an event which commanded attention throughout the worlds of popular commentary and scholarship) and the more subtle and long drawn out (as in the case of the changes in East Asia, which have been the hotly contested concern of more restricted communities of scholarship and policy analysis). However we might come to summarize this spread of changes, it is clear that they have formed the general context within which the present interest in regionalism is being pursued.

The present interest in regionalism has a particular intellectual and political centre of gravity in the international political–economic analysis of shifting geoeconomic patterns. As the old familiar territory of the cold war falls away into history the present becomes not less but more problematical. A series of cross-cutting tendencies have been identified, routinely encapsulated in the trio of notions 'globalization', 'regionalization' and 'localization', which point to a new spread of exchanges between the ongoing American drive to order the global system according to neoliberal nostrums, various projects of regional accommodation and resistance, and the continuing centrality for the bulk of humankind of the local and circumscribed realm of ordinary life. In turn, within this new and shifting intellectual and political context, there is increasing interest in the interchange between the internal dynamics and regional interlinkages of the European Union and East Asia. The exchange has a routine double aspect, as patterns of change within one or other region generate particular interests in the other, which thereafter look to find expression. The fundamental logic of this exchange is not new, and we may recall, for example, that in the nineteenth century the expansion of European colonial power within the East Asian region was driven by domestic material demands, and theorized/legitimated by quite specific discursive constructs, and the response of the various regional elites similarly flowed out of domestic dynamics. In the twenty-first century we can find a similarly complex intermeshing of domestic, regional and international concerns.[1]

SOME RECENT DEBATES RECALLED

I have argued elsewhere that reflexivity is a necessary condition of scholarship.[2] The claim unpacks both procedurally (by calling attention to those habits of reflexive criticism which ensure that arguments are made self-consciously) and comparatively (where the claim can be made that what typifies scholarship is precisely the centrality of this procedure, in contrast, for example, to policy analysts, journalists or political actors, all of whom, it might reasonably be supposed, are driven by more immediately practical concerns).

In the context of the idea of procedural reflection, it can be asserted that it is crucial to enquiry to be clear about the constitutive assumptions of particular lines of argument making. The sets of assumptions which we affirm in order to make our explicit arguments are taken from disciplinary traditions, in turn lodged within wider cultural contexts that are rich in meaning. If we set up our questions without attending to their constitutive assumptions then we are at risk of reproducing schedules of taken-for-granted ideas and prejudices in our own scholarly work. It might also be suggested, relatedly, that the concern for the critical inspection of constitutive assumptions is most acutely necessary, and most readily addressed, when an area of enquiry is in process of establishment. The contemporary discussion of the linkages between Europe and East Asia is of quite recent origin, that is, it postdates the end of the cold war in Europe.³ It can also be noted both that much popular Anglo-American debate is neoliberal, one way or another, and that counter-agendas can be established, both from within the classical European tradition of social theorizing (the tradition which the author inhabits) and from the available resources lodged in the cultures and concerns of others.

Start Point One: Popularly Noted Change(s)

The profound reordering of the global system which marked, in Hobsbawm's terms⁴, the end of the 'short twentieth century' has been grasped most energetically by the Anglo-American proponents of the power of the liberal marketplace whose work finds expression in two lines of commentary; the celebration of 'globalization' and the related explorations of the notion of 'postmodernity'.

It is routinely asserted, at the present time, that the global system has seen sweeping changes in recent years. The proponents of globalization argue that the American neoliberal economic, social and political system (and the political–cultural project both embedded within and constituting this system) is now both intellectually pre-eminent and substantively without alternative (either existing or in prospect).

In a similar fashion, it is routinely asserted that the global system has undergone a fundamental transformation in recent years of its most basic constitutive logics. The proponents of the notion of postmodernism assert that the global economic system has moved far beyond historically familiar problems of material production (with associated problems of scarcity and distribution) into the novel realm of expressive (ideational) consumption.

Start Point Two: Popularly Noted Events

If the notions of globalization and postmodernity, which point to the broadest of systemic and cultural changes, comprise one element of the context of debates about Europe and Asia, then a second element is to be found in the reception of a series of more specific events: the collapse of the USSR, the reforms in China and the recent Asian financial crisis.

The political–cultural project of 'state socialism' was affirmed by the USSR from its inception in 1917 through to its dissolution in 1991. The debate, in respect of the largely unanticipated collapse of the USSR and the Eastern bloc, has produced a series of interlinked lines of explanation, citing, in particular, economic stagnation, political stasis and historical accident. First, in respect of economics, it has been suggested that the Soviet system had become economically stagnant and unable to meet the aspirations of its population, and this structural circumstance was the fundamental occasion of collapse. Second, with respect to politics, the Soviet system became politically moribund and experienced a legitimation/motivation crisis such that the political classes were unable to formulate and deploy effective plans to deal with what might otherwise have been perfectly soluble problems. Third, with respect to historical accident, it might be suggested that whilst the demise of the Soviet system was occasioned by structural circumstances, the precise path of events was influenced by a series of entirely accidental developments, including the over-optimism of the Gorbachev reforms, the revolutions in Eastern Europe and the chaotic rule of Boris Yeltsin.

In China the government has been pursuing 'market-oriented' economic and social reforms since the late seventies. The earliest phases of the programme involved the establishment of Special Economic Zones in a series of coastal locations in southern China, and the programme has subsequently broadened as the Chinese government has pursued its own version of the familiar export-oriented development path overseen by a developmental state. The upshot of the reforms in China has been a long period of rapid economic growth, which has seen extensive reforms in rural and urban areas as domestic and overseas capital has been put to use within a newly market-friendly environment. The reforms in the rural areas have been successful, and the pattern of cooperatives has been largely abandoned as farmers have shifted to family farms and market-oriented production. In urban areas, the reforms have been rather more problematical, with old established industries finding it difficult to renew themselves and the extensive system of state-owned enterprises remaining an area urgently in need of reform.

It is clear that the reform programme established in the late seventies by Deng Xiaoping has been widely successful, notwithstanding problems in the pronounced regional nature of development (where the coastal and eastern regions have prospered while the inland and western regions have not advanced so quickly), with inequality within society increasing and a flow of migrants into the newly burgeoning coastal and eastern towns. One particular aspect of the reforms in China has been the development of linkages with the regional economic system and the wider global system. The Chinese economy has growing links with Japan and with the EU and USA. In this context, it might be noted that the 'Chinese sphere in East Asia (encompassing, for present purposes, China, Hong Kong, Taiwan, Singapore and the Southeast

Asian diaspora of the 'Overseas Chinese') is economically powerful, and, indeed, seems largely to have escaped the more serious impacts of the recent Asian financial crisis.

The recent Asian financial crisis has reinforced recent interest in East Asia. A tangled debate followed, with proponents of neoliberalism speaking in terms of the inevitable costs of crony capitalism whilst those disposed to work with reference to the European tradition have looked to slow patterns of structural change and the deleterious impact of Western-sponsored deregulation and liberalization, which exposed the region to the vagaries of the international money markets. The debate continues but has, interestingly, broadened as the ways in which the global economic system is ordered have come into open question.

All these events have been absorbed into the debate about the global system. The implications of the collapse of the political–cultural project of state socialism for European patterns of political understanding have been profound. The Manichean simplicities of cold war rhetoric, which pitted the realm of Western freedom against the Soviet sphere of state-sponsored 'unfreedom', have fallen away to leave space for new thinking. The reforms in China have reinforced this tendency, notwithstanding residual debates around the nature of the Chinese political system. The American response has, in significant measure, been triumphalist. However, in Europe there has been a political–cultural turn away from Washington (and the whole post-Second World War liberal-trading settlement) towards Brussels (with its developing regionalism). A similar concern for regionalism is evident in East Asia.

Start Point Three: Popularly Drawn Conclusions

A series of more elaborated political/theoretical claims are attached to these interrelated exercises, concerning change and noting certain events: (i) that the West 'won the cold war'; (ii) that the ethico-political end of history has been secured in liberal-democratic capitalist systems; (iii) that the evident diversity of the global system will diminish over time in a process of convergence; and (iv) the post-Second World War aspiration to state-controlled development is now definitively superseded in the final victory of the neoliberal marketplace.

It has been widely asserted that the west 'won the cold war'. The claim has a particular plausibility, in that the cold war saw two elite-ordered systems in broad competition until one unilaterally withdrew, that is the USSR, and thereafter collapsed. The cold war competition had a series of aspects: military (there was a sustained arms race), economic (there was an equally sustained competition in respect of material levels of living), diplomatic (with both sides looking to win allies amongst the non-committed) and ideological (with both sides deploying elaborate official ideologies through a variety of media. The whole exchange could be summarized as a competition between two political–cultural projects, liberalism and socialism, both of which derived from the early phases of the shift to the modern world in Europe.

It might be noted, in this vein, that a routinely unacknowledged corollary of the end of the cold war is that, as East and West mutually defined each other, the West now has no convenient external enemy, or, more strongly, any overriding reason to continue with the political–cultural project of 'the West' (as Westerners have understood it over the long post-Second World War period). It might be noted that the project of the 'West' was orchestrated by the USA, vehicled politically through the rhetoric and institutions of cold war, and ordered economically through the machineries of the Bretton Woods system. That settlement, its associated systems and the political–cultural project which animated them, is now in question. It can be argued that if the project of 'the West' is to continue then it will require a new process of self-definition against external enemies, as the group of countries/regions embraced within the term 'the West' are diverse and home to equally diverse political–cultural projects. The alternative, of course, is that it will collapse in turn and, in this particular context, one notes with interest the developing tension between, on the one hand, the continuing US predilection for its neoliberal market project (as with the WTO, for example) and the increasing regionalization of the global system, including, most relevantly, the increasing disposition evident in European and East Asian political actors to assert their own interests over the routine affirmations of US-sponsored neoliberal goals.

In the wake of the collapse of the political–cultural project of state socialism in Eastern Europe, the theorist Francis Fukuyama[5] announced that the ethico-political end of history had been secured in the worldwide pre-eminence of liberal-democracy. The argument affirmed that, henceforth, all political debate would have to be conducted within the conceptual sphere delimited by liberal-democracy; that is, there are no alternative ways of thinking about political life. The argument gained immediate attention with certain political groups who found the message congenial, though others found it less to their taste. One could revisit the material and affirm both that Fukuyama's intervention was amusing and that, on relatively little reflection, it was implausible. At a distance it seems clear that the work was yet another expression of the familiar (indeed, within the territory encompassed by the political–cultural project of the West, widely taken-for-granted) ideology of Americanism. As the nineties have unfolded, the Fukuyama's latent 'convergence theory' has not found support; indeed, as regions develop, the reverse has been true.

The continuing diversity of the global system has been read in terms of its anticipated decline over time in the face of the unavoidable logic of liberalism. This is a revisited 'convergence theory'. The argument looks to patterns of development lodged within the economic and social world such that the presently imagined end-point of extant processes is a fundamentally unitary neoliberal economic system within which diverse cultures will retain a decorative/expressive function.

A final popularly drawn conclusion has been made; namely, that the post-Second World War aspiration to state-sponsored social engineering (of either state-socialist or mixed-economy forms) is now definitively superseded in a final recognition of the power of the liberal marketplace. The argument neglects the rule-based nature of the market system and the extensive planning that secures its order (the machineries of national governments, with their intimate links to corporate interests and the wider apparatus of the IMF, World Bank, WTO and so on). Any suggestion that the neoliberal market system is the unplanned spontaneous outcome of a myriad of private decisions is simply foolish.

Overall, in sum, one can report that the decade of the nineties was dominated within the Anglo-American sphere (that is, the USA and the English-speaking countries) by a pervasive neoliberalism which found expression both in the high politics of state policymaking and within the sphere of popular culture, where any concern for the future was submerged within a market-vehicled celebration of unrestricted consumption. Yet, viewed in the longer run, the present situation (where economic success is conjoined with political confidence, both marked by relatively quiet public debate) recalls the years of the fifties; the period when, it was claimed, the logic of industrialism was fostering a systemic convergence of social systems in a preference for consumption such that it could be announced that the West had seen the 'end of ideology'. Alastair MacIntyre[6] commented, at the time, that maybe the problem was not that ideology (and thus debate) had come to an end but rather that there were no good ideologies around to debate. Shortly thereafter, of course, the confidence of that post-Second World War period collapsed as the USA entered a period of great domestic and overseas conflict.

It might be sensible, therefore, both to note the confidence of the proponents of globalization, postmodernity and the ethico-political end of history, and also to move on to look for intellectually more secure alternative agendas for the future. A series of counter-positions can be asserted, and here I will consider three, rather disparate, lines of reflection: (i) a counter-position derived formally from the resources of the classical European tradition; (ii) a counter-position derived from reflection upon the debate surrounding the recent Asian financial crisis; and (iii) a counter-position(s) which might be derived from resources local to the region.

Counter-Agenda One (Formally Derived): The Work of the Classical European Tradition of Social Theorizing

All the three starting points of reflection (popularly noted changes, popularly noted events and popularly drawn conclusions), indicate sets of ideas which find expression not merely within the sphere of popular opinion but also within political, policy-analytical and scholarly work. Yet, equally clearly, the neoliberal globalization/postmodernist strategy of analysis which these popular views either embody or express is not unproblematic; indeed many would regard it as deeply unpersuasive.[7]

A counter-position can be asserted that is based in the classical European tradition of social theorizing. The tradition can be characterized in terms of a trio of notions: (i) historical occasion (the sets of circumstances which gave rise to the tradition); (ii) the formal character of work within the tradition (that is, the typical argument machineries deployed); and (iii) substantive preoccupations (the sets of questions asked by theorists working within the tradition).

The historical occasion of the classical European tradition can be found in the late eighteenth- and early nineteenth-century-concerns of intellectuals to grasp selfconsciously the patterns of change enfolding and running through the societies in which they lived. Sydney Pollard[8] speaks of an alliance of interest between the rising commercial and industrial bourgeoisie, on the one hand, and the intellectual theorists, on the other. Quite how this ambiguous relationship played out over time is another matter[9], but the early exchange saw the first attempt to theorize the historical and structural process of the 'shift to the modern world'.[10]

The formal character of the classical European tradition can be summarily characterized as interpretive (where there is a concern to locate arguments within wider cultural contexts), critical (where the work is routinely ethically engaged), dialogic (such that work is oriented to discourse within the public sphere) and interdisciplinary (such that arguments are drawn and deployed from the full range of the sphere of reflection upon the social). The tradition is, therefore, quite different from the more familiar professionalized disciplines of social science which, typically, lay claim to a restricted sphere of technical knowledge that can be made available within the knowledge marketplace. The tradition is also diverse. There are a variety of national traditions in Europe and each has its own preoccupations and typical relations with the central axes of social power in the state, market and polity.[11] Yet, it would also be true to say that the years following the end of the Second World War saw a period when the influence of the USA was strong. However, the strength of that particular influence waned with the emergence of political and intellectual confusions within the USA in the decade of the 1960s.

In substantive terms, the central preoccupation of the classical European tradition is with the analysis of complex change; that is, the ways in which various agent groups have read and reacted to enfolding structural circumstances in the process of the ongoing construction of the modern world of diverse industrial capitalisms. The shift to the modern world has been episodic, uneven and often violent (and these matters should not be confused with the anodyne tales of US 'modernization theory' with its reassuring scheme of the smooth evolutionary movement towards the model of, in effect, the USA). It is a shift which is ongoing in the double sense that the dynamics driving systemic change are still in place and the present global system is not the end of history (so to speak).

A series of recent restatements of the forms and concerns of the tradition can be identified[12], but at the present time the long-established interest of the classical European tradition in the analysis of complex change has found a new influential expression in the work of critical international political economy.[13] In sum, if we turn to the classical European tradition then we generate two lines of reflection: (i) formal (how to analyse patterns of change); and (ii) substantive (what seems to be the case at the present).

In respect of the first issue, it may be asserted that scholars, like citizens, cannot step outside the culture they inhabit. In respect of the liberal theorist's aspirations to a secure grounding of enquiry in the putative givens of human nature, and thus, by extension, a universality of application of the results generated, it is safe to assert, from within the classical European tradition, that the most that can be sought is a reflexive appreciation of the constitutive assumptions of substantive analyses (which will be culturally context-bound) as the basis for dialogue with others.

In respect of the second issue, the debate is one between those who would affirm the power of the putatively universal assumptions of liberalism (the likely unrestricted spread of liberal-market relations) and those who would affirm the preference of the classical European tradition for analysis cast in terms of the historical–structural dynamics of the global system, in which case the dynamics of the system, the nature of the regions within it and the implications of current changes (properly understood) for the governments and citizens of individual countries become key questions.

An agenda derived from formal reflection on the resources of the classical European tradition would look to the analysis of complex change in the ongoing shift to the modern world, which we can unpack in terms of the dynamics of shifting structural changes and agent-group reactions. As elites read and react to changing enfolding structural circumstances they will plot a route to the future and mobilize their populations accordingly. The history of the ongoing shift to the modern world can be told, therefore, in terms of changing structures and the various projects of key agents. It is an episodic history, a series of discontinuous phases, and it is ongoing.

Counter-Agenda Two (Substantively Derived): The Crisis, the Nature of Regions and the Issue of Global Regulation

A counter-agenda is available in recent debate about the Asian financial crisis. The episode has been addressed in a variety of ways within the region.[14] It has been addressed within the Western community in terms of two sharply differing diagnoses: (i) a liberal-market analysis, which has spoken of failings in the development of the market in the region and diagnosed the root of the crisis in terms of a notion of crony capitalism; and (ii) an international political–economic analysis, which has spoken of the unfortunate and destabilizing effects of ill-advised liberalization upon the distinctive 'high-debt' models of the region.

The first line of argument, deeply informed by the nostrums of the Washington Consensus, has suggested that rapid growth in recent years fostered a peculiarly ill-disciplined version of capitalism, so called 'crony capitalism'. In this perspective, the root cause of the Asian financial crisis was to be found in fundamentally corrupt Asian business and political practices. The crisis was, therefore, seen as a necessary corrective, an occasion for the implementation of more liberal-market rational institutional structures and policy stances.

The second line of argument, informed by the resources of international political economy, looks to the intermeshing of two different economic logics – that of the competitive capitalism of the USA and the developmental capitalism of East Asia – in the particular context of financial market liberalization (urged upon East Asian governments by the proponents/ institutions of the Washington Consensus). In this perspective, the root cause of the crisis was an inappropriate financial liberalization, which exposed otherwise successful economies to the vagaries of the international speculative financial market.

It should be noted, in order to move discussion forwards, that the Asian financial crisis was only one of a series of economic, social and political crises which have occurred within the global system in the years following the collapse of the broadly social-democratic Bretton Woods settlement in the early 1970s. It is clear that the era of neoliberal enthusiasm has seen a series of acute crises: (i) the problems of the European exchange rate mechanism; (ii) the Mexican currency crisis; (iii) the Asian financial crisis; (iv) the emerging markets crisis; and (v) the Long Term Capital Management hedge fund crisis in the USA. These financial crises have occasioned a debate about revising the residual machineries of the old Bretton Woods system in order to fashion a set of institutions which could govern the global economic system of today. In this context, the claims of the neoliberals to the inevitability of deregulation, liberalization and ever-freer trade (the Washington Consensus position) have been challenged by those who would claim that the global system comprises a diversity of forms of life with differing economic logics, patterns of social organization and cultural expectations, and who therefore suggest that any revision to the residual machineries of the Bretton Woods system might best be secured dialogically.

Overall, an agenda derived from debate surrounding the Asian financial crisis suggests that there is something to argue about in respect of the following: (i) the fundamental logics of diverse regions; (ii) their interlinkages and role within the overall global system; and (iii) the way in which that system might best be managed.

Alternative Agendas Noted

It is possible to identify alternative political–cultural projects for the region. We could speak of the political–cultural projects of a variety of regional elites but, to simplify, we can look at the regional core economy (Japan), at the second tier of NICs, at the third tier of the ASEAN countries and, finally, at the rapidly emerging former-state-socialist countries of the region (in particular, China). On the basis of these distinctive understandings, agendas are developed that express different projects for the development of particular countries and the wider region. Thereafter, it is on the basis of these projects and shared concerns that the political–cultural project of an East Asian region is developing.[15]

Japan is home to the earliest indigenous conceptualization of East Asia. The reforms undertaken by the Meiji oligarchy were extensive but revolved around two key concerns: first, development at home; and, second, security within the Northeast Asian region. The pursuit of development and security involved an extensive process of conceptual relocation, as the Japanese moved out of their secluded historical development trajectory and into the mainstream of a European- and American-dominated global industrial capitalism. An element of this relocation related to their situation *vis-à-vis* the historically long-established regional core; that is, China. As the Japanese elites rethought their situation, they both affirmed the legacy of China, now placed in Japanese hands, and modulated it in terms taken from the West; that is, they deployed a notion of the Orient. On this basis, they laid claim to a priority within the Asian region.[16] The orientation established in the late nineteenth century modulated over the years following the Great War into the militaristic nationalism of the interwar years. However, notwithstanding the reforms inaugurated in the years of SCAP administration, it remains the case that the

Japanese elite, the system they animate and the population which they lead all have a distinctive view of their place in the region and in the wider global system.

This being so, we might note that the enthusiastic neoliberal market theorists, who have read the recent Japanese economic downturn and the subsequent Asian financial crisis as the occasion of a necessary reordering of the Japanese economy, have been resisted by Japanese commentators, who take the view that whatever the precise detail of the reasons for Japanese success over the post-Meiji period these reasons resided in the particularity of the Japanese historical development experience and that, accordingly, it is to these intellectual and institutional resources that the modern Japanese should look.[17]

The second tier of NICs have developed within the context of a market-oriented sphere centred upon the USA, where Japan has been the key local representative, so to say, and has simultaneously offered a distinctive variant of the industrial-capitalist model. The four NICs evidence distinctive forms of life, as each has had its own route to the modern world. In brief, to recapitulate well-known material, South Korea and Taiwan have developed on the basis of Japanese colonial legacies and fairly direct American involvement, at least in the early postwar years, such that they both now have highly developed economies, local populations displaying nationalist sentiment and advancing programmes of political reforms. In contrast, the territories of Hong Kong and Singapore developed, historically, as colonial entrepots of the empire of the British. The two territories have had different experiences over the postwar years, with Singapore attaining an early and unexpected independence, the basis for a rational authoritarian national development project, and Hong Kong pursuing a rather more superficially business-friendly orientation, a stance that appears to have been sustained in the 1997 process of becoming a Special Administrative Region (SAR) of the People's Republic of China. It is in the particular context of the record of the Asian NICs that we meet the notions of the 'developmental state' and the somewhat wider notion of 'developmental capitalism'.[18]

In the third tier, the countries of ASEAN, to simplify once again, emerged in the postwar period from the dissolution of the colonial empires and confronted the dual task of both establishing distinctive identities and pursuing development (the whole business of 'nation-building'). The task was made more difficult by the slow and reluctant final withdrawal of the Europeans and the catastrophic cold-war-inspired involvement of the Americans in Indo-China. In brief, political stability in Southeast Asia was not secured without struggle. The same might be said in respect of the economic development of the countries of the region, where an initial concern for development, cast in the terms current in the 1960s and 1970s (that is, some mix of Keynesian-inspired growth theory, dependency theory derived import substituting industrialization and Third Worldist solidarity) generated a modest success, which has subsequently been significantly built upon with the development of export-oriented industrialization strategies. The role of Japanese aid, trade and foreign direct investment has been important. In this matter, it should be acknowledged that regionally-based capitals and states have been active participants, not merely passive recipients of foreign largesse.[19] In this context, by way of an example, we can note that Malaysia's Prime Minister, Dr Mahathir, has been active in pursuing a model of development that draws on the Japanese experience and, more broadly, has argued an 'Asia for the Asians' case, in which we can note particularly the proposal for an EAEC, the assertion of 'Asian values' and the recent rejection of the US/IMF view of the nature of the regional financial crisis in his decision to reintroduce capital controls.

The Chinese government continues to affirm a distinctive project. The reform programme inaugurated by Deng Xiaoping in 1978 has continued to move forwards. An initial focus on a series of Special Economic Zones (SEZs) has broadened to embrace countrywide economic reform, in both rural and urban areas. Over the last two decades, China has recorded very high growth rates. However, alongside this rapid growth a series of problems have developed; in particular: (i) the movement of population from rural into urban areas; (ii) the emergence of social problems associated both with inward migration to urban areas and the dislocations of the process of marketization; (iii) the development of rising inequalities, both within the economy in general and between regions; and (iv) the changing nature of the Chinese government; in particular, in its dealings with provincial authorities and in its general legitimation with the Chinese population. At the present time, the Chinese government remains committed to an ongoing programme of economic and social reform (the latest expression of this commitment being the talks in respect of Chinese accession to the WTO). The schedule of reforms will be overseen by the machineries of the state.

As we review, in simple fashion, the ongoing dynamics of change within the region it is clear that we can identify a variety of discrete starting points from which to analyse change within East Asia. All of these would be, of course, essentially political–cultural projects.[20] However, the further elaboration of these materials will not be pursued here. Rather the issue is one of identifying key starting points for reflection.

A Start Point for Reflections

All the foregoing reflections can be reduced to a few key ideas. The central claim is that all social scientific analysis is lodged within given intellectual traditions. This being so, a necessary condition of scholarship is reflexive criticism; that is, the selfconscious location of the theorist within the tradition inhabited. The reflections presented in this chapter are lodged within the classical European tradition of social theorizing. The central concern of the classical traditions is with the emancipatory elucidation of the dynamics of complex change. In this perspective, the notion of change becomes a central and difficult concept (in contrast to the evolutionary simplicities of globalization theory), and amongst the repertoire of concepts we can note the ideas of logics of change, phases of development, breaks in development trajectories, political–cultural projects and the notion of the ongoing shift to the modern world, and so on.[21] This repertoire of concepts lets us grasp and characterize both the individual historical trajectories of countries as they shift into the modern world and the overall global pattern thereby generated. The overall pattern generated by countries is of a diversity of forms of industrial capitalisms interacting variously within the global system.

In the perspective of the classical tradition the present circumstances of the global system can be discussed under a series of headings, after the style of Susan Strange[22], which grasp the present pattern generated by the ongoing exchange of structures and agents (in particular, here, states): (i) production (that there has been some regionalization and internationalization of production); (ii) finance (that parts of the global financial system have been significantly internationalized); (iii) security (that post-cold war security agendas are in the process of construction; and (iv) knowledge (that the distribution of scientific knowledge is increasingly uneven. All this can be summed up, after Hirst and Thompson[23], as 'internationalization'. This is an historically contingent configuration; it flows from present patterns of structural power and agent response, and generates a global pattern of diverse, interacting, industrial capitalisms. This is the most general context within which particular agent groups will pursue their future projects. The liberal expectations of a unilinear evolutionary movement towards a single encompassing industrial capitalism - namely globalization - are without foundation.

One aspect of the present global system is its pronounced regional character. In the case of Asia/Europe, all this generates two broad areas of questions: (i) the business of the constitution of regions; and (ii) the business of the linkages between regions.

REGIONS AND INTERREGIONAL LINKAGES

The crucial claim in these debates is that a region is more than a geographical territory; it is a social construct. It can be argued, in a very general fashion, that a region is constituted in the exchange of political–economic, social–institutional, cultural and political structures and the prospective responses of key agent groups. In the present context, the key agent groups will typically be states, multinational companies, firms which trade outside their home base, and, of growing significance, ordinary tourists. The agency of the state might well involve a spread of personnel; politicians and civil servants, plus, of course, related contingents of journalists, advisors and academics. It is clear that there is scope for a multiplicity of contacts between the variously engaged agents and it is from these contacts that the notion of a region, thereafter read into routine practice, will emerge.

Available Analyses of the Logic of Regions

The available literature offers a series of ways of addressing the logic of regionalism, in brief: (i) theories about economic systems; (ii) theories about the necessary logics of interstate relations; (iii) theories about civilizations and societies; (iv) theories about cultural processes; and (v) structural theories detailing historical patterns of development. All these intellectual resources have been deployed at one time or another to grasp the nature of both Europe and East Asia.

(i)   Economic analyses

In the case of the European Union the key agreement has been the Single European Act, which came into force in July 1987, establishing the programme and timetable for the establishment of a single market. In the Treaty of Maastricht, signed in February 1992, a programme of political union was established, and economic and monetary union timetabled. The European Central Bank was established, along with the euro currency, in January 1999. The overall intellectual style of the economic aspects of these treaties, and the debates which surrounded them, is in dispute. It has been claimed that while the overall project of the European Union is distinctively European, in the sense of social or Christian Democratic, the economic machineries are distinctly neoliberal in style. However this debate plays out, it is the case that regional economic integration has been growing within Europe and has been further encouraged by the sequence of recent treaties. In global terms, the European Union is now one of a trio of powerful 'economic spaces' within the global system. It might be added that there has been a long-established debate around the functionalist expectation that economic integration will lead to political integration, the idea of 'spillover'. However, this debate now seems somewhat passé, as the drive for unification within Europe is clearly centrally political and not mechanically derivative of economic changes.[24]

In the case of East Asia, Bernard[25] reports that the available economic approaches include: (i) an ahistorical neoliberalism which looks at economic transactions between national economies and argues for freeing up exchanges; (ii) an ahistorical product cycle theory which looks at slowly evolving regional divisions of labour where a high-tech core slowly offloads outmoded technology, which is then passed down to the periphery (flocks of 'flying geese'); and (iii) an apolitical neo-institutionalism which looks at networks of companies within the region.

It is clear that the lines of analysis all have merit, but none have the intellectual weight to contribute plausibly to an appreciation of the dynamics of the construction of a regional economic space. The neoliberal celebration of liberal-market exchange discards all reference to an idea of historical trajectories, and affirms a notion of the benefits of trade which is oblivious to either the complexities of actually existing patterns or the implausibility of reducing international exchanges to this simple axis. Product-cycle theory correctly points to the rhythms of technological innovation but incorrectly assumes a simple 'well-spring model' of technological innovation; that is, in one central place from which all other users in due course receive benefit when the history of technological innovation reveals a more historically nuanced picture (as with Japanese borrowings from the USA in the 1950s in order to leapfrog the USA, and so on). Neo-institutionalism, which correctly looks to network construction, fails to look at the exchange of companies and governments in the process of building international networks. However, against these approaches, Bernard[26] looks to 'region formation in terms of a number of complex interrelationships: the way the region is linked to both the global and the local; the social relationships that exist both between and within states; the relationship between the material and ideational; and the tensions between forces of integration and disintegration in region formation'.

(ii)   International relations analyses
The main traditions of international relations analysis can be summarized as realist, rationalist and critical.[27] The realist tradition is, it seems safe to suggest, the core tradition. It asserts that state power is the key instrument in identifying and securing state interests within an essentially ruleless global environment. A corollary is that stability requires a hegemonic power. The two remaining strands of reflection point, respectively, to the sets of ethical rules embedded within institutional structures, which thus constrain the use of state power, and to a deep-seated ethical aspiration to progress, which finds expression in various strands of talk about a global community. In the light of these available international-relations traditions, the case of the European Union in the post-Second World War period presents two rather obvious areas of concern: first, the construction of US hegemony in the post-Second World War period, which was associated with the apparatus of cold war; and, second,

the domestic European drive for unification, which has run over the entire postwar period. It is evident that the accidents of war left the USA able to assert its interests over a war-damaged Europe; an exercise legitimated theoretically by realism, politically by the machineries of the cold war and socially (that is, popularly) by the material prosperity associated with the Bretton Woods system. It is also equally evident that the assertion of US priority has been resisted by Europeans. The slow development of the juridical, administrative and political apparatus of the European Union evidences both European determination and caution in respect of American agendas. At the present time the European Union remains militarily dependent upon the USA, a key concern in international relations whatever theoretical line is used, but the economic, social, cultural and political dominance of the USA is diminishing.

In the case of East Asia these debates run rather differently. The main realist tradition of international relations, which looks to the necessary logics of interstate relations, generates the view that regional stability requires a hegemonic power. In East Asia the security system that was in place over the long years of the cold war saw two major powers confronting each other and the USA hegemonic within the richer dynamic market-oriented sphere. The theory thus seems to be vindicated by the practice. And if realism looks to states reaching intergovernmental agreements, then a related line of analysis, which considers the functional demands of economic activity, looks to the slow supranational ordering of regions. Once again, the line of analysis concludes that regional integration requires a hegemonic power to order this economic sphere. And, in the case of East Asia, it is possible to point to the role of the USA, in particular as a market for export-oriented development projects, and to regional organizations, such as APEC, which acknowledge the sphere of economic exchange.

However, it would be true to say that the extent of formal regional integration remains slight and sharply contested. The continued security role of the USA, the regional role of Japan, and the role of China are all in question. The nature of regional economic integration is similarly in question, with some suggesting that it is very advanced while others suggest it has hardly begun. A newer debate might, conceivably, be starting where the participants are East Asians; one thinks of the Japanese concern to establish an Asian variant of the IMF. Overall, the sanguine US view of their hegemonic role in East Asia seems increasingly insecure.

(iii)   Analyses of civilizations
In the case of the European Union, we can point to a recent welter of talk about 'Europe'. We have flags and anthems, symbolic sites (ambiguously gestured to through the images on the first euro banknotes); distinctions between

Europeans and Slavs; or between Western Catholic Europe and Eastern Orthodox Europe. Delanty[28] argues that there have been a series of 'invented Europes' and that a new one (which he does not much care for) is in process of construction around the project of the European Union. In the case of Europe it is possible to point to two areas of concern related to the use of the notion of civilization; first, that the strategy of analysis seems to involve abstract claims about patterns of life which may not stand up to scrutiny when questioned[29], and second, that the talk is redolent of colonial days, when broad claims to the superiority of European civilization in contrast to the cultures of the colonized were made.

In the case of East Asia, the territory of theories about civilizations and societies is similarly awkward, as it involves making very broad comparisons between cultural spheres and claiming for large geographical areas a received cultural coherence. It is a problematical area insofar as it can quickly take on the guise of ideological myth making.[30] Thus, there have been many attempts to distinguish the typically Asian from the typically European. Indeed, these attempts date from the nineteenth century, when the driving logic of industrial-capitalist expansion brought European and American traders to Asia.[31] In the case of contemporary East Asia it is perhaps worth noting that there is an indigenous line of resistance to Western political ideas expressed via the notion of 'Asian values', which reports that the polities of Asia are more naturally consensual than the individualistic polities of the West and that this finds appropriate expression in disciplined and hierarchical societies and polities.[32] In the same vein, an influential external view of Asia has characterized it as a coherent cultural bloc along with several others, all of which are taken by the author to be potential competitors with the West.[33]

A general reply to arguments from 'civilizations' would be to suggest that a disaggregated concern for real historically-embedded social processes might be expected to generate a more sophisticated understanding of contemporary patterns of life. It is clear that the peoples of Europe are diverse, as the routes to the modern world taken by the respective countries have all been different, and, indeed, the continent has a history of warfare. At the present time, in Europe, arguments to either national essentials or continent-wide essentials (the talk about a 'shared Judaeo-Christian heritage') do not have a central role within either intellectual or public political life, and to the extent that such arguments are made they belong to marginal groups. And in a similar way, if we turn to the case of East Asia, the arguments from 'civilizations' are also unhelpful. The region is large and diverse, encompassing the legatees of the Malay maritime empires in Southeast Asia; the internally differentiated territory of modern China, with its various regions; the sometime tributary states of premodern China; through to the particular patterns of life in

Northeast Asia, Japan and Far Eastern Russia. It might be argued that if we can find any commonality in this territory at the present time, it is to be found in developing regional interlinkages, themselves derived from national bases. In this sense, we can speak of a nascent East Asian region, rather than an 'Asian civilization'.

In all, the talk about 'civilizations' is not easy.[34] An alternative way of easing into the same territory of concern (that is, the sets of ideas carried within tradition) can be accessed, it seems to me, through the notion of culture.

(iv) Cultural analyses

Bauman[35] argues that there are a series of meanings of the notion of culture in familiar usage: culture as tradition, an inherited set of ideas; culture as the product of social learning, a spread of acquired sensibilities and skills; and, more interestingly, culture as praxis, the patterns of ideas and actions found in an everyday life taken to be lodged within a wider context, group or nation, itself having a discrete historical trajectory. It is this last interpretation that Bauman finds useful, rejecting the others as variously flawed. Once again, we are pointed to the realm of routine social practice. It is, of course, an area of enquiry that has been extensively developed in recent years, such that there is now an elaborate repertoire of concepts whereby cultural practices can be analysed.[36]

If we turn to the case of Europe, we can ease our way into these debates by drawing a distinction between the European world prior to the outbreak of the Second World War and that same world in the postwar period. In respect of the postwar period we can point to three areas of debate which endeavour to grasp the ways in which the inherited patterns of life extant in the autumn of 1939, 'the world we left behind'[37], have been remade: (i) the extensive, yet declining, influence of the USA (including here the effects of the end of the cold war); (ii) the continuing influence of the accumulated prosperity of the post-Second World War period; and (iii) the growing influence of the European Union.

In the case of East Asia, in the area of cultural analysis, the story is rather more complex. In anthropological terms, the area is very diverse, with many distinct groups.[38] The indigenous pattern was overlain and altered by the process of colonization. The dissolution of the formal colonial empires following the Pacific War generated both a spread of new nation-states and a region-wide cold war division. The impact of the cold war machineries was severe. It could be argued that it was not until the 1970s (in particular with Deng's 1978 reforms) that East Asia began to develop the sorts of routine social exchanges that worked over many years to foster integration in Europe.

At the present time, reports Bernard[39], some commentators 'argue that a region-wide civil society is now emerging ... [which] constitutes the basis for the region to be a new kind of "imagined community"'. However, matters are more complex and it is necessary to look at how local areas are situated within regional patterns. The movement towards a common civil society could include: (i) regionalized urban spaces, such that the region's cities have increasingly common patterns of production and consumption[40]; (ii) regionalized tourism, for example, intraregional travel and the passion for golf amongst newly affluent elites; and (iii) the networks of Chinese urban bourgeoisie, which stretch through much of the region. But all this is tentative and speculative. Bernard[41] concludes by recording both that there has been a growth in interconnectedness within the region and that the prospects for further integration are fraught with difficulties and tensions.

(v)   Historical structural analyses

The classical European tradition of social theorizing is concerned with elucidating the dynamics of complex change. The contemporary approach of structural international political economy, which recalls this material, offers a strategy which embraces many of the particular elements noted above in order to grasp the long-term historical dynamics of change within the region in question. It is clear that regions have existed in a myriad of historical contexts, and taken a variety of forms.

In the case of Europe, the slow shift to the modern world is described by Delanty[42] and could be unpacked for the more recent period in terms of Eric Hobsbawm's sequence of histories: the early-sixteenth-century shift to the modern capitalist world; the rise of nation-states in the nineteenth century; the 1914–45 era marked by two world wars; the 1945–89 period of what E. P. Thompson has called 'bloc time'; and, finally, the present post-1989 phase, which has seen the political–cultural project of the European Union come to assume a central role.

In the case of East Asia, an historical structural analysis would look to the successive ways in which the region has been configured and to the ways in which the peoples of the region understood themselves and have thereafter acted. The idea of an Eastern Asian region has existed since its invention by Japanese theorists in the late nineteenth century. It was constituted in expansionary Japanese military practice in the years up to 1941, and through the war years, but at the end of the Pacific War the region was sharply reconfigured. The new pattern owed much to the USA. The US security structure helped underpin the region, whilst the economy of Japan provided the core of a regionalized economy and the USA provided an ever-open market. Overall, Bernard[43] argues that the 'regionalized production structure ... has fostered an awareness of the regional nature of production, particularly through the crystallization of a region-wide bloc of state and business elites, and a cadre of technicians who have been the prime beneficiaries of regionalized manufacturing'. However, he[44] adds that the Japan-centred network is not the only one, and there are Chinese networks, taking in Hong Kong, Taiwan and Southeast Asia, which are establishing 'regional structures built around different kinds of economic activity – such as those related to agribusiness, property development or services – [and] with different spatial contours including a proliferation of ties with state and party elites in coastal China'.

Logics of Interregional Linkages

In the years following the end of the cold war, as received certainties have fallen away, the importance of regions has been acknowledged. The related business of regional interlinkages has come to be widely discussed. The idea of linkages points to specific patterns of relationships between more or less ordered units. In other words, it only makes sense to speak of linkages in particular circumstances; that is, when the system has units which can thereafter operate in various connections. A system of interlinked elements could be contrasted, for example, with a network, where there can be multiple and shifting connections. Or, indeed, a system of interlinked elements could be contrasted, more radically, with a single system comprising multiple shifting crosscutting linkages. The argument line followed in this chapter has granted the notion of more or less discrete regional blocs which thereafter generate interlinkages. The construction of a European Union region is well advanced. There is available evidence which points to the emergence of a nascent East Asian region. The chapters in this volume have shown that any analysis of these matters is a difficult task. An historical/structural analysis entails a wide spread of enquiries.

The interlinkages of the two regions can be grasped in terms of material links, discursive readings and formal mechanisms. The material linkages of the two regions embrace both patterns of ancient trade (the old Silk Road), the more recent episode of colonial rule (with its characteristic admixture of development and exploitation), and their continuing economic, social, cultural and political legacies. The depth of the historical interchange between the two regions of Europe and Asia is very significant. Indeed, cast in terms of the period covering the rise of the modern world, the exchange between Europe and Asia has been central. A. G. Frank[45] has offered a recent persuasive illustration of this claim in his analysis of the displacement of Asia by Europe over this time period. The intermingling of the European and Asian worlds in the long process of the shift to the modern world; the business of the remaking of economies, societies and polities in Europe and Asia in line with the demands of the mercantile and later industrial capitalist systems; reached an apogee in the establishment of the formal colonial systems.[46] At the turn of the twentieth century, the Asian world was subject to an externally determined process of extensive systemic change. The route to the modern world for the bulk of the peoples of East Asia has been through the experience of colonialism or quasi-colonialism. The legacies of this period continue down to the present day; in Asia, in patterns of economic development and trade, patterns of law, language and political institutions, and, in Europe, in similar ways. It is this deep historical experience that provides the background to contemporary exchanges; the further business of cultural exchange, learning and the creation of memory.

The contemporary linkages embrace the economic (trade, investment and financial flows), the social (migration, including labour and tourism), the cultural (law, language, custom and memory) and the political (patterns of informal linkages and loyalties). The Second World War caused great damage to both Europe and East Asia. In both regions there were extensive military campaigns, large numbers of casualties, enormous social dislocation and severe economic damage. These circumstances did not obtain in the USA, which emerged from the wartime episode as the largest single economy in the global system. However, over the last fifty years or so both regions have engineered economic reconstruction, recovery and success. The global pattern now embraces three macro-regions, North America (essentially the USA), the European Union and East Asia. As we have noted earlier, each region is economically autonomous, which is to say that economic activity is largely internal to the region and can be sustained on the basis of domestic resources of capital, people and knowledge. Nonetheless, the regions are not autarchic zones and the interlinkages are extensive. Over much of the early postwar period the USA figured as the key economic partner of the market-oriented economies of East Asia. However, as the European and East Asian economies advanced, the interregional linkages also began to develop (or, in historical perspective, recover), and the economic interchange between Europe and East Asia is now large and growing. The patterns of exchange spill over into social, cultural and political linkages, as not merely goods and services move back and forth but also people, whose presence not merely expresses contemporary preoccupations but also recalls and reanimates the cultural residues of those longer historical exchanges.

The material interlinkages of the two regions have been read into the ordinary practical activities of both groups; that is, understandings of the other become routine elements of definition of self. These discursive constructs are subtle and pervasive. In the case of Europe/Asia we can point to contemporary discursive linkages in three areas of social activity: memory (the collective recollection of selective aspects of the past); ignorance (the cognitively demobilizing effects for Europe–Asia discursive linkages of the long period of US hegemony); and consumption (the realm of material goods, cultural goods and travel/tourism).

As we noted earlier, Bauman speaks of 'culture as praxis', the realm of practical activity and routine understandings. In the case of Europe–Asia linkages, such practical activity embraces an economic exchange that is drawing in ever-greater numbers of people. As Europe–Asia linkages develop and deepen, received discursive constructs might be expected to change. The central arena of these discursive constructs is memory, understood as an active social process of the creation of meaning. It is no simple recollection of 'times past'.[47] In the social world, memory is a subtle and powerful force: it shapes the ways in which individuals and groups understand their everday routines, and the present which they happen to inhabit. It has been made clear in recent years that memory is not a simple accretion of facts, one piled upon another; rather it is a fluid contested social construct. This being so, we can speak of the memories carried informally amongst social groups (folk memory, thereafter), the more explicitly articulated sets of ideas that constitute an agreed national past, and, most formally, one might speak of the official ideologies of states.[48] The counterpart to memory, of course, is ignorance, the process of collective forgetting (either engineered or merely adventitious, a matter of how things turn out). In the case of Europe–Asia, the material taken variously into memory looks to the long experience of colonialism, decolonization and, to a lesser extent, cold war. It is these patterns of events that provide the materials to be read into a series of national pasts. The deepening linkages between Europe and Asia will see these pasts interrogated, not merely transregionally but, more immediately, intraregionally, where one immediate concern is likely to be with the legacies of the Second World War and Pacific War.[49] The national past is a subtle construction that serves to link individuals to the ordered political realm. As such, it is a matter of intense concern to state-regimes, and any revisions to a given national past are likely to have not merely domestic but also intraregional and transregional ramifications. It might be noted that there are strong signs of such debates and discussions taking place within Europe alongside the project of the European Union, but in East Asia there are various domestic and intra-regional difficulties. Nonetheless, the continuing development of linkages within regions and between Europe and Asia, with the concomitant movement of people and ideas, is likely to help keep these matters in view within the official, public and private realms.

The final area of concern relates to those formal linkages which embrace interstate relations, treaty organizations and consultative fora. These mechanisms play a significant role not merely in generating interregional linkages but also in establishing regional identities.

CONCLUSION: RESEARCHING EUROPE–ASIA LINKAGES

The current discussion of regions, their character and interrelations is relatively new, as it postdates the end of the cold war. In the case of Europe, the abrupt collapse of the cold war bloc system left the institutional structures and political project of the European Union both intact and without immediate competitors. In the case of East Asia, the emergence from cold war has been more drawn out and problematical, with economic changes progressing, on the one hand, and political changes rather less obvious. If we grasp these matters in terms of an idea of unfolding regional logics, then it is clear that both are advancing within the context of a still vigorous American-sponsored neo-liberal project (IBRD, IMF, WTO and so on). It is in this context that the development of Europe–Asia linkages attains a clear political significance, and this is likely to keep these issues high on the research agendas of policymakers and scholars. It is the last-noted group who are best placed to appreciate the full depth and richness of the developing interlinkages of Europe–Asia.

NOTES

1. See, for example, Julie Gilson's piece on the implications for East Asian regional identities of the ASEM process, J. Gilson (1999), 'Japan's role in the Asia–Europe Meeting', *Asian Survey*, **XXXIX**.
2. P. W. Preston (1985), *New Trends in Development Theory: Essays in Development and Social Theory*, London: Routledge, pp. 102–5. The idea of reflexivity is thereafter pursued through subsequent work. It has also become a key issue in cultural studies; see, for example, Dick Pels (2000), 'Reflexivity: one step up', *Theory, Culture and Society*, **17** (3), 1–25. See also Michael Lynch (2000), 'Against reflexivity as an academic virtue and source of privileged knowledge', *Theory, Culture and Society*, **17** (3), 26–54.
3. There are, of course, other agendas which we could note: the work of Orientalists and the critique recently made by Edward Said, the work of cultural critics in the area of postcolonial literature, and the recent 'New Asianism' discussed above by John Clammer.
4. E. Hobsbawm (1994), *The Age of Extremes: The Short Twentieth Century*, London: Michael Joseph.
5. F. Fukuyama (1992), *The End of History and the Last Man*, London: Hamish Hamilton.
6. See A. MacIntyre (1971), *Against the Self Images of the Age*, London: Duckworth.
7. See, for example, Z. Bauman (1992), *Intimations of Postmodernity*, London: Routledge; P. Hirst and G. Thompson (1996), *Globalization in Question*, Cambridge: Polity; C. Hay and D. Marsh (eds) (2000), *Demystifying Globalization*, London: Macmillan; D. Harvey (1989), *The Condition of Postmodernity*, Oxford: Blackwell; A. Callinicos (1989), *Against Postmodernism*, Cambridge: Polity; A. Woodiwiss (1993), *Postmodernity USA*, London: Sage.
8. S. Pollard (1971), *The Idea of Progress*, Harmondsworth: Penguin.
9. See, for example, Zygmunt Bauman (1987), *Legislators and Interpreters*, Cambridge: Polity, who argues that an early progressive alliance of bourgeoisie and intellectuals rather quickly collapsed into an elite-sponsored concern to order the new social world, a shift to a

positivistic aspiration to 'legislation' which the author suggests must be set aside in order to recover a richer idea of 'interpretation'.

10. This is an idea that I borrow from Barrington Moore.

11. This is an idea that I take from Geoffrey Hawthorn (1976), *Enlightenment and Despair*, Cambridge University Press, who suggests (and I report here very schematically), that we can identify a preference in Britain for small-scale contributions to a range of audiences (in the state, in particular, and thereafter market and polity); a preference in France for independent theorizing as the community of scholars has developed independently of the centralized state; and a preference in Germany for a notion of science deployed within the public sphere.

12. One might readily access these debates through the earlier work of Anthony Giddens, which saw, amongst other things, an English-language representation of the materials of hermeneutics, critical theory and structuralism, and an acknowledgment of the broad twentieth-century concern for language.

13. A schematic but useful introduction to this work is provided by Susan Strange (1988), *States and Markets*, London: Pinter.

14. For example, the episode is referred to as 'the IMF crisis' in Korea, and 'the monetary crisis' in Indonesia. See Kuan-Hsing Chen and Beng Huat Chua (2000), 'An Introduction', *Inter-Asia Cultural Studies*, **1** (1), 10–11.

15. M. Bernard (1996), 'Regions in the Global Political Economy', *New Political Economy*, **1** (3).

16. For an international-political-economy informed discussion of Japan's shift to the modern world, see P. W. Preston (2000), *Understanding Modern Japan: A Political Economy of Development, Culture and Global Power*, London: Sage; on the way in which Japanese elites understood themselves, see Stefan Tanaka (1993), *Japan's Orient: Rendering Pasts Into History*, Berkeley, University of California Press and see also, Ge Sun (2000), 'How Does Asia Mean?', *Inter-Asia Cultural Studies*, **1** (1), 13–48.

17. See, for example, F. Gibney (ed.) (1998), *Unlocking the Bureaucrats Kingdom: Deregulation and the Japanese Economy*, Washington, Brookings Institution; and K. Sheridan (ed.) (1989), *Emerging Economic Systems in Asia*, St Leonards: Allen & Unwin.

18. This later expression is mine, but there are any number of theorists who have pointed to the same general phenomena, a state committed to national development, local capital obedient to that goal, with efforts serviced by a mobilized population, where the whole ensemble can be tagged as a distinctive variant of industrial capitalism. A useful characterization is that of 'plan rational'; see R. P. Appelbaum and J. Henderson (eds) (1992), *States and Development in the Asian Pacific Rim*, London: Sage.

19. See P. Phongpaichit (1990), *The New Waves of Japanese Investment in ASEAN*, Singapore: Institute for Southeast Asian Studies.

20. However, a further alternative agenda is available in the rather different work of the theorists of postcolonialism and the proponents of the idea of New Asianism. On this see the chapter above by John Clammer.

21. All of this is further explained in Preston (1998), chapters 1 and 2.

22. Strange (1988).

23. P. Hirst and G. Thompson (1996), *Globalization in Question*, Cambridge: Polity.

24. For a brief review, see Juliet Lodge (ed.) (1989), *The European Union and the Challenge of the Future*, London: Pinter.

25. M. Bernard (1996), 'Regions in the Global Political Economy', in *New Political Economy*, **1** (3), 339.

26. Ibid.

27. There are a number of ways of summarizing debates within international relations, and this one is rather simple. It is derived from Andrew Linklater (1990), *Beyond Realism and Marxism: Critical Theory and International Relations*, London: Macmillan.

28. G. Delanty (1995), *Inventing Europe*, London: Macmillan.

29. For example, if one appeals to 'Western European/Catholic Europe' one runs into the problem that much of northern Europe is Protestant and, more broadly, that Christian

doctrine has, over the centuries, been so flexible as to make it difficult to speak of a coherent tradition – a thought I take from Alasdair MacIntyre (1967), *A Short History of Ethics*, London: Macmillan.

30. E. Said (1978), *Orientalism*, London: Routledge and Kegan Paul; S. Tanaka (1993), *Japan's Orient: Rendering Pasts into History*, Berkeley, University of California Press.

31. See, for example, E. Wilkinson (1983), *Misunderstanding: Europe Versus Japan*, Harmondsworth: Penguin; J. Goody (1996), *The East in the West*, Cambridge University Press.

32. See, for example, Mahathir Mohamad and Ishihara Shintaro (1995), *The Voice of Asia*, Tokyo: Kodansha.

33. S. P. Huntington (1993), 'The Clash of Civilizations', *Foreign Affairs*.

34. It might also be added that the term 'civilizations', and the implication that there are different civilizations which might, thereafter, be compared, makes modern Europeans uneasy. The intellectual and moral legacies of the nineteenth and twentieth centuries continue to exercise contemporary thinkers and political actors.

35. Z. Bauman (1976), *Culture as Praxis*, London: Sage.

36. For a short review, see Chris Jenks (1993), *Culture*, London: Routledge.

37. R. Kee (1984 [1939]), *The World We Left Behind*, London: Cardinal.

38. G. Evans (ed.) (1993), *Asia's Cultural Mosaic*, Singapore: Prentice Hall.

39. Bernard (1996), p. 346.

40. J. Clammer (1997), *Contemporary Urban Japan*, Oxford: Blackwell.

41. Bernard (1996), p. 346.

42. Delanty (1995).

43. Bernard (1996), p. 343.

44. Ibid.

45. A. G. Frank (1998), *Re-Orient: Global Economy in the Asian Age*, University of California.

46. The scale of the process is captured in Peter Worsley (1984), *The Three Worlds: Culture and World Development*, London: Weidenfeld.

47. See R. Samuel (1994), *Theatres of Memory: Volume I Past and Present in Contemporary Culture*, London: Verso.

48. This takes us into the territory of cultural studies, history from below and ideological critique. For a brief sophisticated statement, see the introductory essay in Patrick Wright (1985), *On Living in an Old Country*, London: Verso.

49. On this see I. Buruma (1994), *The Wages of Guilt: Memories of War in Germany and Japan*, London: Cape; see also B. Cummings (1999), *Parallax Visions: Making Sense of American East Asian Relations at the End of the Century*, Duke University Press, especially chapter 2 which deals with American exterminism in the air war against Japan.

Index